John
Paul II

THE GREAT MERCY POPE
BEATIFICATION EDITION

D1466478

John Paul II

THE GREAT MERCY POPE
BEATIFICATION EDITION

Fr. George W. Kosicki, CSB
with David C. Came

Foreword by Fr. Kazimierz Chwalek, MIC

MARIAN  PRESS
STOCKBRIDGE   MA 01263

2011

IMPRIMI POTEST:
Very Rev. Kazimierz Chwalek, MIC
November 13, 2011
Provincial Superior
The Blessed Virgin Mary, Mother of Mercy Province
Stockbridge, Massachusetts

Library of Congress Catalog Number: 2011940909
ISBN 978-1-59614-241-1

Editing: David C. Came
Proofreading and Photo Insert: Andrew Leeco
Cover and Page Design: Kathy Szpak
Cover Photo of Pope John Paul II: Joseph Romagnano
Back Cover: Tapestry of Blessed John Paul II is unveiled at his
beatification on Divine Mercy Sunday, May 1, 2011, in St. Peter's
Square. Photo by Joseph Romagnano.
Photo of Pope John Paul II for page design: Marie Romagnano

Special Thanks: To Mr. Shaun Hillary,
for his generous help and prayers

Beatification Edition: Updated through 2011

Published by
John Paul II Institute of Divine Mercy
An Imprint of Marian Press

DEDICATION

To Blessed John Paul II, the Great Mercy Pope,
for leaving us an enduring legacy of Divine Mercy.

TABLE OF CONTENTS

APPENDIXES

IN CHRONOLOGICAL ORDER:

ACKNOWLEDGMENTS

A special thanks to the Very Rev. Fr. Kazimierz Chwalek, MIC, provincial superior of the Blessed Virgin Mary, Mother of Mercy Province, for writing the Foreword to the Beatification Edition. Special thanks as well to David C. Came, my coauthor and the executive editor of Marian Press, for writing the new chapters in Part I on the beatification of Blessed John Paul II, helping me with the Introduction, and developing further in chapter 3 of Part V the influence of Pope John Paul II on his successor, Pope Benedict XVI.

Further, I wish to thank Andrew Leeco, associate editor of Marian Press, for proofreading the text, preparing the photo insert, expanding the Chronology of the Great Mercy Pope, and updating the Index of Papal Writings and Addresses. Finally, I thank Kathy Szpak, a designer at the Marian Helpers Center, for designing the cover and the pages.

MERCY GEMS FROM
JOHN PAUL II

- "Right from the beginning of my ministry in St. Peter's See in Rome, I considered this message [of Divine Mercy] my special task. Providence has assigned it to me in the present situation of man, the Church and the world. It could be said that precisely this situation assigned that message to me as my task before God" (November 22, 1981, Shrine of Merciful Love in Collevalenza, Italy).

- "On the threshold of the third millennium, I come to entrust to Him once more my Petrine ministry — 'Jesus, I trust in You!' ... I took with me [the message of Divine Mercy] to the See of Peter and which in a sense forms the image of this Pontificate" (Shrine of Divine Mercy, Krakow-Lagiewniki, Poland, June 7, 1997).

- "John Paul II, who said that he felt spiritually 'very near' to Sr. Faustina, had been 'thinking about her for a long time' when he began writing *Dives in Misericordia*" (George Weigel, *Witness to Hope*, 1999).

- "I will sing of the mercies of the Lord forever" (Psalm 89:2, John Paul II repeated on important occasions of his papacy, including the canonization of St. Faustina, April 30, 2000).

- "Sister Faustina's canonization has a particular eloquence: by this act, I intend today to pass this message on to the third millennium" (Homily of Canonization of St. Faustina, April 30, 2000).

- "This is the happiest day of my life" (the Pope's words to Dr. Valentin Fuster — the cardiologist who investigated the miraculous healing of the heart of Fr. Ron Pytel through the intercession of St. Faustina — on the day of her canonization, April 30, 2000).

- "[The] fire of mercy needs to be passed on to the world" (Solemn Act of entrustment of the world to Divine Mercy, Aug. 17, 2002, Krakow-Lagiewniki, Poland).

- "The Eucharist is a mystery of faith: a great mystery, a mystery of mercy" (Encyclical *Ecclesia De Eucharistia Vivit*, II, Holy Thursday, 2004).

- "Christ crucified and risen, just as He appeared to Sister Faustina [as the image of Divine Mercy], is the supreme revelation of this truth: 'God is Love' " (*Memory and Identity*, chapter on the Mystery of Mercy, p. 55, the last book John Paul wrote, 2005).

- "*How much the world needs to understand and accept Divine Mercy! ... Jesus, I Trust in You, have mercy upon us and upon the whole world. Amen.*" These are John Paul II's concluding words of his final Divine Mercy Sunday message, written earlier and delivered the day after his death (Divine Mercy Sunday, April 3, 2005). They are a summary of John Paul II's life and message of Divine Mercy: his entrustment to Divine Mercy and constant prayer (see Shrine of Divine Mercy, Krakow, June 7, 1997).

FOREWORD TO THE BEATIFICATION EDITION

It gives me great joy to write the Foreword to the Beatification Edition *of John Paul II: The Great Mercy Pope.*

There are two reasons for this joy. First, I had the privilege of attending the beatification of John Paul II on Divine Mercy Sunday, May 1, 2011, in St. Peter's Square.

Second, Blessed John Paul II was someone special to my religious community, the Marian Fathers of the Immaculate Conception. What brought us together, in part, was a shared mission to proclaim God's extraordinary love and mercy for all people. It is a mission of salvation and peace for humanity. "Mankind will not have peace until it turns with trust to My mercy," Jesus tells St. Faustina, as recorded in her *Diary* (300).

REFLECTIONS ON THE BEATIFICATION

Let me start by sharing some of my reflections from the beatification of Blessed John Paul II. (See chapter 3 of Part I for a more complete account of the beatification. Also, some of my personal reflections on the beatification appear in that chapter.)

First, the beatification was a dream come true for the Marian Fathers — especially Fr. Seraphim Michalenko, MIC, who has spent his whole life promoting this message of hope and God's merciful love. At the beatification celebration, the Marians were overjoyed to see The Divine Mercy Image displayed on the main altar, to hear the Divine Mercy Chaplet prayed before the solemn Mass, and, of course, to witness John Paul II being beatified on Divine Mercy Sunday.

What joy, what a fulfillment, what a special gift for us from God to witness personally this great event together with a number of our Marian Helpers who came with us on pilgrimage. It was truly a crowning moment for Blessed John Paul II's legacy of

Divine Mercy and a resounding confirmation of our many efforts to share this urgent message of salvation, following his lead.

Other personal highlights of the beatification included the moment when the Holy Father, Pope Benedict XVI, processed to the altar and then took his chair amidst beautiful music and loud cheering as the Mass began. After attending the vigil the night before in the Circus Maximus and then braving the long wait for the beatification through the early morning hours on the day itself — as pilgrims filled St. Peter's Square as well as the surrounding streets and piazzas in Rome — it was a moment of great joy for me and for all in attendance when the liturgy finally began.

Then, immediately after the Penitential Rite, Cardinal Agostino Vallini, the vicar general for the Diocese of Rome, asked the Holy Father to beatify the Venerable Servant of God and gave testimony to the holiness of John Paul II's life. Cardinal Vallini had given witness to John Paul II's life at the vigil.

I particularly remember being overcome with joy when Pope Benedict declared John Paul II blessed, and the crowd exploded with a thunderous cheer of thanksgiving. "Oh, God," I exclaimed in prayer, "You are so gracious to us!"

There was also the solemn, silent procession with the relic of Blessed John Paul II as it was moved to the main outdoor altar. The relic was his blood contained in a cruet. It was poignantly symbolic of the way he had poured out his life in service to Christ and the Church.

Finally, I was especially touched by Pope Benedict's homily when he said:

> I would like to thank God for the gift of having worked for many years with Blessed Pope John Paul II. I had known him earlier and had esteemed him, but for twenty-three years, beginning in 1982 after he called me to Rome to be Prefect of the Congregation for the Doctrine of the Faith, I was at his side and came to revere him all the more. My own service was sustained by his spiritual depth and by the richness of his insights.

His example of prayer continually impressed and edified me: he remained deeply united to God even amid the many demands of his ministry. Then too, there was his witness in suffering: the Lord gradually stripped him of everything, yet he remained ever a "rock," as Christ desired. His profound humility, grounded in close union with Christ, enabled him to continue to lead the Church and to give to the world a message which became all the more eloquent as his physical strength declined. In this way he lived out in an extraordinary way the vocation of every priest and bishop to become completely one with Jesus, whom he daily receives and offers in the Church. Blessed are you, beloved Pope John Paul II, because you believed!

These personal reflections by Pope Benedict are moving because he shares about his longtime collaboration with Pope John Paul II and the deep influence the newly blessed had on him spiritually. The Holy Father also speaks eloquently of John Paul II's heroic witness in suffering and his example of extraordinary faithfulness to his vocation as a priest and bishop.

THE MARIANS FOLLOW THE LEAD OF BLESSED JOHN PAUL II

In his enduring legacy of Divine Mercy, Blessed John Paul II has inspired the Church and the Marians in significant ways. Here are some mercy milestones for him that included the Marians following his lead.

Early in his pontificate, in 1980, Pope John Paul II published his famous encyclical, *Rich in Mercy*. John Paul shows how God the Father is "rich in mercy" through a masterful exposition of the Gospel parable of the prodigal son (5-6). He roots the message of mercy in Scripture and Catholic theology, speaking of how the love of the Father is revealed in Christ as the "Incarnation of Mercy" and "the inexhaustible source of mercy" (8).

Publishing an important work on Divine Mercy was also

on the minds of the Marians in the early 1980s. In 1981, we prepared and published the original Polish edition of the *Diary of Sr. Faustina*, whose cause of beatification was initiated by John Paul when he was still Archbishop of Krakow. The *Diary* is the source book of The Divine Mercy message and devotion as revealed by Jesus to St. Faustina. Pope John Paul II quoted from it on a visit to Sr. Faustina's tomb, at her beatification and her canonization, and when he entrusted the world to The Divine Mercy.

Over the next several years, the Marians published other editions of the *Diary* in English, Spanish, Portuguese, and Russian. Today, Marian Press is known the world over as the publisher of the *Diary* in English and Spanish. This work of mystical literature has helped to ignite the Divine Mercy movement — one of the greatest grassroots movements in the history of the Church.

It is worth noting here that Fr. George. W. Kosicki, CSB, the author of this book, assisted the Marians in our publishing of the *Diary* in English. In 1987, he headed our Divine Mercy Department in Stockbridge, Massachusetts, which was responsible for editing and proofing the English translation of the *Diary*.

Sister Faustina's cause of beatification was a priority for Pope John Paul II even when he was Archbishop of Krakow. This is borne out by a telling entry in *The Making of the Pope of the Millennium: Kalendarium of Karol Wojtyla*. On Aug. 21, 1965, Rev. Dr. Michael Sopocko, who had been Sr. Faustina's confessor and spiritual director, met with Archbishop Karol Wojtyla and asked when the diocesan process for Sr. Faustina's cause of beatification would start. "This matter is foremost in my mind," the Archbishop answered. "Maybe we will still be able to begin it this year" (Fr. Adam Boniecki, MIC, Author; Fr. Kazimierz Chwalek, MIC, English-language Editor, *The Making of the Pope of the Millennium: Kalendarium of Karol Wojtyla*. Stockbridge, Mass.: Marian Press, 2000, p. 253).

On Oct. 21, 1965 — two months to the day after the meeting — Sister Faustina's cause was launched in the Archdiocese of Krakow.

Following Pope John Paul II's lead, Fr. Seraphim

Michalenko, MIC, served as a vice-postulator for Sr. Faustina's cause for some 20 years. In his role, he was pivotal in securing the documentation and testimony needed for a miracle to be recognized for the nun's beatification, and then another one for her canonization.

In fact, Fr. Michalenko even witnessed the first miracle on March 28, 1981, when Maureen Digan was healed of the incurable disease of lymphedema at the tomb of Sr. Faustina in Poland.

Maureen and Fr. Michalenko were present in Rome on Divine Mercy Sunday, April 18, 1993, when Pope John Paul II beatified Sr. Faustina. "O Faustina, how extraordinary your life is!" John Paul exclaimed in the beatification homily. "Precisely you, the poor and simple daughter ... of the Polish people were chosen by Christ to remind people of this great mystery of Divine Mercy!"

Then, the healing in 1995 of Fr. Ron Pytel, a priest with a serious heart condition, paved the way for the blessed's canonization in 2000. In considering the cure of Fr. Pytel, the Vatican required greater scientific scrutiny. Father Michalenko located Valentin Fuster, MD, a world-renowned cardiologist, to review the case. His testimony advanced the case quickly, with Fr. Michalenko providing Vatican officials with the needed documentation. So, on Divine Mercy Sunday, April 30, 2000, Pope John Paul II canonized St. Faustina in Rome as the first saint of the Great Jubilee Year 2000. Father Michalenko, Fr. Pytel, and Dr. Fuster were all present for the big day.

Pope John Paul II even attended the reception after the canonization. He told Dr. Fuster, "This is the happiest day of my life."

What made April 30, 2000, the happiest day of John Paul II's life?

The Pope said and did some truly remarkable things at St. Faustina's canonization. First came his surprise announcement in his homily about Divine Mercy Sunday. "It is important that we accept the whole message that comes to us from the word of God on the Second Sunday of Easter, which from now on

throughout the Church, will be called 'Divine Mercy Sunday,' "
he said.

Second, he did something that has great relevance to our
world's need for Divine Mercy in these times wracked by terrorism and war. "Saint Faustina's canonization has a particular
eloquence," the Pope said. "By this act I intend to pass this
message [of Divine Mercy] on to the new millennium." Pope
John Paul II was underscoring The Divine Mercy message St.
Faustina was given as *the* message of the third millennium.

Interestingly, the Pope's establishing Divine Mercy Sunday
for the whole Church came as no surprise to Fr. Michalenko.
The evening before the canonization, Fr. Michalenko was
informed by Monsignor Stanislaus Dziwisz, John Paul II's
personal secretary, of the decision.

It was recognition of the Marians' "Feast of Divine
Mercy Petition" drive, which was announced on the EWTN
Cable Network and to the Marian Helpers in the Spring 2000
issue of *Marian Helper* magazine. In the petition, the faithful
asked Pope John Paul II to declare Divine Mercy Sunday a
universal feast.

The grassroots response was overwhelming. The Marians
received thousands upon thousands of signed petitions by mail
and fax from the faithful around the world. For months that
spring, the Marians kept on sending the Holy See box after box
of signed petitions.

To help the faithful understand these new developments,
the Marians asked Fr. Kosicki — one of our close collaborators
in promoting Divine Mercy — to write two new publications.
Both were published by Marian Press before Divine Mercy
Sunday 2001. Father Kosicki's booklet *Why Mercy Sunday?*
provided a Q&A guide to celebrating the universal feast day.
Meanwhile, in the first edition of this book, Fr. Kosicki chronicled
the rich mercy legacy of John Paul.

After the momentous developments surrounding St.
Faustina's canonization, the faithful barely had time to catch
their breath before the Mercy Pope acted again.

In June of 2002, under Pope John Paul II's direction, the

Church granted a plenary indulgence for the faithful who fully participate in Divine Mercy Sunday. The indulgence was available for the first time on Mercy Sunday 2003. Pope John Paul II wanted the indulgence to be available on Divine Mercy Sunday "in order to impress deeply on the souls of the faithful the precepts and teachings of Christian faith" regarding the mercy of God, according to a Vatican announcement.

Then, in August of 2002, Pope John Paul II entrusted the world to The Divine Mercy when he consecrated the Basilica of Divine Mercy in Lagiewniki, a suburb of his beloved Krakow in Poland. This shrine is located where St. Faustina lived and worked.

"In this shrine, I wish solemnly to entrust the world to Divine Mercy," he said in his homily. "I do so with the burning desire that the message of God's merciful love, proclaimed here through St. Faustina, may be made known to all the peoples of the earth and fill their hearts with hope."

The Marians supported these new developments by publishing before Divine Mercy Sunday 2003 pamphlets with the text of John Paul's entrustment homily and the plenary indulgence.

The Great Mercy Pope encouraged the Marians to spread Divine Mercy when we gathered for our General Chapters in Rome. At our Chapter in 1993, he charged us, "Be apostles of Divine Mercy under the maternal and loving guidance of Mary." Then, in a written message to the Marians at our Chapter in March 2005, he echoed this charge when he said, "Be apostles and witnesses of Divine Mercy for everyone."

One important way the Marians spread The Divine Mercy message is through our John Paul II Institute of Divine Mercy, which is headquartered in Stockbridge. Inspired by its name-sake, John Paul II, the Institute teaches clergy and lay leaders about the message through its seminars and publications. In March 1996, Pope John Paul II signed an apostolic blessing for its dedication.

Along with naming our Institute after him, we have a special sign of Blessed John Paul II's presence with us on Eden Hill here in Stockbridge at the National Shrine of The Divine

Mercy. It is a first-class relic of Blessed John Paul II — a drop of his blood on cloth. It's an extraordinary gift to our Shrine. Alongside the first-class relics of St. Faustina and her confessor, Blessed Michael Sopocko, at the Shrine, we now have one of the third great promoter of Divine Mercy, Blessed John Paul II.

As a sign of appreciation for the Marians' promotion of The Divine Mercy message and devotion since 1941, the relic was given to us by Cardinal Dziwisz, Archbishop of Krakow, Poland, at the second World Apostolic Congress on Mercy, which was celebrated at the Basilica of Divine Mercy in Lagiewniki on October 1-5, 2011.

TO PRESERVE HIS LEGACY FOR FUTURE GENERATIONS

In light of this history involving the Great Mercy Pope, Blessed John Paul II, and the Marian Congregation, I am pleased to highly recommend the Beatification Edition of *John Paul II: The Great Mercy Pope* by Fr. Kosicki. It follows on the heels of the Second Edition, which covered John Paul's entire papacy through the prism of Divine Mercy and was published in 2006, the year after his death. Building on that edition, Fr. Kosicki and his coauthor, David Came, in this new edition have developed masterful chapters on John Paul II's cause for beatification, the miracle recognized for his beatification, and the beatification itself. Further, they bring us up-to-date on John Paul II's influence on his successor, Pope Benedict XVI, in promoting Divine Mercy. Moreover, they make the chronology of the Great Mercy Pope current to include events through 2011 that are part of John Paul's legacy. Here is an invaluable resource for every apostle of Divine Mercy who wants to understand and embrace the Great Mercy Pope's special mission of proclaiming God's merciful love to all humanity.

As our publishing apostolate, Marian Press, produces this new edition, it represents another milestone for the Great Mercy Pope, helping to ensure that his legacy of Divine Mercy is preserved for future generations. For both Fr. Kosicki and the Marians, it represents a labor of love dedicated to his beloved memory and our continuing efforts to promote his legacy.

Very Rev. Kazimierz Chwalek, MIC
Provincial Superior
The Blessed Virgin Mary, Mother of Mercy Province
Marian Fathers of the Immaculate Conception

INTRODUCTION TO THE
BEATIFICATION EDITION

On January 29, 1989, in a private meeting in the papal household with Pope John Paul II's personal secretary, Msgr. Stanislaus Dziwisz, I was encouraged when he told me "that the message of Divine Mercy was very much a part of his own life as it was of the Holy Father's."

Then on March 10, 2006, as Archbishop of Krakow, Msgr. Dziwisz wrote to me, "Divine Mercy was an important subject in the teaching of John Paul II and the *key to understanding the life and teaching of Peter in our time*" (emphasis added).

It's important to emphasize here that Divine Mercy was not only a personal message and devotion of Pope John Paul II, but it was also a message and devotion for his homeland of Poland and for the whole world so desperately in need of Divine Mercy.

The message of trust in God's mercy was the essence of John Paul II's teaching and ministry from his very first public address on the day of his papal inauguration, October 22, 1978, to his very last written word, written some two or three weeks prior to his death on the vigil of Divine Mercy Sunday, April 2, 2005. That final message was read the next morning to the faithful at the Mass of Divine Mercy Sunday in St. Peter's Square.

In fact, this last message was highlighted nearly a year after the death of John Paul II on March 26, 2006, when Pope Benedict XVI was visiting the Roman parish of God the Merciful Father on the Fourth Sunday of Lent. He was speaking of the importance of "a personal encounter with the Crucified and Risen Christ," based on the Sunday readings, when he turned to the testament of mercy that John Paul left the Church in his last words:

> In meditating on the Lord's mercy that was revealed totally and definitively in the mystery of the Cross, the

text that John Paul II had prepared for his meeting with the faithful on April 3 [Divine Mercy Sunday], the Second Sunday of Easter, comes to my mind.

In the divine plan it was written that he would leave us precisely on the eve of that day, Saturday, April 2 — we all remember it well — and for that reason he was unable to address his words to you. I would like to address them to you now, dear brothers and sisters, "To humanity, which sometimes seems bewildered and overwhelmed by the power of evil, selfishness, and fear, the Risen Lord offers his love that pardons, reconciles, and reopens hearts to hope. It is a love that converts hearts and gives peace."

The Pope, in this last text which is like a testament, then added: "How much the world needs to understand and accept Divine Mercy!" (*Regina Caeli* message, read by Archbishop Leonardo Sandri, Substitute of the Secretariat of State, to the faithful gathered in St. Peter's Square, April 3, 2005).

In this poignant remembrance of John Paul II's last words, Pope Benedict singles out John Paul's powerful cry of the heart to the world — which includes each of us — "to understand and accept Divine Mercy." These words are like a testament we can turn to whenever we are "bewildered and overwhelmed by the power of evil," as we were on September 11, 2001. He identifies what we truly *need* most of all. (See David Came, *Pope Benedict's Divine Mercy Mandate*. Stockbridge, Mass.: Marian Press, 2009, pp. 60-62.)

Thus, Blessed John Paul II, in this "testament" and now through his beatification, has left us an enduring legacy of Divine Mercy. This is especially the case with the beatification because it was celebrated on Divine Mercy Sunday, May 1, 2011. (In chapter 3 of Part I, David Came and I cover the significance of John Paul II being beatified on Divine Mercy Sunday.) It is the rationale behind the subtitle for the Beatification Edition: "An Enduring Legacy of Divine Mercy."

WHAT'S NEW IN THIS EDITION?

Essentially, we chronicle Pope John Paul II's legacy of Divine Mercy in this book through analyzing his writings, addresses, and homilies on Divine Mercy. Drawing upon what he said and wrote throughout his papacy, we explore his life in his roles as a teacher and a model of mercy. Further, we examine key mercy themes in John Paul's thought as well as aspects of his legacy of mercy, such as his strong influence on his successor Pope Benedict XVI.

The second half of the book provides the Vatican translation in English of his words of mercy, arranged in chronological order. We also include a chronology of the Great Mercy Pope and an index to his writings.

New material for the Beatification Edition includes:

- A foreword by Fr. Kazimierz Chwalek, MIC, provincial superior of the Marian Fathers of the Immaculate Conception in the United States and Argentina;
- A new Part I on the beatification;
- More on Pope John Paul II's influence on Pope Benedict XVI, his successor;
- An up-to-date chronology of the Great Mercy Pope;
- The full text of Pope John Paul II's last message for Divine Mercy Sunday;
- Pope Benedict's homily at John Paul II's beatification;
- And a 12-page color photo insert.

Now let me talk about these additions to the book in more detail.

FOREWORD: In his Foreword, Fr. Chwalek shares some of his own personal highlights of the beatification for John Paul II, which he attended. He also shows how John Paul II, as the Great Mercy Pope, achieved milestones in spreading the message of God's mercy. With these milestones, he points out how the Marians have followed John Paul II's lead in promoting the message of Divine Mercy.

PART I: BEATIFICATION: In this new part to the book, David Came and I start in chapter 1 looking at the genesis of John Paul II's beatification cause. Interestingly, it really started at his funeral in St. Peter's Square on April 8, 2005, with the faithful crying out "*Santo subito!*" (Saint now!) and "*Magnus!*" (Great!). Learn how the official Church had to play catch up by waiving the usual five-year waiting period for the start of the beatification process.

Then, in chapter 2 of this part, we learn of a French nun's healing from Parkinson's disease as the miracle that is recognized for the beatification. Pope John Paul II himself had suffered in his last years from Parkinson's disease, which makes this healing through his intercession poignant.

Finally, in chapter 3 of Part I, we have provided a more detailed account of the beatification itself, including some important developments leading up to it. For example, in the lead-up to the beatification, we hear of the Pope and Vatican officials remarking on the significance of the date set for it, namely, Divine Mercy Sunday, May 1, 2011. We also hear in 2010 about the importance of a new book on John Paul II by papal biographer George Weigel. With the beatification itself, we draw from the firsthand reflections of Fr. Chwalek, various news sources, and quote extensively from Pope Benedict's homily.

JOHN PAUL II'S INFLUENCE ON POPE BENEDICT: In Part V: The Legacy of Pope John Paul II, chapter 3, we bring you up-to-date on how John Paul II has had a deep and lasting influence on his successor and longtime collaborator, formerly Cardinal Joseph Ratzinger, now Pope Benedict XVI. For example, we chronicle how Pope Benedict approved and participated in the first World Apostolic Congress on Mercy in Rome during 2008, which was inspired by the Great Mercy Pope. Further, we develop how Pope Benedict often includes mention of John Paul II and St. Faustina in his homilies for Divine Mercy Sunday and to mark the anniversary of John Paul II's death.

CHRONOLOGY OF THE GREAT MERCY POPE: Since the last edition of my book was published by Marian Press in 2006, it was necessary to update this chronology on the Divine Mercy legacy of John Paul II through 2011. The chronology now ends with the second World Apostolic Congress on Mercy, which was held in Krakow, Poland, on October 1-5, 2011.

THE FULL TEXT OF POPE JOHN PAUL II'S LAST MESSAGE FOR DIVINE MERCY SUNDAY: In the previous edition, I had only drawn the key words from John Paul II's last message, which was shared on Divine Mercy Sunday, April 3, 2005, the day after his death. So in the Beatification Edition, I wanted to include the full text for the record.

POPE BENEDICT'S HOMILY AT JOHN PAUL II'S BEATIFICATION: Since this is the Beatification Edition of my book, I thought many of my readers would want to read the full text of the Holy Father's homily for the occasion.

TWELVE-PAGE COLOR PHOTO INSERT: This insert takes us from the start of John Paul II's papacy through his close relationship with the Marian Fathers, his funeral, beatification, and finally the second World Apostolic Congress on Mercy, inspired by his enduring legacy. It even includes a photo of myself with the Marians making a special presentation to Pope John Paul II while filming a movie on Divine Mercy.

SOME OF MY OWN MEMORIES WITH POPE JOHN PAUL II

Working on the three editions of this book and getting to know Pope John Paul II more personally have left a deep impression on my life. He was truly a Pope of mercy who lived the message that he preached.

Here, I share some personal recollections of him to help you appreciate more the man behind the words.

FIRST OF ALL, I remember during his first pastoral visit to the United States in 1979, being present on October 1, when he was at Holy Cross Cathedral in Boston, Massachusetts. It was the feast day of St. Thérèse of Lisieux. Traveling from Rhode Island with some fellow clergy, I arrived late at the event. We found seats in the back of the cathedral. When the Pope arrived, he turned toward me, looking right at me, with his hand raised in blessing. It was an extraordinary moment.

However, it took me several years to realize that it was also a unique moment of my call to promote the message and devotion of Divine Mercy. For that moment of him blessing me marked the beginning of my full-time involvement in spreading Divine Mercy.

A HUMOROUS MOMENT with Pope John Paul II came on November 13, 1986. It was after the Holy Father had celebrated Holy Mass in his private chapel. I was there in the Vatican with the Marians and the whole production team filming for the movie *Divine Mercy — No Escape*. After the filming in the Vatican, a "thank you" to the Holy Father, and the presentation of a Divine Mercy Image to him, we wanted to film him signing the guest book.

Since I had been assigned to ask guests to sign it, I asked the Holy Father to sign and handed the book to Msgr. Dziwisz, along with my pen. John Paul reached out to sign it with an orange ballpoint pen. Someone then nudged me and said, "He shouldn't sign with a ballpoint pen." So I went up the desk where the Holy Father was seated and picked up my gold-top Parker 51 pen. Then, in my best Polish, I said, "Your Holiness, this is real ink!"

"Oh!" Pope John Paul II said, and then he signed the book with my Parker 51 pen.

IN ANOTHER SPECIAL MOMENT related to the film, it was September 15, 1987, and Pope John Paul II was in San Francisco addressing the religious of the area at the cathedral. I was in Hollywood, California, for the premiere of the film *Divine Mercy — No Escape* at Grauman's Chinese Theatre.

So after the premiere, I drove up to San Francisco with a group of others to attend the Holy Father's presentation to the religious. We arrived early, and I sat in the front pew of the center isle. To my great joy, the Pope shook my hand upon entering and upon leaving.

A PARTICULARLY POIGNANT MOMENT with Pope John Paul II came on January 9, 1989. It was at the Holy

Father's daily Mass in his private chapel at the Vatican.

At the Mass, I was assigned by Msgr. Dziwisz to a place right next to John Paul II's kneeler. For some 15 minutes before Mass, I observed him and was distracted by my question, "What is John Paul II praying for so intently?"

What kept coming to my mind during that quarter of an hour of prayer in preparation for the Mass was that the Holy Father was praying, "Have mercy on us and on the whole world." As a confirmation for this intuition, I found out almost a decade later on June 7, 1997, that Pope John Paul II said, "I pray unceasingly — Have mercy on us and on the whole world." The occasion was his visit to the Shrine of The Divine Mercy in Lagiewniki, Poland, where he prayed before the tomb of then-Blessed Faustina.

What a great witness to the power of intercessory prayer the Great Mercy Pope gave me that day!

'MAKE JOHN PAUL II'S LEGACY OF DIVINE MERCY YOUR OWN'

The hope I have for you, the readers, is that the Beatification Edition of my book would help form you into apostles of Divine Mercy. I encourage you to share it with your fellow apostles of Divine Mercy and with those in your family, circle of friends, and parish who would be open to learning about Blessed John Paul II's legacy of Divine Mercy.

My prayer is that you would make John Paul II's legacy of Divine Mercy your own. You can best do this by applying his teachings on Divine Mercy, following his example in living this message, and letting his zeal for spreading it inspire you. Make his testament of mercy a cry of your heart to the Lord, "How much the world needs to understand and accept Divine Mercy!"

Then, while you embrace this call, seek the powerful intercession of this great apostle of Divine Mercy by frequently invoking his aid with the prayer: Blessed John Paul II, pray for us. Amen.

PART I
BEATIFICATION

Discover how the faithful unofficially launched John Paul II's cause for beatification at his funeral on April 8, 2005. Read the inspiring account of a French nun's healing from Parkinson's disease, which was recognized as the miracle for John Paul's beatification. Savor highlights from the Great Mercy Pope's beatification on Divine Mercy Sunday, May 1, 2011.

CHAPTER I
THE CAUSE

On April 8, 2005, only six days after the death of Pope John Paul II, the faithful unofficially launched his cause for beatification in a way that was unprecedented for the Church in modern times. The occasion was the funeral Mass of the beloved Pontiff in St. Peter's Square, and the signal moment came after the distribution of Holy Communion. At that time, the faithful in the square and down the Via della Conciliazione spontaneously took up the cry of "*Magnus, Magnus!*" (Great, Great!) and "*Santo subito!*" (Saint now!). Many also raised and waved signs emblazoned with these words. The cries were so loud that they could be heard from the Janiculum Hill, which overlooks Vatican City.

To put it in historical context, you have to go back to the early centuries of the Church for a time when saints were recognized by public acclaim. And you have to go back more than 1,400 years to the funeral of Pope Gregory I in 604 for a time when the faithful acclaimed a Pope as "Great."

Cardinal Joseph Ratzinger, who was the principal celebrant at John Paul's funeral as the dean of the College of Cardinals, took it all in stride by waiting several minutes for the cries to subside before he began the Mass's dismissal rites. Many of the media covering the funeral observed that the chants and cries of the crowd seemed to come in response to Cardinal Ratzinger's homily. In his remarks, the Cardinal stressed that John Paul was in the Father's house and called for future generations to recognize him as "John Paul the Great." (See George Weigel, *The End and the Beginning: Pope John Paul II — The Victory of Freedom, the Last Years, the Legacy.* New York, N.Y.: Doubleday, 2010, pp. 394-5.)

Even before the cries of "*Magnus!*" and "*Santo subito!*" filled the square, another aspect of the funeral seemed to confirm John Paul II's holy life: "At the funeral Mass, when the Book of the Gospels was placed on his coffin, the wind started blowing the pages one by one. It was as if the Holy Father's life was passing by right in front of us. Finally, the book was closed by the wind." This was shared in the Summer 2005 issue of *Marian Helper* magazine by Br. Andrew Maczynski, MIC — a Marian brother who attended the funeral and who enjoyed a number of private audiences with Pope John Paul II because of his work for the Marian community and their Association of Marian Helpers.

Since wind is symbolic of the Holy Spirit, commentators at the funeral wondered if this was a sign of the Spirit's seal on John Paul II's life, confirming his holiness.

To add to the luster of the occasion, an estimated 4 million mourners made their way to Rome to pay tribute to their Pope of beloved memory. The funeral Mass drew about 400,000 pilgrims to St. Peter's Square, with millions watching on large TV screens in the piazzas and streets of Rome. An estimated 4 billion more around the world watched via television, cable, and the Internet.

THE CAUSE OFFICIALLY STARTS

The official Church had to catch up with the unofficial jumpstart of John Paul II's cause at the funeral. Citing the "exceptional circumstances," Pope Benedict XVI dispensed with the usual five-year waiting period for the cause to start. The Vatican announced his decision on May 13, 2005, the feast of Our Lady of Fatima, and the 24th anniversary of the assassination attempt on John Paul II in St. Peter's Square. Poignantly, John Paul II had credited Our Lady with guiding the bullet and preserving his life on that day.

Then, on June 28, 2005, the cause for John Paul II officially got under way with the edict issued by Cardinal Camillo Ruini, vicar general for the Diocese for Rome, in the Lateran Basilica, which is the cathedral of the Diocese of Rome. This opened the diocesan inquiry, with the gathering of testimonies and documents related to the life and virtues of the Servant of God John Paul II.

In the opening sentence of the edict, Cardinal Ruini mentioned how Pope John Paul II had been called to the Lord on "the Octave of Easter and Divine Mercy Sunday":

On Saturday, April 2, 2005, upon entering the Lord's Day, the Octave of Easter and Divine Mercy Sunday, the Lord called to Himself, from the Vatican Apostolic Palace, the Holy Father John Paul II. The Servant of God, a Man who lived an intense life of prayer, a tireless Pastor of the universal Church and courageous Witness of the Gospel of Christ, entrusting himself completely to God's will and to the Virgin Mary, confirmed in his vast and rich Magisterium the centrality of the Mystery of the Eucharist in the life of the Church. He indicated to every baptized person each one's primary commitment to holiness, defined as the "high standard of ordinary Christian living." At the moment of his death with the formal request to begin the Cause for Beatification and Canonization of the Servant of God, in making it known to the Ecclesial Community, we invite each and every one of the faithful to communicate with us directly or through the Diocesan Tribunal of the Vicariate of Rome any information that could be favorable to the fame of holiness of the aforementioned Servant of God.

The diocesan inquiry closed on April 2, 2007, which was the second anniversary of the death of Pope John Paul II. The cause was now taken up by the Vatican Congregation for the Causes of the Saints, which launched its own investigation. This always includes the writing of the *Positio*, which is a critical biography of the Servant of God and a summary of the testimonies collected during the diocesan inquiry. The *Positio* argues that the candidate for beatification lived a heroic and virtuous life.

The *Positio* was submitted to the Vatican Congregation for the Causes of the Saints in 2008. The key figure in coordinating the writing of the *Positio* and advocating for the beatification of

John Paul II was Msgr. Slawomir Oder, who is the postulator for John Paul's cause. Since September 2001, he has served as judicial vicar of the court of appeal for the Diocese of Rome.

Even while the life of John Paul II was being examined by the Vatican in 2008-9, claims of possible miracles through his intercession began to surface. For example, Cardinal Stanislaus Dziwisz, the Archbishop of Krakow, Poland, and longtime personal secretary of Pope John Paul II, shared with the media a possible miracle worked through the intercession of the Servant of God. He related on April 2, 2009, the fourth anniversary of John Paul II's death, the case of a 9-year-old Polish boy from Gdansk. The boy, who was suffering from kidney cancer and completely unable to walk, had visited with his parents the tomb of the Servant of God in St. Peter's Basilica. Upon leaving the basilica, the boy reportedly told his parents, "I want to walk." He then began walking normally.

Returning to the progress of John Paul II's cause, the theological consultors in the Congregation for the Causes of the Saints voted to approve the *Positio* on June 30, 2009. On November 16, 2009, the Cardinals and Bishops of the Congregation then voted unanimously that Pope John Paul II had lived a life of virtue to a heroic degree, based on the *Positio*. Finally, the Congregation submitted the Decree on Heroic Virtues of the Servant of God John Paul II to Pope Benedict XVI, who then signed it on December 19, 2009. Thus, John Paul II can now be called a Venerable Servant of God, since he practiced the virtues to a heroic degree, living a truly holy life that all the faithful are encouraged to emulate.

EXAMPLES OF JOHN PAUL II'S HOLY LIFE

On the basis of his work on John Paul II's cause, Msgr. Oder wrote the book, *Why He Is a Saint — The Life and Faith of Pope John Paul II and the Case for Canonization*. In his book, he recounts John Paul's life, accomplishments, and sanctity through the eyewitness accounts of those who knew him best.

Monsignor Oder emphasizes in particular Karol Wojtyla's (John Paul II's) extraordinary devotion to the Eucharist, which included long periods of time adoring Jesus in the Most Blessed Sacrament:

> [I]t was not uncommon for Wojtyla to spend part of the night in prayer before the altar, stretched out on the floor, his arms spread in the sign of the cross. As one eyewitness put it, "The presence of Christ in the tabernacle allowed him to have a very personal relationship with Him: not merely to speak to Christ, but actually converse with Him" (Msgr. Oder, *Why He Is a Saint*. New York, N.Y.,: Rizzoli, 2010, p. 35).

Along with his love of the Eucharist, Wojtyla was sustained by a deep prayer life that had a mystical quality to it. As one witness points out in Msgr. Oder's book:

> "I am convinced that John Paul was favored by a special grace of prayer, which allowed him to penetrate the mysteries of faith in a way that was not accessible to ordinary people," a person close to him declared. "So many times I saw his face after contemplation and adoration, visibly changed and happy. During prayer, he seemed to be in continual conversation with God, like Moses who spoke with God face to face. During prayer, Wojtyla did not notice anything that happened around him. He seemed to lose all sense of time, to the extent that his secretary at a certain point would have to shake him out of this extraordinary state of concentration because other commitments awaited him" (Msgr. Oder, *Why He Is a Saint*, p. 151).

Interestingly, these examples of the importance of the Eucharist and mystical prayer in the life of John Paul II are also highlighted by the Marian Fathers in their book, *The Making of the Pope of the Millennium: Kalendarium of the Life of Karol Wojtyla*. For example, shortly after Fr. Karol Wojtyla is nominated an auxiliary bishop of the Archdiocese of Krakow in 1958, we find him in a convent chapel conversing for many

hours with the Lord before the Blessed Sacrament. The entry
in the *Kalendarium* is dated August 12, 1958, and reads:

> [O]ne day towards the evening, an unknown man
> dressed as a priest, hence a priest, knocked at the gate
> of the house of the sisters' convent. "Could I enter
> your chapel to pray?" He was led into the chapel and
> left alone. When he did not emerge for some time,
> they looked in on him. He lay prostrate on the ground.
> The sister stepped back, filled with respect. "He must
> have an important matter, perhaps he's a penitent."
> After another while, the sister looked into the chapel
> again. The priest still lay prostate. But the hour was late.
> The sister went up to him and shyly asked: "Perhaps,
> Father, would be so kind as to come to supper?" — The
> stranger responded: "My train to Krakow isn't until
> after midnight. Allow me to stay here. I have much to
> discuss with the Lord. Do not disturb me." ... Today
> this man is called John Paul II, the Pope (Fr. Jan Zieja,
> "Pewien czlowiek," Weiz, no. 11, November 1978) (Fr.
> Adam Boniecki, MIC, Author; Fr. Kazimierz Chwalek,
> MIC, English-Language Editor, *The Making of the Pope
> of the Millennium*. Stockbridge, Mass.: Marian Press,
> 2000, pp. 171-172).

Pope John Paul II was also known for his great love and
pastoral care for others, especially those in families. He made
people feel special by giving them his undivided attention. This
love and mercy for others flowed seamlessly from his love of
the Lord.

Consider this testimony by Paulette Kardos, a Marian
Helper, which involves both her family and more personal
encounters with the late Holy Father. She shared it in the
Summer 2005 issue of *Marian Helper* magazine.

> I will never forget Jan. 13, 2002, the feast of the Baptism
> of the Lord. On that day, Pope John Paul II baptized
> my granddaughter Anya Francesca in the Sistine Chapel.

Among all the infants, she was the only American to be baptized by the Holy Father. What a privilege!

I was totally overwhelmed with emotion. How blessed I was to have the Vicar of Christ bring my grandchild into the Church! It was such a blessing for my entire family. Seventeen of my family members were present, and Maren, one of my other granddaughters, was asked to bring up the gifts at the offertory.

When Maren presented the Holy Father with the ciborium filled with hosts, he could tell she was nervous. So, he took her head in his hands and kissed her. Maren came back and told us, "I was a little scared."

Then, around Easter in 2003, I had the privilege of an audience with the Holy Father and brought photos of my granddaughter Anya. I showed him the photos and said, "Holy Father, this is the baby that you baptized. And we all love you."

Another special moment came earlier, in 2001. I was asked to serve as lector at the Holy Father's daily Mass in his private chapel. I had to walk right up past the Holy Father to reach the lectern. As I read, I noticed that the Pope was listening intently to every word!

As I look back, I treasure the fact that I was presented to the Holy Father many times. One time, all I could say was, "Holy Father, Holy Father, thank you." I couldn't get anything else out.

At each audience, when I knelt before the Holy Father, he made me feel special.

All of my personal encounters with Pope John Paul II filled my heart with love for Christ, Our Lady, and the Church. The Holy Father gave me so much.

May these testimonies to the holiness of John Paul II inspire us all to cry from the heart, *"Magnus!"* and *"Santo subito!"* Most importantly, may they inspire us to emulate his holy life, especially his love of the Lord and heart of concern for others.

Blessed John Paul II, John Paul the Great, pray for us.

CHAPTER 2
THE MIRACLE

Pope John Paul II suffered from the debilitating effects of Parkinson's disease in his last years, as he struggled with slurred speech, trembling in his hands, and stooped posture. He even had to put up with the indignity of being transported on a platform. According to papal biographer George Weigel in *Witness to Hope: The Biography of Pope John Paul II*, John Paul was first diagnosed with the disease in 1994. The Vatican would go public with the diagnosis several years later.

Especially in the closing weeks of his life, John Paul was rendered almost completely silent in his suffering from the disease. Who can forget, for example, how he was unable to speak and could only bless the crowd in St. Peter's Square on his last Easter Sunday in 2005?

What makes John Paul II's struggles with advanced Parkinson's — which was a contributing factor in his death — so poignant is the nature of the miracle recognized for his beatification. The miracle involved a French nun who says she was instantly healed of Parkinson's through his intercession two months to the day after his death. As we consider his legacy as the Great Mercy Pope, the crowning irony of this is that he was able to relieve someone else of Parkinson's through his intercession while he himself struggled with the cross of the disease to the end.

The nun involved is Sr. Marie Simon-Pierre Normand of the Congregation of the Little Sisters of Catholic Motherhood. She works as a nurse in a Paris maternity clinic and had been diagnosed with Parkinson's in June 2001 at the age of only 40. She reports of the disease that it affected the whole left side of her body, creating great difficulty for her, as she was left-handed. After three years, she said that the initial phase of the disease, slow but progressive, was followed by an aggravation of the symptoms, which included an increase of the trembling, more rigidity, pain, and insomnia.

Tellingly, she said that watching Pope John Paul II deteriorate from the effects of Parkinson's disease, "I saw myself in the years to come" (Catholic News Service report, March 30, 2007).

When John Paul II passed to the Lord on April 2, 2005, Sr. Simon-Pierre reported that her condition began to worsen week by week. She was unable to write and if she attempted it, what she wrote was unintelligible. She could drive only for short trips because her left leg would stiffen and her rigidity would impede her driving. Further, to do her work at the maternity clinic, it took more time than usual. She says that she was exhausted. (This comes from her testimony, written in 2006, which formed part of John Paul II's cause for beatification.)

Members of Sr. Simon-Pierre's congregation began to pray for her healing from the disease through the intercession of John Paul II, following the Vatican dispensing with the five-year waiting period for John Paul II's cause on May 13, 2005.

SISTER SIMON-PIERRE'S TESTIMONY

She reports further in her testimony of 2006 about her miraculous healing:

On June 1, I was finished; I struggled to stand and to walk. On June 2 in the afternoon, I went to find my superior to ask her if I could leave my work. She encouraged me to endure a bit longer until my return from Lourdes in August, and she added: "John Paul II has not yet said his last word" (John Paul II was surely there, in that meeting, which passed in serenity and peace). Then, Mother Superior gave me a pen and told me to write: "John Paul II." It was 5 o'clock in the afternoon. With effort, I wrote: "John Paul II." We remained in silence before the illegible letters, then the day continued as usual.

At the end of the evening prayer, at 9 o'clock at night, I went to my office before going to my room. I felt the need to pick up the pen and to write, just as if someone within me was saying: "Pick up the pen and write." It was between 9:30 and 9:40 at night. To my great surprise, I saw that the writing was clearly legible. Not understanding anything, I went to bed. Two months exactly had gone by since John Paul II's departure to the House of the Father. I woke up at 4:30 a.m., surprised that I was able to sleep, and I leapt out of bed: My body was no longer insensitive, rigid, and interiorly I was not the same.

Then, I felt an interior call and the strong impulse to go to pray before the Most Blessed Sacrament. I went down to the Oratory and prayed before the Most Blessed Sacrament. I felt a profound peace and a sensation of wellbeing; too great an experience, a mystery difficult to explain with words.

Later, before the Most Blessed Sacrament, I meditated on John Paul II's Mysteries of Light. At 6 o'clock in the morning, I went out to meet with the sisters in the chapel for a time of prayer, which was followed by the Eucharistic celebration.

I had to walk some 50 meters, and at that very moment I realized that, as I walked, my left arm was moving, it was not immobile next to my body. I also felt a physical lightness and agility that I had not felt for a long time.

During the Eucharistic celebration, I was full of joy and peace; it was June 3, the feast of the Sacred Heart of Jesus. Coming out from Holy Mass, I was sure of my cure; my hand did not shake any more. I went to write again, and at midday I stopped taking my medicines.

On June 7, as planned, I went to my neurologist, my doctor for the past four years. He was also surprised to see the disappearance of all the symptoms of the disease, despite my having interrupted the treatment five days earlier. The next day, the Superior General entrusted an act of thanksgiving to all our communities, and the entire congregation began a thanksgiving novena to John Paul II (testimony written in 2006 for John Paul II's cause for beatification).

In this account of Sr. Simon-Pierre's healing, there's an intriguing connection with the exact time of John Paul II's death, 9:37 p.m. on April 2, 2005, and the time two months later on June 2 "between 9:30 and 9:40 at night" when Sister says someone within her urged her to try again to write John Paul's name. Was this someone within her John Paul II, coming to her aid, perhaps two months to the minute after his death? After all, she notes that this time her writing of his name, to her "great surprise," was "clearly legible."

APPROVAL FOR THE MIRACLE

The diocesan inquiry on a miracle for the Servant of God John Paul II began in 2006. It included submission of the testimony of Sr. Simon-Pierre's possible miraculous healing through the intercession of John Paul II. Such a miracle is required for beatification, along with proof that the candidate lived a virtuous life to a heroic degree. (This was covered in our first chapter.)

In the case of the miracle for the cause, it is investigated by both medical experts and theological consultants. Theological consultants weigh the evidence for determining that the alleged miracle occurred through the intercession of the candidate for beatification.

Usually, a possible miracle involves a physical healing, such as was the case with Sr. Simon-Pierre. This is where the medical investigators weigh in with their expertise to determine whether the healing is inexplicable on scientific and medical grounds.

In the case of the healing of Sr. Simon-Pierre, the medical consultants voted their approval on October 21, 2010. The theological consultants followed suit with their approval on December 14, 2010. The miracle was then approved by the Cardinals and Bishops of the Congregation for the Causes of the Saints on January 11, 2011. Finally, approval by Pope Benedict XVI and publication of the Decree on the Miracle came on January 14, 2011.

Now the way was cleared by the Vatican to schedule the date for the Venerable Servant of God's beatification.

'I SAW GOD'S GLORY'

Following the beatification, which we will cover in our next chapter, Sr. Simon-Pierre has committed herself to sharing her testimony involving the miracle. For instance, at the second World Apostolic Congress on Mercy celebrated in Poland on October 1-5, 2011, she gave her testimony in Wadowice, the hometown of John Paul II.

On that occasion, she mentioned how "my congregation did pray for the mercy of my healing." She also said that she "saw God's glory" at the beatification of John Paul:

> Since May 14, 2005, [the day after the Pope dispensed with the five-year waiting period for John Paul II's cause to start] a certain verse from the Gospel of John has been deep inside me and has not left: "Did I not tell you that if you believe, you will see the glory of God?" (Jn 11: 40). I saw God's glory in St. Peter's Square on May 1, 2011, on the Sunday of Divine Mercy when John Paul II was declared Blessed. Six

years had just passed since I stopped my therapy. ... My congregation did pray for the mercy of my healing from Parkinson's disease, so that I could work and serve in my maternity clinic, as a nurse taking care of mothers and newborns. I was young then [in my 40s]. To take part in the Church's mission, arms, hands, eyes, and hearts are needed so that all families — all families regardless of their problems — can be told about the divine love of our Father. We hope that this healing miracle has made at least a small contribution to the beatification of Pope John Paul II ... . We deeply loved the Pope, seeing in him the Shepherd of God's Heart and the Pope of the Family.

For Sr. Simon-Pierre and the rest of us, Blessed John Paul II's merciful intercession for her and his faithfulness to the Lord during his struggles with Parkinson's stand as a testament to God's mercy and John Paul's heroic virtue. They inspire us to do likewise, interceding for those in need and bearing our own crosses in fidelity to our merciful Savior's will for our lives. Such a testament to God's mercy can inspire us to see the glory of God shining through our lives, as it did for Sr. Simon-Pierre at the beatification.

O merciful Savior, You told Martha before raising her brother Lazarus from the dead, "Did I not tell you that if you believe, you will see the glory of God?" (Jn 11:40). Give us eyes of faith to see Your glory shining through our lives. Grant this prayer through the intercession of Your servant, Blessed John Paul II. Amen.

CHAPTER 3
BLESSED JOHN PAUL II

As the miracle for the Venerable Servant of God John Paul II's beatification was vetted by the Vatican in late 2010, the media speculated about the date for the beatification. Would it be as early as May 1, Divine Mercy Sunday, or would it be scheduled in October, perhaps around the anniversary of John Paul's election as Pope on October 16, or October 22, the anniversary of his papal inauguration?

The news came with surprising speed. On January 14, 2011, Pope Benedict XVI signed the decree recognizing the healing of Sr. Marie Simon-Pierre Normand from Parkinson's disease as a miracle through the intercession of John Paul II. On that same day, the Vatican announced that Pope Benedict XVI would beatify John Paul II on May 1, Divine Mercy Sunday, in St. Peter's Square.

Then on January 16, Pope Benedict said of the news:

> On May 1, I'll have the joy of beatifying Venerable Pope John Paul II, my beloved predecessor. The date that has been chosen is very significant: It will be the Second Sunday of Easter, which he himself entitled "Divine Mercy." ... Those who knew him, those who esteemed and loved him, cannot but rejoice with the Church for this event. We are happy!

This remarkable statement by Pope Benedict pinpoints Divine Mercy Sunday as a significant aspect of John Paul II's enduring legacy of Divine Mercy. Benedict points to the date as "very significant" because it will be the Second Sunday of Easter, which John Paul himself titled "Divine Mercy."

But there's more to the connection between John Paul II and Divine Mercy Sunday than his instituting of the feast, important as that was. Significantly, John Paul died on the vigil of the feast day after receiving *Viaticum*, his final Holy Communion — aware of the great graces promised to those who receive Holy Communion worthily on the feast day. Further, he beatified and canonized St. Faustina on Divine Mercy Sunday. Also, starting on Divine Mercy Sunday 1993, he began sharing with the world an annual Divine Mercy Sunday message — his last message was shared posthumously the day after his death in 2005. Thus, Divine Mercy Sunday is like the linchpin that holds together his legacy of mercy.

VATICAN TAKES NOTE OF SIGNIFICANCE

Tellingly, Jesuit Father Federico Lombardi, director of the Vatican press office, on January 14, 2011, said of the beatification being set for Divine Mercy Sunday:

[John Paul II's] life and his pontificate were characterized by the passion to make known to the world in which he lived — the world of our tragic history in the course of two millennia — the consoling and enthusiastic greatness of God's mercy. This is what the world needs. That is why we will have the joy of celebrating the solemn beatification on the day in which he himself wanted the whole Church to fix her gaze and prayer on this Divine Mercy.

Father Lombardi's remarks about John Paul II were made on an edition of Vatican Television's "Octava Dies."

Not only did the Vatican press office take note of the beatification and its significance but the preacher for Pope Benedict's 2011 Lenten retreat, Discalced Carmelite Fr. François-Marie Lethel, said in a March 17 interview published by *L'Osservatore Romano*:

After the Pope asked me to preach these spiritual exercises, I recollected myself in prayer and it became clear to me the direction I should give the meditations: a spiritual preparation for the beatification of John Paul II. [It] will take place on May 1, the Sunday of the octave of Easter, the feast of Divine Mercy, the beginning of the Marian month, and also the feast of St. Joseph the Worker. I am convinced that it is an event of enormous significance for the Church and for the world. [It] calls for a profound spiritual preparation on the part of the whole people of God, and in an exemplary manner on the part of the Holy Father and his closest collaborators. John Paul II's beatification is like the crowning of his extraordinary pontificate precisely under the sign of sanctity.

These developments show officials in the Vatican following Pope Benedict's lead in recognizing the significance of the beatification and the date chosen for it.

DIVINE MERCY AS A SOURCE OF RENEWAL AND A GUIDING PHILOSOPHY OF LIFE

Even before the announcement about the beatification being scheduled for Divine Mercy Sunday, John Paul II's preeminent biographer George Weigel touted the late Pope's legacy of Divine Mercy in his new book *The End and the Beginning* (Doubleday), which is the sequel to his bestselling *Witness to Hope: The Biography of Pope John Paul II*. Published in 2010, his new book shows how John Paul's Divine Mercy legacy has included the renewal of devotional life in thousands of Catholic parishes worldwide and has given the Church a rationale or philosophy for living mercifully in the third millennium.

Let's consider first how Weigel assesses Divine Mercy as a major theme of what he calls John Paul's "evangelical" papacy:

The divine mercy, manifest in God the Father of mercies, was … an element of the Christian *kerygma*, or proclamation, that was of consequence [for Pope John Paul II and the universal Church] far beyond Krakow and Poland. To proclaim the compassion of the Father who welcomes home his prodigal children and restores them to the dignity they have squandered was to meet a universal need, after a century in which humanity had turned its creations upon itself and turned the world into a slaughterhouse in the process. That was why John Paul II, the evangelical pope, made divine mercy one of the focal points of his teaching: in the 1980 encyclical, *Dives in Misericordia* (*Rich in Mercy*); in lifting up the healing riches of sacramental confession and penitential practice in the 1984 post-synodal apostolic exhortation, *Reconciliatio et Paenitentia* (*Reconciliation and Penance*), in beatifying Sr. Faustyna in 1993 and making her the first saint of the new millennium in 2000; and by decreeing that the Octave of Easter should be celebrated throughout the Church as Divine Mercy Sunday. That the Divine Mercy devotion outlined by Saint Faustyna Kowalska became, during the pontificate of John Paul II, a means for the recovery of devotional life in Catholic parishes throughout the world suggested that John Paul II's pastoral intuitions about the imperative of the Church's preaching God's mercy at the turn into a new millennium were squarely on target (Weigel, *The End and the Beginning: Pope John Paul II — The Victory of Freedom, the Last Years, the Legacy*, p. 438).

In unpacking this quote from *The End and the Beginning*, it's helpful to notice the foundation Weigel lays for assessing John Paul's Divine Mercy legacy. First, the Divine Mercy message that Pope John Paul II proclaimed focused on revealing "God the Father of mercies" as an element of the Gospel message or "Christian *kerygma*." After all, Jesus' fundamental mission was and is restoring our relationship with the Father, who is "rich in mercy." So, as Pope, John Paul proclaimed "the compassion of the Father who welcomes home his prodigal children and restores them to the dignity they have squandered." John Paul II set forth this message in its most complete form in his 1980 encyclical, *Rich in Mercy*, which Weigel highlights as one of John Paul's mercy milestones.

Second, John Paul's proclamation of Divine Mercy "was of consequence" for the Church far beyond his native Poland precisely because it addressed "a universal human need" — our need for Divine Mercy in addressing the horrors of the 20th century that had "turned the world into a slaughterhouse." Weigel enumerates these horrors earlier as "the slaughters of World Wars I and II, the mass murders of the Gulag, the Holocaust, the Ukrainian terror famine, Mao's Great Leap Forward, and so on."

Along with these foundational points for understanding John Paul's emphasis on Divine Mercy, it's worth studying Weigel's final sentence in this quote. There, he astutely observes that Pope John Paul II was right on target to preach God's mercy at the turn of the millennium. The fruit of John Paul's "pastoral intuitions" is that the Divine Mercy devotion he promoted has led to "the recovery of devotional life in Catholic parishes throughout the world."

One thinks here, for instance, of the millions of Catholics who now pray the Chaplet of Divine Mercy every day at 3 p.m., the Hour of Great Mercy. Or the thousands of Divine Mercy prayer groups in parishes whose members perform works of mercy in their local communities.

Now let's turn to another quote from *The End and the Beginning*. It's particularly interesting because Weigel shows how Pope John Paul II connected two major themes of his papacy in his homily at the canonization of St. Faustina on April 30, 2000: "the Law of the Gift" and the call to live mercifully, inspired by God the Father of mercies. The exciting point is that understanding this connection can yield the beginnings of a philosophy of life to guide us in living mercifully in the third millennium.

Here's the quote (Note: Except for the summary from Vatican II, all quoted matter is from the canonization homily):

> John Paul concluded his homily by returning to two themes that had been prominent throughout his pontificate. He had spoken frequently about the Law

of the Gift — the law of self-giving — built into the human person; the Second Vatican Council's summary of this law, that "man can fully discover his true self only in a sincere giving of himself," had been one of the two most cited Vatican II texts in his magisterium. The Law of the Gift was not, however, easy to live. For "it is not easy to love with a deep love, which lies in the authentic gift of self. This love can only be learned by penetrating the mystery of God's love. Looking at him, being one with his fatherly heart, we are able to look with new eyes at our brothers and sisters, with an attitude of unselfishness and solidarity. All this is mercy!" And the embrace of that mercy was essential if the third millennium was to be spared the worst experiences of the second:

> It is this love which must inspire humanity today, if it is to face the crisis of the meaning of life, the challenges of the most diverse needs, and especially the duty to defend the dignity of every human person. Thus the message of Divine Mercy is also implicitly a message about the value of every human being. Each person is precious in God's eyes; Christ gave his life for each one; to everyone the Father gives his Spirit and offers intimacy (Weigel, *The End and the Beginning: Pope John Paul II — The Victory of Freedom, the Last Years, the Legacy*, pp. 229-230).

In reflecting on these words of Pope John Paul II, notice first how he honestly admits that "it is not easy to love with a deep love, which lies in an authentic gift of self." Sustaining such deep love in giving of ourselves to others just isn't possible because of our human limitations. This is precisely why we need to learn how to love deeply "by penetrating the mystery of God's love" and mercy.

How do we do that? By looking at the Father of mercies, whom Jesus has revealed, and by seeking to be one with His "fatherly heart." Only then are we empowered "to look with new eyes at our brothers and sisters, with an attitude of unselfishness and solidarity." Then, God's mercy can flow through us to our brothers and sisters in need.

To gaze at the Father and learn mercy from Him, we recommend that you meditate on the figure of the merciful father in Jesus' parable of the Prodigal Son (see Lk 15:11-32), especially in his relationship with his two sons. This is the central Scripture in John Paul II's encyclical *Rich in Mercy*.

But before you do that, let's return to the words of John Paul II to draw out a significant implication that can guide us in living the message of Divine Mercy and even aid our meditation on the parable. Namely, when we look at our brothers and sisters through the eyes of God the Father, we discover that His mercy excludes no one. It seeks to embrace, for example, not only the wayward prodigal but the older, judgmental brother in the parable. As John Paul II put it, "Thus the message of divine mercy is ... a message about the value of every human being. Each person is precious in God's eyes; Christ gave his life for each one; to everyone the Father gives his Spirit and offers intimacy."

This merciful outlook can become our guiding philosophy of life. It means we should strive to value and love each person in our lives, looking at the person through the eyes of the Father of mercies and realizing how precious he is.

Weigel's astute analysis of John Paul II's embrace of Divine Mercy as a philosophy of life and a source of renewal showed the world, as the beatification approached, that God's mercy was key to understanding John Paul and his papacy.

CELEBRATING THE NEW BLESSED, HIS LIFE, AND HIS LEGACY

The celebration of John Paul II's beatification actually began on Saturday, April 30, with the vigil at the Circus Maximus. The ancient chariot-racing stadium created a type of World-Youth-Day atmosphere for the celebration. Scenes from his life and travels and video clips from his talks were shown on huge screens. Music from contemporary Christian groups to choral and symphonic productions serenaded the audience of an estimated 200,000 participants. Everyone joined in praying the Rosary, which created a nostalgic longing for him, since he was known as Mary's Pope and introduced the Luminous Mysteries.

"Some of his words — scenes from the past — moved many, including me, to tears. Many times, both the flood of memories and hearing his unique and powerful voice from the younger days of his pontificate produced chills in my body," said the Very Rev. Fr. Kazimierz Chwalek, MIC, the Marians' provincial superior in the United States and Argentina, who attended the beatification and wrote the Foreword to this book.

Along with the powerful music, words, and images of John Paul II, key highlights involved the personal witnesses given by those who knew him well. The three main witnesses were: Joaquín Navarro-Valls, who was John Paul II's spokesman for 21 years; Sr. Marie Simon-Pierre Normand, who received the miracle cure from Parkinson's through John Paul's intercession; and Cardinal Stanislaus Dziwisz, Archbishop of Krakow and John Paul II's longtime personal secretary.

Father Chwalek reported on these witnesses.

Joaquín Navarro-Valls explained that to understand John Paul II, one must understand Divine Mercy, because he lived it and witnessed to it. He said, "To see him pray was to see a person who was in conversation with God."

Sister Simon-Pierre, spoke very candidly about her relationship with John Paul II, especially as he was her inspiration and model of how to live with Parkinson's disease. She also said that the sisters in her community prayed for her healing.

Cardinal Dziwisz spoke of the two loves of John Paul II, "God and people, and in particular the young. He loved people, and all felt loved by him." Young people in the crowd of 200,000 responded to the Cardinal's remarks with loud cheers.

As the big day arrived on May 1, hundreds of thousands began streaming toward the Vatican. By early morning, St. Peter's Square was full and the crowd could be seen filling up the Via della Conciliazione, the boulevard leading up to the square.

By the time the ceremony started, there was a crowd of an estimated 1.5 million pilgrims with many in the piazzas and streets viewing the festivities on video screens. In fact, it was the largest crowd Rome had seen since John Paul II's funeral in 2005.

There are two other interesting facts about the beatification worthy of mention. First, according to the Vatican, it was the largest crowd ever for a beatification. Also, it was the first time in 10 centuries that a Pope had beatified his immediate predecessor.

Before the beatification liturgy started, the Divine Mercy Chaplet was chanted in five languages with unique melodies — all prayed before a large image of The Divine Mercy displayed at the main outdoor altar. "This was the first time the Divine Mercy Chaplet was prayed by such a huge crowd in St. Peter's Square, along with the reading of quotes from the *Diary of St. Maria Faustina Kowalska*," said Fr. Chwalek.

The big moment on the big day came when Pope Benedict XVI read the formula of beatification for John Paul II:

> We grant that the Venerable Servant of God John Paul II, Pope, henceforth be called Blessed and that his feast may be celebrated in the places and according to the regulations established by law, every year on October 22.

At that moment, a huge round of applause rose up from St. Peter's Square, passing along the Via della Conciliazione and side streets to the Circus Maximus — where thousands followed the celebration on video screens. People raised banners in the air, and lifted their hands in celebration as they applauded. The applause lasted for several minutes.

A smiling portrait of Pope John Paul II, from a 1995 photograph, was uncovered at that moment on a large banner that hung from the main loggia of St. Peter's Basilica. The pilgrims, many from Poland, were unable to hold back their tears.

As set forth in the formula of beatification, Blessed John Paul II was assigned October 22 — the date of his papal inauguration — as his feast day.

Sister Simon-Pierre, whose inexplicable healing from Parkinson's disease made it possible to conclude the beatification process — along with Sr. Tobiana, the Polish nun who assisted John Paul II's physician — carried in procession a relic of the newly Blessed John Paul II, a cruet of his blood (Zenit News Service, May 1, 2011).

The blood was taken from Pope John Paul II at Gemelli Hospital in case a blood transfusion was needed in his final days.

HIGHLIGHTS OF POPE BENEDICT'S HOMILY

In his homily to mark the occasion, Pope Benedict opened with these words:

Six years ago we gathered in this Square to celebrate the funeral of Pope John Paul II. Our grief at his loss was deep, but even greater was our sense of an immense grace which embraced Rome and the whole world: a grace which was in some way the fruit of my beloved predecessor's entire life, and especially of his witness in suffering. Even then we perceived the fragrance of his sanctity, and in any number of ways God's People showed their veneration for him. For this reason, with all due respect for the Church's canonical norms, I wanted his cause of beatification to move forward with reasonable haste. And now the longed-for day has come; it came quickly because this is what was pleasing to the Lord: John Paul is blessed! ...

Today is the Second Sunday of Easter, which Blessed John Paul II entitled Divine Mercy Sunday. The date was chosen for today's celebration because, in God's providence, my predecessor died on the vigil of this feast (see Appendixes, page 281 for the complete text of the homily).

Notice how the Holy Father, as he had in commenting on the date of the beatification, highlights the significance of it being the Second Sunday of Easter, which Pope John Paul II titled Divine Mercy Sunday. He further remarks that the date was chosen because "in God's providence my predecessor died on the vigil of this feast." These words of Pope Benedict helped to confirm the Great Mercy Pope's enduring legacy.

In his homily, Pope Benedict focused on John Paul II's deep devotion to the Blessed Virgin Mary, which was informed by his participation in the Second Vatican Council:

> Karol Wojtyla took part in the Second Vatican Council, first as an auxiliary Bishop and then as Archbishop of Krakow. He was fully aware that the Council's decision to devote the last chapter of its Constitution on the Church to Mary meant that the Mother of the Redeemer is held up as an image and model of holiness for every Christian and for the entire Church. This was the theological vision which Blessed John Paul II discovered as a young man and subsequently maintained and deepened throughout his life. A vision which is expressed in the scriptural image of the crucified Christ with Mary, His Mother, at His side. This icon from the Gospel of John (19:25-27) as taken up in the Episcopal and later the papal coat-of-arms of Karyol Wojtyla: a golden cross with the letter "M" on the lower right and the motto "*Totus tuus,*" drawn from the well-known words of St. Louis Marie Grignion de Montfort in which Karol Wojtyla found a guiding light for his life: "*Totus tuus ego sum et omnia mea tua sunt. Accipio te in mea omnia. Praebe mihi cou tuum, Maria* — I belong entirely to you , and all that I have is yours. I take you for my all. O Mary, give me your heart" (*Treatise on True Devotion to the Blessed Virgin,* 266).

It's interesting to note here how Pope Benedict, as Cardinal Joseph Ratzinger, connected John Paul II's devotion to Mary to that of Divine Mercy on an earlier occasion. The occasion was John Paul's funeral Mass at which then-Cardinal Ratzinger presided. In his homily on that occasion, he said:

Divine Mercy: the Holy Father found the purest reflection of God's mercy in the Mother of God. He, who at an early age had lost his own mother, loved his divine mother all the more. He heard the words of the crucified Lord as addressed personally to him: "Behold, your Mother." And so he did as the beloved disciple did: "He took her into his own home" (Jn 19:27) — *Totus tuus.* And from the mother he learned to conform himself to Christ.

Later in his homily, Pope Benedict singled out the enormous contributions Pope John Paul II made to the Church and the world during his reign, including leading the Church into the third millennium and passing on the patrimony of the Second Vatican Council. Indeed, Benedict described John Paul II as having "the strength of a titan" in opening wide the systems of the world to Christ:

In his Testament, the new Blessed wrote: "When, on October 16, 1978, the Conclave of Cardinals chose John Paul II, the Primate of Poland, Cardinal Stefan Wyszynski, said to me: 'The task of the new Pope will be to lead the Church into the Third Millennium.'" And the Pope added: "I would like once again to express my gratitude to the Holy Spirit for the great gift of the Second Vatican Council, to which, together with the whole Church — and especially with the whole episcopate — I feel indebted. I am convinced that it will long be granted to the new generations to draw from the treasures that this Council of the twentieth century has lavished upon us. As a Bishop who took part in the Council from the first to the last day, I desire to entrust this great patrimony to all who are and will be called in the future to put it into practice. For my part, I thank the Eternal Shepherd, who has

enabled me to serve this very great cause in the course
of all the years of my Pontificate." And what is this
"cause"? It is the same one that John Paul II
presented during his first solemn Mass in St. Peter's
Square in the unforgettable words: "Do not be afraid!
Open, open wide the doors to Christ!" What the newly-
elected Pope asked of everyone, he was himself the first
to do: society, culture, political, and economic systems
he opened up to Christ, turning back with the strength
of a titan — a strength which came to him from God
— a tide which appeared irreversible. By his witness of
faith, love, and apostolic courage, accompanied by great
human charisma, this exemplary son of Poland helped
believers throughout the world not to be afraid to be
called Christian, to belong to the Church, to speak of
the Gospel. In a word: he helped us not to fear the
truth, because truth is the guarantee of liberty. To put
it even more succinctly: he gave us the strength to
believe in Christ, because Christ is *Redemptor
hominis*, the Redeemer of man. This was the theme
of his first encyclical, and the thread which runs
though all the others.

Toward the end of his homily, the Holy Father became
more personal in describing his longstanding relationship with
Pope John Paul II as one of his closest collaborators, as well as
highlighting his predecessor's eloquent "witness in suffering":

> Finally, on a more personal note, I would like to thank
> God for the gift of having worked for many years with
> Blessed Pope John Paul II. I had known him earlier
> and had esteemed him, but for twenty-three years,
> beginning in 1982 after he called me to Rome to be
> Prefect of the Congregation for the Doctrine of the
> Faith, I was at his side and came to revere him all the
> more. My own service was sustained by his spiritual
> depth and by the richness of his insights. His example
> of prayer continually impressed and edified me: he

remained deeply united to God even amid the many demands of his ministry. Then too, there was his witness in suffering: the Lord gradually stripped him of everything, yet he remained ever a "rock," as Christ desired. His profound humility, grounded in close union with Christ, enabled him to continue to lead the Church and to give to the world a message which became all the more eloquent as his physical strength declined. In this way he lived out in an extraordinary way the vocation of every priest and bishop to become completely one with Jesus, whom he daily receives and offers in the Church.

'ICONS OF DIVINE MERCY'

In his *Regina Caeli* message after the beatification liturgy, Pope Benedict gave the pilgrims in attendance and all of the faithful a charge inspired by the newly Blessed John Paul II. He said, "May [Blessed John Paul II's] example of firm faith in Christ, the Redeemer of Man, inspire us to live fully the new life which we celebrate at Easter, to be icons of Divine Mercy, and to work for a world in which the dignity and rights of every man, woman, and child are respected and promoted. Trusting in his prayers, I cordially invoke upon you and your families the peace of the Risen Savior!"

Observe how Pope Benedict encourages us to take to heart the example of John Paul's "firm faith" in Christ the Redeemer, so it would inspire us to "live fully" the new life we receive at Easter. This new life enables us to become images or icons of Divine Mercy — like the crucified and Risen Savior depicted in the Image of The Divine Mercy — radiating mercy to others in our needy world. He speaks of it as a call "to work for a world in which the dignity and rights of every man, woman, and child are respected and promoted." This commitment to protect the dignity of every person flows from our resolute faith in Christ, the One who redeemed us and now gives us the grace to radiate His mercy to others.

Interestingly, we saw this connection between Divine Mercy and defending the dignity of every human highlighted earlier in Pope John Paul II's homily for St. Faustina's canonization on April 30, 2000 — in our excerpt from papal biographer George Weigel in *The End and the Beginning*. It's worth repeating here to underscore the common thread uniting Blessed John Paul II's beatification with the canonization of St. Faustina:

> It is this love which must inspire humanity today, if it is to face the crisis of the meaning of life, the challenges of the most diverse needs, and especially the duty to defend the dignity of every human person. Thus the message of Divine Mercy is also implicitly a message about the value of every human being. Each person is precious in God's eyes; Christ gave his life for each one; to everyone the Father gives his Spirit and offers intimacy.

Blessed John Paul II, pray for us that we may be given the grace to be icons of Divine Mercy in our needy world. Then, as we radiate the Lord's mercy to others, may we seek to protect and defend the dignity of every human person. May we cherish each person as precious in the eyes of God our Father, "who is rich in mercy" (Eph 2:4). May we always remember that Christ gave His Life for each one. Amen.

PART II
TEACHER OF MERCY

Study the Great Mercy Pope's masterwork on Divine Mercy, his encyclical *Rich in Mercy*. Immerse yourself in his homilies and addresses on Divine Mercy. Also, discover the thread of Divine Mercy in many of his writings other than *Rich in Mercy*.

CHAPTER I
THE ENCYCLICAL RICH IN MERCY

The opening line of John Paul II's second encyclical sets the tone and summarizes the document:

It is God, who is "rich in mercy" (Eph 2:4) whom Jesus Christ has revealed to us as Father.

The encyclical concludes that the mission of Christ is also the mission of His Church.

The reason for her existence is, in fact, to reveal God, the Father who allows Himself to be "seen" in Christ (see Jn 14:9).

This encyclical is a teaching and proclamation on the nature of Divine Mercy that builds up to an exhortation to pray for mercy for the whole world and concludes with John Paul II leading us in a strong prayer for mercy. This special prayer of the Pope will be discussed in chapter four of Part III.

The origins of the knowledge and concern of Pope John Paul II for the message of Divine Mercy came from his personal involvement with the message of Divine Mercy revealed to Sister Faustina Kowalska (1905-1938) in his home archdiocese of Krakow, Poland. During the 1930s, Sister Faustina received revelations from our Lord telling her of His infinite mercy for mankind. He asked that His mercy be made known to everyone now, "while it still is the time for mercy." As Archbishop of Krakow, then Karol Wojtyla introduced Sister Faustina's cause for canonization. He was instrumental in conscripting the leading Polish theologian, the Rev. Professor Ignacy Rózycki, to prepare a definitive study of her writings and of the heroic virtues of her life. After 10 years of exhaustive study, Professor Rózycki submitted a highly favorable document of support for the cause of her canonization.

George Weigel in his *Witness to Hope*, the biography of Pope John Paul II, recorded a remarkable statement of the Holy Father, associating Sr. Faustina and his encyclical on Divine Mercy:

As Archbishop of Krakow, Wojtyla had defended Sister Faustina when her orthodoxy was being posthumously questioned in Rome, due in large part to a faulty Italian translation of her diary, and had promoted the cause of her beatification. John Paul II, who said that he felt spiritually "very near" to Sister Faustina, had been "thinking about her for a long time" when he began *Dives in Misericordia*.

A TRILOGY OF ENCYCLICALS:

Three encyclicals of Pope John Paul II form a trilogy, as he himself expressed in the third letter. The first letter, *Redeemer of Man*, points to Jesus Christ as "the center of history and the universe" who reveals to each and every person his identity and dignity. He further points out that the Church is the link and the way to Christ for every person in every circumstance of life. The second letter of the trilogy is *Rich in Mercy*, in which John Paul II points to the Father as "rich in mercy." The Father's mercy is revealed in Christ Jesus, Mercy Incarnate, the only hope for peace in the world. In the third letter of the trilogy, *Lord and Giver of Life*, John Paul II shows that it is the Holy Spirit who converts us from our greatest sin, namely, the practical atheism of the world. At the same time, he shows that the Holy Spirit brings our souls to the cross to be washed in the blood of Jesus, so that we might receive His saving love and mercy and inherit eternal life.

This trilogy is a clear response to the greatest problems of our day. Sin is the issue of our day, and mercy is the answer.

SUMMARIES OF THE ENCYCLICAL ON DIVINE MERCY

Because of its importance, three kinds of summaries of the encyclical on Divine Mercy are presented here as aids to understanding the message:

An "Abstract" which gives the sequence of the topics and the flow of the main concepts;

A "Schematic Summary" which gathers the key points in sweeping statements that can be used to teach, preach, and be reminders of this message of mercy; and

A "Sense-line Summary" which stresses the main points of each section in short phrases, conveying the strength of the message.

✝ ABSTRACT

The theme of the encyclical letter *Dives in Misericordia* is Divine Mercy. Pope John Paul II develops the thesis that *to practice, proclaim, and pray for mercy is the mission of the Church and the whole world.* The letter is divided into eight chapters with fifteen subtopics.

In Chapter One, the Pope expands the biblical text John 14:9, "He who sees Me sees the Father," by discussing the revelation of mercy through Christ, the incarnation of mercy. He encourages us all to open our minds and hearts more widely to Christ.

"The Messianic Message" of Chapter Two describes "when Christ began to [minister] and to teach." The Messiah is a clear sign of God who is love. Through His lifestyle and through His actions, Jesus revealed that love is present in the world.

"The Old Testament" is the topic of Chapter Three. The concept of mercy and its history are developed. Mercy is contrasted with God's justice.

"The Parable of the Prodigal Son" is the topic of Chapter Four. It brings focus to the relationship between justice and love that is manifested as mercy. In this parable, love is transformed into mercy. A particular focus on human dignity is presented, as well as the faithfulness of a Father's love.

In "The Paschal Mystery," Chapter Five, mercy is revealed in the Cross and Resurrection. It emphasizes that love is present in the world and that this love is more powerful than any kind of evil. Believing in this love means believing in mercy. "Love more powerful than death, more powerful than sin" is expanded. A discussion of Mary, the Blessed Mother of Jesus and the "Mother of Mercy" concludes the chapter.

Chapter Six proclaims "Mercy ... from generation to generation" and discusses the need for mercy in our generation. There are sources of uneasiness and a lack of peace attributed to our times. The question, "Is justice enough?" is raised. The Pope calls for a deeper power of love, for justice is *not* enough.

"The Mercy of God in the Mission of the Church" stresses the Church's role to profess and proclaim the mercy of God, the most stupendous attribute of the Creator and Redeemer. "The Church seeks to put mercy into practice" for "blessed are the merciful, for they shall obtain mercy." True mercy is, so to speak, the most profound source of justice. Mercy is also the most perfect incarnation of "equality" between people. All people are invited to proclaim and introduce into life the mystery of mercy supremely revealed in Jesus Christ. "It is precisely in the name of this mystery that Christ teaches us to forgive always. ... he who forgives and he who is forgiven encounter one another at an essential point, namely, the dignity or essential value of the person ... ."

The encyclical letter ends with "The Prayer of the Church in Our Times." Prayer is needed to overcome modern man's lack of courage to utter the word "mercy." The Pope exhorts us to call upon the God who loves all people and desires every true good for each individual. He prays that the Love, which is in the Father, may once again be revealed at this stage of history. He concludes by pointing out that the very reason for the Church's existence is to reveal God, who is Love and Mercy Itself.

✝ SCHEMATIC SUMMARY OF *RICH IN MERCY*

The Papal Letter "Rich in Mercy" proclaims mercy as:
The revelation of the Father, who is rich in mercy.
The prophetic word for our times.
The power and mission of Christ and His Church.
The summary of the Gospel: "Blessed are the merciful, for they shall obtain mercy."
The parable of mercy: the Prodigal Son — the essence of mercy in the restored value of man.

The answer to the anxiety of "a lack of peace."
The summons to the Church and by the Church to practice,
preach, and plead for mercy.
The revelation of Jesus, Mercy Incarnate, centered in the
crucified and risen Jesus, and continued in the Heart of Mary.
The prayer for the presence of love, which is greater than evil,
sin, and death.
The plea for mercy for us and the whole world.

✝ A SENSE-LINE SUMMARY OF *RICH IN MERCY*

I. *He Who Sees Me Sees the Father*

Jesus has revealed God
who is rich in mercy
as the Father.

Christ crucified
is the center of all;
He reveals to us
the mercy
of the Father. (1)

God is visible
in and through Christ,
visible in His mercy.
Christ is mercy,
incarnate and personified.
Is mercy a threat?
No.
God is the Father of mercies
especially to the suffering.
This letter is a summons
TO the Church and
BY the Church
for mercy. (2)

II. *The Messianic Message*

When Christ began
to do [minister] and teach,
He proclaimed
liberty to the oppressed.
The words and actions of Jesus
make the Father present,
the Father who is love and mercy.
Jesus demanded from the people
the same love and mercy
as a condition of mercy:
"The merciful ... shall obtain mercy." (3)

III. *The Old Testament*

The Hebrew Bible
is a history of special experiences
of the mercy of the Lord.
Mercy is a special power of love
that prevails over the sin
and infidelity of the chosen people.
Mercy is the content of the
experience of intimacy
with their Lord.
Mercy is *Hesed*:
goodness, grace, love, fidelity.

Mercy is *Rahamim*:
love of a mother, tender, the heart's womb.
The Old Testament
encourages the suffering to appeal to mercy.
Mercy is more powerful
and more profound than justice.
Mercy is love vis-a-vis justice.
Mercy is involved in the mystery of creation
and in the mystery of election. (4)

IV. The Parable of the Prodigal Son

Mary's canticle brings Old Testament mercy
to the New Testament:
"mercy ... from generation to generation."
Zachariah's canticle remembers
God's covenant of mercy,
both *hesed* and *rahamim*.
The parable of the Prodigal Son
expresses the essence of Divine Mercy.
Each of us
in each age
is the prodigal.
The dignity of the son
in the father's house
is greater than his possessions
or their lack.
The son's turning point
is the awareness
of the loss of his dignity
as his father's son.
Love is transformed into mercy
as it goes beyond
the precise norm of justice. (5)

The father is faithful
to his fatherhood.
The son's humanity is saved.
Mercy has the interior form
of agape-love.
The son is restored
to value
and not humiliated.

Conversion
is the most concrete working of mercy
in the human world.

Mercy restores value,
promotes good,
draws good from evil,
causes rejoicing.
Mercy is the fundamental
content and power
of Christ's mission. (6)

V. The Paschal Mystery

The Father in Christ's Paschal Mystery
reveals the depth of love
and the greatness of man.
The Paschal Mystery
is a superabundance
of justice
that bears upon sin and
restores love.
It reveals mercy in its fullness.
The Cross is the final word
of Christ's messianic mission,
speaking unceasingly of God
the Father as merciful.
Believing in the crucified Son
is believing in love
present in the world.
Believing in the crucified Son
is believing in mercy.

The Cross is witness
to the strength of evil
in the world.
In Christ on the Cross
Justice is done
to sin and death
at the price
of sacrifice and death.

The Cross is
the radical revelation
of mercy.
The Resurrection perfects
the revelation of mercy and
foretells a new heaven.
In this our time,
love is revealed as mercy.
In the end,
mercy will be revealed as love.

The Church's program,
like Christ's mission is mercy.
With the Cross at the center,
Christ crucified is the Word
that does not pass away.
He is the one who stands at the door
and knocks. (7)
Our love of God
is an act of mercy
toward the incarnate Son of the Father.
"Blessed are the merciful,
for they shall obtain mercy"
is a synthesis
of the whole Good News.
By the Resurrection
Jesus experienced mercy —
the very love of the Father —
more powerful than death!
In the Paschal Mystery
Christ reveals Himself
as the inexhaustible source
of mercy —
He is the definitive incarnation
of mercy;
its living sign. (8)

In this age, too,
"His mercy is from generation to generation ..."
Mary, who obtained mercy
like no other
shares in revealing
God's mercy
by the sacrifice of her heart.
Mary experienced
the mystery of mercy
and also has the deepest knowledge
of mercy.
She knows its price.
She received into her heart
the mystery of mercy.
Mary is the Mother of Mercy.
What Jesus came to reveal,
her heart continues to reveal
as the merciful love
of a mother. (9)

VI. *Mercy ... from Generation to Generation*
Our generation, too,
is included
in His mercy.
This age has tremendous potential
but
there is a lack of peace and
a sense of powerlessness
in regard to the situation
in the world. (10)

There is increasing fear
of destruction
because of atomic stockpiles;
fear of oppression
because of materialism
and abuse of power.

There is a gigantic remorse
over inequity
between rich and poor nations.
This is why
the moral lack of peace
is destined to become
even more acute.
This lack of peace
reaches out for solutions.
This lack of peace
is stronger
than all emergency measures. (11)

Justice alone
is not enough!
The Church shares with the people
the desire for a just life.
Often programs that start
with the idea of justice
suffer in practice
from distortions.
The Church shares
in the lack of peace
caused by the decline
of fundamental values,
the crisis in truth,
desacralization of relationships
and the common good. (12)

VII. *The Mercy of God in the Mission of the Church*

In the face of the lack of peace,
the Church must witness
to mercy
by professing
and proclaiming it.

Mercy is
the greatest attribute of God

towards His people.
The Heart of Christ
is the center of the revelation
of the merciful love
of the Father.
The Church lives an authentic life
when she draws near
to the source, Christ's Heart,
and dispenses
and professes mercy.
Mercy is
the most stupendous attribute
of the Creator and Redeemer.
The sources
of the Savior's mercy are:
the Word of God;
Eucharist — love more powerful than death;
Reconciliation — love greater than sin.
God, who is love
cannot reveal Himself
other than as Mercy.
Mercy, like God,
is infinite —
infinite in readiness
and power to forgive.
Conversion —
consists in the discovery
of mercy and
a rediscovery of the Father. (13)

"Blessed are the merciful,
for they shall obtain mercy."
Man attains God's mercy
as he is merciful.
Mercy is
reciprocal and bilateral —
the one who gives

is also the beneficiary.
As man respects
the dignity of man,
Christ receives mercy
as done unto Himself.
Mercy is the most profound source of justice
and the most perfect incarnation
of the "equality" of justice.
Mercy makes
the world more human
because it introduces
forgiveness.
The Church must proclaim
and introduce mercy —
the source of forgiveness
from our wellspring, the Savior.
Forgiveness is for everyone —
for all time —
not a cancellation
of the requirement of justice,
not an indulgence
toward evil,
but the love necessary so that
man may affirm himself
as man —
as the father affirmed
the dignity
of his prodigal son. (14)

VIII. The Prayer of the Church in Our Times

The Church must proclaim
and practice mercy.
Yet,
in these critical times,
she cannot forget
the right and duty
to appeal for mercy —

especially when the world
moves away from mercy.
"Loud cries" for mercy
ought to be the cry
of the Church of our times.
Modern man is anxious
about the solution
to the terrible tensions
of our times, and lack of courage
to cry for mercy.
So all the more
the Church must cry:
"MERCY!"
Everything said in this encyclical
must be continually transformed
into an ardent prayer for mercy
for all of mankind,
even if the world deserves
another "flood,"
as in the time of Noah.

Let us appeal to God
through Christ,
mindful of the words of
Mary's Magnificat
which proclaims:
"Mercy ... from age to age;"
let us cry out
to the God of Mercy Himself
for this present generation!
Let us offer our cry
with Christ on the Cross:
"Father, forgive them."
Let us offer our cry
for the love of God
and for the love of man.

May the love of the Father
be revealed again
by the work of the Son
and the Holy Spirit.
May that love be shown
to be present
in the modern world
and to be more powerful
than evil, sin, and death.
We pray through the intercession of Mary
who does not cease to proclaim:
"Mercy ... from generation to generation." (15)

CHAPTER 2

HOMILIES AND ADDRESSES ON DIVINE MERCY

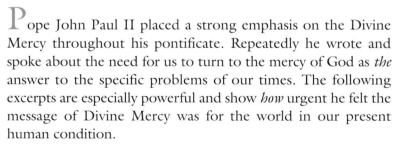

Pope John Paul II placed a strong emphasis on the Divine Mercy throughout his pontificate. Repeatedly he wrote and spoke about the need for us to turn to the mercy of God as *the* answer to the specific problems of our times. The following excerpts are especially powerful and show *how* urgent he felt the message of Divine Mercy was for the world in our present human condition.

On April 6, 1986, these are the words of the Holy Father, Pope John Paul II, to pilgrims in St. Peter's Square, Rome, at the noonday recitation of the *Regina Caeli*:

I direct now my affectionate greeting to all the groups of pilgrims present in St. Peter's Square; in particular,

I express a cordial welcome to the group of Roman supporters of The Divine Mercy, according to the message of Sister Faustina Kowalska, who celebrate today the feast of The Divine Mercy.

In a series of talks from 1981 to 1997, John Paul II spoke of the need to experience Divine Mercy in order to "be merciful just as your Father is merciful" (Lk. 6:36). For example, on November 22, 1981, Feast of Christ the King, Pope John Paul II made his first public visit outside of Rome following a lengthy recuperation from his bullet wounds, to the Shrine of Merciful Love in Collevalenza near Todi, Italy, where, within a few days, an international congress was to be held to reflect on the encyclical *Dives in Misericordia* (*Rich in Mercy*) one year after its publication. After celebrating the Holy Sacrifice of the Eucharist, he made a strong public declaration about the importance of the message of mercy:

> A year ago I published the encyclical *Dives in Misericordia*. This circumstance made me come to the Sanctuary of Merciful Love today. By my presence I wish to reconfirm, in a way, the message of that encyclical. I wish to read it again and deliver it again.
>
> Right from the beginning of my ministry in St. Peter's See in Rome, I considered this message my special task. Providence has assigned it to me in the present situation of man, the Church and the world. It could be said that precisely this situation assigned that message to me as my task before God."

Then in a series of addresses on *Divine Mercy Sunday* over the years he continued to call us to the experience of God's mercy:

✝ **APRIL 10, 1991:** Pope John Paul II spoke about Sister Faustina, showing his great respect for her, relating her to his encyclical *Rich in Mercy*, and emphasizing her role in bringing the message of mercy to the world:

The words of the encyclical on Divine Mercy (*Dives in Misericordia*) are particularly close to us. They recall the figure of the Servant of God, Sister Faustina Kowalska. This simple woman religious particularly brought the Easter message of the merciful Christ closer to Poland and the whole world ... .

And today? ... Is it perhaps not necessary to translate into the language of today's generations the words of the Gospel, 'Blessed are the merciful, for they shall obtain mercy' (Mt. 5:7).

(See the *Appendixes*, "The Easter Message of the Merciful Christ," April 10, 1991, for fuller text.)

✝ **APRIL 18, 1993:** Sister Faustina was beatified by Pope John Paul II in Rome on the Second Sunday of Easter, which our Lord had revealed to her as the "Feast of Mercy":

"I clearly feel that my mission does not end with death, but begins," Sister Faustina wrote in her diary. And it truly did! Her mission continues and is yielding astonishing fruit. It is truly marvelous how her devotion to the merciful Jesus is spreading in our contemporary world and gaining so many human hearts! This is doubtlessly a sign of the times — a sign of our 20th century. The balance of this century which is now ending, in addition to the advances which have often surpassed those of preceding eras, presents a deep restlessness and fear of the future. Where, if not in The Divine Mercy, can the world find refuge and the light of hope? Believers understand that perfectly.

Give thanks to the Lord, for He is good. Give thanks to the Lord, for He is merciful.

(See the *Appendixes* for a fuller text of the homily and the General Audience, April 19, 1993.)

✝ **APRIL 10, 1994:** Second Sunday of Easter, *Regina Caeli* Address:

> What is mercy if not the boundless love of God, who confronted with human sin, restrains the sentiment of severe justice and, allowing Himself to be moved by the wretchedness of His creatures, spurs Himself to the total gift of self, in the Son's cross? 'O happy fault ... which gained for us so great a Redeemer!' (Easter Proclamation).

> Who can say he is free from sin and does not need God's mercy? As people of this restless time of ours, wavering between the emptiness of self-exaltation and the humiliation of despair, *we have a greater need than ever for a regenerating experience of mercy* (April 10, 1994, emphasis added).

In this address, John Paul II made a strong appeal for an *experience of mercy* that is regenerating. This means we need a revival of God's life within us. Then in the following year, again on Mercy Sunday, he made another strong appeal to all people to *personally* experience the tender mercy of the Father.

(See the *Appendixes*, p. 211, for the full text.)

✝ **APRIL 23, 1995:** Pope John Paul II celebrated Divine Mercy Sunday in Holy Spirit Church, the Shrine of The Divine Mercy in Rome. (*L'Osservatore Romano*, English Edition, April 26, 1995). In his homily he challenged us to "trust in the Lord and be apostles of Divine Mercy":

> Sister Faustina Kowalska's mystical experiences were all focused on the mystery of the merciful Christ. ... [Her] mystical experience and her cry to the merciful Christ belong to the harsh context of our century's history. As people of this century which is now coming to an end, *we would like to thank the Lord for the message of Divine Mercy* (emphasis in the text). ... I would like to say to

all: trust in the Lord! Be apostles of Divine Mercy and, following the invitation and example of Blessed Faustina, take care of those who suffer in body and especially in spirit. Let each one feel the merciful love of the Lord who comforts and instills joy.

In his *Regina Caeli* address, he spoke of this Octave of Easter as one day and this Sunday as the day of thanksgiving for God's mercy, called the Sunday of Divine Mercy. He also stressed learning to forgive:

> Dear brothers and sisters, We must *personally experience* this [tender-hearted mercy of the Father] if, in turn, we want to be capable of mercy. *Let us learn to forgive!* The spiral of hatred and violence which stains with blood the path of so many individuals and nations can only be broken by the *miracle of forgiveness.* (italics in the text)

Here we have one of the great exhortations of the Mercy Pope calling us to personally experience the mercy of God that revives us and makes it possible for us to forgive.

(See the Appendixes, p. 219, for the full text.)

THE PERSONAL EXPERIENCE OF THE MERCY POPE

✝ **JUNE 7, 1997:** At the Shrine of The Divine Mercy in Lagiewniki, outside of Krakow, Poland, where the relics of Sister Faustina are kept, John Paul II addressed the Sisters of Our Lady of Mercy. It was a personal testimony of his own involvement with the message of Divine Mercy and a sweeping summary of both the message and devotion to The Divine Mercy.

The following excerpts highlight the Pope's personal experience of Divine Mercy:

Purpose of his pilgrimage: "I have come here 'to sing of the mercies of the Lord forever'" (Ps 89:2).

Urgency: "There is nothing that mankind needs more than Divine Mercy."

The Message: Divine Mercy is "that love which is benevolent, which is compassionate, which raises man above his weakness to the infinite heights of the holiness of God."

The Image: "Those who gaze on the image of the merciful Jesus hear, like Blessed Faustina, 'Fear nothing, I am with you.'"

Trust: "Those who sincerely say 'Jesus, I trust in You' will find comfort in all their anxieties and fears."

The Church: regards the message of Divine Mercy as "the light of hope" and "unceasingly implores mercy for all."

Commends: "the concerns of the Church and humanity to the merciful Christ."

Entrusts to The Divine Mercy: "once more [his] Petrine ministry, *'Jezu Ufam Tobie!'* [Jesus, I trust in You!]."

Personal Witness: "The message of Divine Mercy has always been near and dear to me."

Pontificate: "I took with me [the message of Divine Mercy] to the See of Peter and which in a sense *forms the image of this pontificate*" (emphasis added).

Divine Mercy Sunday: "I give thanks to divine Providence that I have been enabled to contribute personally to the fulfillment of Christ's will through the institution of the *Feast of Divine Mercy*" [in Poland in 1995] (emphasis added).

Chaplet of The Divine Mercy: "I pray unceasingly that God will 'have mercy on us and on the whole world' " (Chaplet).

Challenge to the Sisters of Our Lady of Mercy: "Accept the responsibility of your extraordinary vocation! The people of today need your *proclamation* of Divine Mercy, your *works* of mercy, and your *prayer* for mercy."

Prayer for all: "May The Divine Mercy transform hearts. ... We all need it so much as the third millennium approaches."

"I cordially bless all those devoted to The Divine Mercy." (See the Appendixes for the full text.)

✝ **APRIL 19, 1998:** Again, on Divine Mercy Sunday, the Mercy Pope calls us to "accept Divine Mercy with an open heart." (See the *Appendixes* for the full text.)

✝ **APRIL 11, 1999:** John Paul II called the Octave Day of Easter Divine Mercy Sunday. He encouraged all to be apostles of Divine Mercy like Blessed Faustina. He invited us to intensify our prayer for peace as a gift of mercy.

(See the *Appendixes* for the full text of "Silence the Arms and Return to Dialogue.")

Cardinal Fiorenzo Angelini celebrated Divine Mercy Sunday in St. Peter's Square with some 30,000 faithful from around the world.

✝ **APRIL 30, 2000:** Before some 250,000 pilgrims and the media of the world on Mercy Sunday, Pope John Paul II canonized Sr. Faustina Kowalska, "the great Apostle of Divine Mercy." In this way, he also "canonized" The Divine Mercy message and devotion, and further declared the Second Sunday of Easter as "Divine Mercy Sunday" for the universal Church:

> It is important that we *accept the whole message* that comes to us from the Word of God on this Second Sunday of Easter, which from now on throughout the Church will be called "Divine Mercy Sunday." (Divine Mercy Sunday, April 30, 2000, emphasis added)

In one of the most extraordinary homilies of his pontificate, Pope John Paul II repeated three times that Sr. Faustina is "God's gift to our time." She made the message of Divine Mercy the "bridge to the third millennium." He then said:

> By this act of canonization of Sr. Faustina, I intend today to pass this message on to the third millennium. I pass it on to all people, so that they will learn to know even better the true face of God and the true

face of their neighbor. In fact, love of God and love of one's neighbor are inseparable.

He exhorted all of us to join our voices to Mary, Mother of Mercy, and St. Faustina "who made her life a hymn to mercy" and "sing the mercies of the Lord forever" (Ps 89:2).

He further exhorted us to make her prayer of trustful abandonment our own and say with firm hope:

Jesus I trust in You!

(See the *Appendixes*, p. 233, for the full text.)

✞ **APRIL 22, 2001:** On **Divine Mercy Sunday**, John Paul II celebrated the first anniversary of the canonization of St. Faustina. (See *Appendixes*, p. 241, for the text.)

✞ **APRIL 7, 2002: Divine Mercy Sunday, Day of Prayer for Peace in Middle East.** Vatican City, April 4, 2002 (VIS) — Made public this afternoon was Pope John Paul II's Letter to Cardinal Angelo Sodano, Secretary of State, in which he asks the *entire Church to dedicate Sunday, April 7, Divine Mercy Sunday,* to prayers for peace in the Middle East. Following is the text of that Letter:

> The dramatic situation in the Holy Land induces me to once again urgently appeal to the entire Church, asking all believers to intensify their prayers for those populations now being lacerated by forms of unheard of violence. Precisely in this period, in which the hearts of Christians turn towards the places where the Lord Jesus suffered so much, died and arose, we receive ever more tragic news that adds to the growing dismay of public opinion, provoking the impression of an unstoppable tendency for inhuman brutality.
>
> In the face of the stubborn determination with which both sides continue to go forth on the road of revenge and vendetta, what appears to the anguished souls of believers is the prospect of recourse to prayer

to that God who, alone, can change the hearts of men, even the most obstinate.

Next Sunday, April 7, the Church will celebrate with special fervor the mystery of Divine Mercy, and will give thanks to He who took upon Himself the afflictions of our humanity. What could be a more suitable occasion to raise to heaven a choral invocation of pardon and mercy that implores the Heart of God for a special intervention upon all those who have responsibility and power to undertake the necessary steps, even if they cost a great deal, to put the parties that are fighting on the path towards just and dignified accords for all?

I would therefore, dear brother, be grateful if you could be the intermediary, in a manner you believe to be opportune, to convey this desire of mine to the pastors of the various particular Churches, inviting them all to offer, next Sunday, a unified plea in such a serious hour for all of mankind. May the message of a stable and lasting peace reach that land that is so dear to the three monotheistic religions.

With this hope, that comes from the deepest part of my heart, I send you and all my brothers in the episcopacy a special apostolic blessing.

✝ **AUGUST 16-19, 2002: Holy Father's Apostolic** *Pilgrimage to Poland: Glory to God, Rich in Mercy*. (See Appendixes, p. 258, for full text.)

Welcome Ceremony, August 16, John Paul II explains the purpose of his pilgrimage:

> On Friday evening, August 16, at 6:30 p.m., the Holy Father landed at the International airport of Krakow-Balice, to begin his apostolic visit of Poland. After the President of Poland and the Primate of Poland, Archbishop of Warsaw welcomed him, the Holy

Father gave an extended greeting to the civil and religious authorities and to all of Poland, stressing he came as a messenger of mercy and hope at this time of social and economic transition for Poland. "This time I shall stay only in Krakow, but with affection I embrace the whole of Poland and all its people."

The Holy Father greeted the children, the young people, and those who are suffering. "In these days I will continue to commend to God's mercy your sufferings, and I ask you to pray that my apostolic ministry will be fruitful and meet every expectation." The Holy Father also greeted the Orthodox, other Christians, the Jewish Community, the followers of Islam and people of good will. The Pope then set forth the motto of his pilgrimage, "God, rich in mercy." He listed the three stages of his visit:

> *Motto of the pilgrimage is "God, rich in mercy" as stressed by the Shrine of the Merciful Christ.*
>
> Brothers and Sisters! "God , rich in mercy." This is the motto of this pilgrimage. This is its proclamation. It comes from the encyclical *Dives in Misericordia*, but its source is here, in Krakow, at Lagiewniki. Because from here, thanks to the humble efforts of an unusual witness — St. Sister Faustina — the Gospel message of God's merciful love rings out. That is why the first stage of my pilgrimage and its chief purpose is my visit to the Shrine of The Divine Mercy. I am happy to be able to dedicate the new building, which is becoming a world center of devotion to the merciful Christ. [John Paul II also entrusted the world to The Divine Mercy!]

Beatification

The mercy of God is reflected in human mercy. For centuries, Krakow has found glory in great figures who, trusting in God's love, bore witness to mercy through practical deeds of love of neighbour. It is enough to mention Saint Hedwig, Saint John of Kety, Father Piotr Skarga or, closer to our time, Saint Brother Albert. They will be joined by the Servants of God whom — with God's help — I shall have the joy of raising to the glory of the altars at Holy Mass in Blonie Park. The beatification of Sigismund Felix Felinski, Jan Beyzym, Santia Szymkowiak and Jan Balicki are the second reason for my pilgrimage. Already I hope that these new Beati, who have given an example of the practice of mercy, will remind us of the great gift of God's love and predispose us for the daily practice of love of our neighbour.

Kalwaria Zebrzydowska

There is also a third reason for my pilgrimage which I wish to mention. It is the prayer of thanksgiving for the four hundred years of the Shrine of Kalwaria Zebrzydowska, which I have been associated with from childhood. It was there, praying as I walked along its paths, that I sought light and inspiration for my service of the Church in Krakow and in Poland, there that I made various difficult pastoral decisions. It was precisely there, among the faithful people at prayer, that I came to know the faith that guides me also on the Chair of Peter. Through the intercession of Our Lady of Kalwaria I want to thank God for this gift.

✝ **AUGUST 17, 2002: John Paul II Entrusted the World to The Divine Mercy.** (See *Appendixes*, p. 263, for the full text.)

On August 17, 2002, John Paul II dedicated the newly built Shrine of The Divine Mercy in Lagiewniki-Krakow, Poland. On the same occasion at the end of his homily, he solemnly entrusted the world to Divine Mercy. Listen carefully to the strong words he uses in this entrustment to The Divine Mercy (the full homily is given in the *Appendixes*):

> Today, therefore, in the Shrine, I wish *solemnly to entrust the world to Divine Mercy.* I do so with the burning desire that the message of God's merciful love, proclaimed here through St. Faustina, *may be made known to all the peoples of the earth* and fill their hearts with hope. May this message radiate from this place to our beloved homeland and throughout the world. May the binding promise of the Lord Jesus be fulfilled: From here there must go forth "the spark which will prepare the world for [Jesus'] final coming" (*Diary*, 1732).

> This spark needs to be lighted by the grace of God. This fire of mercy needs to be passed on to the world. *In the mercy of God, the world will find peace and mankind will find happiness!* I entrust this task to you, dear Brothers and Sisters, to the Church in Krakow and Poland, and to all the votaries of Divine Mercy who will come here from Poland and from throughout the world. *May you be witnesses to mercy!*

> *God, merciful Father, in Your Son, Jesus Christ, You have revealed Your love and poured it out upon us in the Holy Spirit, the Comforter. We entrust to You today the destiny of the world and of every man and woman.*

> *Bend down to us sinners, heal our weakness, conquer all evil, and grant that all the peoples of the earth may experience Your mercy. In You, the Triune God, may*

they ever find the source of hope. Eternal Father, by the Passion and Resurrection of Your Son, have mercy on us and upon the whole world! Amen.

The strength of John Paul II's entrustment radiates with power and energy through his words:

- I wish solemnly to entrust the world to Divine Mercy.
- I do so with a burning desire that all the peoples of earth may know the message of Divine Mercy.
- From here must come "the spark which will prepare the world for [Jesus'] final coming" (*Diary of St. Faustina*, 1732).
- This spark, this fire of mercy, needs to be passed on to the world.
- In the mercy of God mankind will find peace and happiness.
- I ENTRUST this task to you!
- May you be witnesses to mercy!

(See the *Appendixes* for the complete text of "John Paul II's Solemn Entrustment of the World to The Divine Mercy.")

✝ **AUGUST 18, 2002: John Paul II's Pilgrimage to Poland (Rich in Mercy). Four New Blesseds: "Creative Messengers of Mercy"** (See *Appendixes*, p. 265, for full text.)

On Sunday, August 18, at Blonie Park in Krakow, the Holy Father celebrated the Mass of Beatification to raise to the glory of the altars four Servants of God, Sigismund Felinski, Jan Balicki, Jan Beyzym, and Santia Szymkowiak. The Pope held them up as heroic witnesses to God's mercy in their generous outreach to their neighbour in need in the most difficult circumstances of modern history. The Holy Father could then insist on the need to respond today to the limitless generosity of Divine Mercy.

Once we recognize this truth, we become aware that Christ's call to love others even as He has loved us calls all of us to that same measure. We feel in some sense impelled to make our lives a daily offering by showing mercy to our brothers and sisters, drawing upon the gift of God's merciful love.

The Holy Father called for a new creativity in charity:

Faced with the modern forms of poverty that, as we all know, are not lacking in our country, what is needed today is — as I called it in my apostolic letter *Novo Millennio Ineunte* — "a new 'creativity' in charity" (50), in a spirit of solidarity towards our neighbour, so that the help we lend will be a witness of "sharing between brothers and sisters" (ibid.) May this "creativity" never be lacking in the residents of Krakow and in all the people of our homeland. It represents the pastoral plan of the Church in Poland. May the message of God's mercy be reflected always in works of human mercy!

Here is a translation of the homily of the Mass of Beatification in part: (See the *Appendixes* for the full text.)

The message of merciful love needs to resound forcefully anew. The world needs this love. The hour has come to bring Christ's message to everyone: to rulers and the oppressed, to those whose humanity and dignity seem lost in the *mysterium iniquitatis.* The hour has come when the message of Divine Mercy is able to fill hearts with hope and to become the spark of a new civilization: the civilization of love.

These four Blesseds proclaim mercy with their lives.

The Church desires tirelessly to proclaim this message, not only by convincing words, but by the ready practice of mercy. This is why she ceaselessly holds up stupendous examples of individuals *who out of love for God and for man "went forth and bore fruit."* Today she adds four new Beati to their number. They lived at different times and led very different lives. But they are united by that particular feature of holiness which is *devotion to the cause of mercy.* (See more in *Appendixes.*)

Never separate from the love of God the cause of man who needs to experience Divine Mercy.

During my 1979 pilgrimage to Poland, here in Blonie I said that "when we are strong with the Spirit of God, we are also strong with faith in man — strong with faith, hope, and love, which are inseparable — and we are ready to bear witness to the cause of man before those who really have this cause at heart" (Homily at Mass at Blonie Kraskowie, 10 June 1979, 4). Therefore, I asked you: "Never disdain charity, which is 'the greatest of these' and which shows itself in the Cross. Without it, human life has no roots and no meaning" (*ibid.*, 5).

Brothers and Sisters, today I repeat this invitation: open yourselfs to God's greatest gift, to His love that, through the Cross of Christ, has revealed itself to the world as merciful love. Today, living in different times, at the dawn of the new century and millennium, continue to be "ready to bear witness to the cause of man." Today, with all my strength, I beseech the sons and daughters of the Church, and all people of good will: never, ever separate "*the cause of man" from the love of God.* Help modern men and women to *experience God's merciful love!* This love, in its splendour and warmth, will save humanity!

✝ **APRIL 27, 2003: Divine Mercy Sunday and Beatification of Six Servants of God: New Blesseds show God's mercy to the world.**

The following is an extract of the translation from Italian of the Holy Father's Homily at the Mass of Beatification on

Divine Mercy Sunday, April 27, in St. Peter's Square:

"Give thanks to the Lord for He is good, His love endures forever" (Ps117 [118]:1). This is what the Church sings today on this Second Sunday of Easter, *Divine Mercy Sunday.* In the Paschal Mystery, the comforting design of salvation, God's merciful love whose privileged witnesses are the saints and blesseds in Heaven, is fully revealed.

By a providential coincidence, I have the joy of raising six new Blesseds to the honours of the altars on this very *Sunday on which we celebrate The "Divine Mercy."* Each one of them, in a different way, expressed the Lord's tender and wonderful mercy: James Alberione, a priest, founder of the Pauline Family; Mark of Aviano, a priest of the Order of Friars Minor Capuchin; Maria Christina Brando, virgin, Foundress of the Congregation of the Sisters, Expiatory Victims of Jesus in the Blessed Sacrament; Eugenia Ravasco, virgin, Foundress of the Congregations of the Daughters of the Sacred Hearts of Jesus and Mary; Maria Domenica Mantovani, virgin, Co-Foundress of the Institute of the Little Sisters of the Holy Family; Julia Salzano, virgin, Foundress of the Congregation of the Catechist Sisters of the Sacred Heart.

The Good News is for all people in all epochs

"These (signs) are written ... that believing you may have life in His Name" (Jn 20:31). The Good News is a universal message destined for the people of all times. It is personally addressed to each one and asks to be expressed in his lifestyle. When Christians become "living Gospels," they are transformed into eloquent "signs" of the Lord's mercy and their witness touches others' hearts more easily. As docile instruments in the hands of divine Providence, they have a profound effect on history. This is how it was with these six new Blesseds, who come from beloved Italy, a land rich in saints.

Blessed Alberione, a beacon of truth in a world with few beacons of truth.

Blessed Mark called for a Europe based on common Christian roots.

Blessed Maria Brando instilled awareness of God's merciful love.

Blessed Eugenia Ravasco cared for those who had fallen away.

Blessed Maria Mantovani had steadfast faith in God's will.

Blessed Julia Salzano combined apostolic activity with prayer.

Eternal is the mercy of God, who never abandons His faithful.

"*Eternal is God's mercy*" which shines in each one of the new Blesseds. Through them God has worked great marvels! Truly eternal, O Lord, is Your mercy! You never abandon those who turn to You. With these new blesseds let us repeat to You with filial confidence: "Jesus, I trust in You! *Jezu, ufam, Tobie!*" the words of St. Faustina Kowalska.

Help us, Mary, Mother of Mercy, to proclaim with our lives that "*God's love endures for ever*. Now and forever. Amen! Alleluia!

✝ **APRIL 27, 2003,** at the *Regina Caeli* talk following the Mass of Divine Mercy Sunday and the beatifications, John Paul II spoke of the Easter gifts of peace and mercy, meditating on the day's holy Gospel:

Truly Jesus offers us Divine Mercy as the effective remedy for our times. Divine Mercy and Christ's peace spring from reconciled hearts.

The risen Jesus encounters the disciples in the Upper Room and offers them the *Easter gifts of peace and mercy.* Meditating on today's holy gospel, it is well to understand that true peace springs from a heart that is reconciled, and that we who have experienced the joy of forgiveness must therefore be ready to pardon. The Church, also absorbed in prayer today spiritually in the Upper Room, presents to our Lord the joys and hopes, the sorrows and the anguish of the whole world, and He offers as an effective remedy *Divine Mercy,* asking His ministers to be His generous and faithful instruments.

Mary, Queen of the apostles and of all the Saints, is spiritually present among us, together with the newly Beatified, who show us the road to follow and always put their trust in the help of the Lord. Today I invoke in particular the Mother of Divine Mercy, praying for the entire human family, knowing that only in the mercy of God can the world find peace. We entrust to Mary in a special way the Eastern Church that is celebrating the Easter Resurrection this Sunday.

✟ **APRIL 18, 2004:** After the celebration of the Mass of Divine Mercy Sunday, at the *Regina Caeli* John Paul II gave a meditation on the testimony of forgiveness given us by Jesus on the Cross:

Jesus is the perfect manifestation of Divine Mercy. By His victory peace results.

1. On Good Friday, as He hung on the Cross, Jesus bequeathed to us His testament of forgiveness: "*Father, forgive them for they know not what they do*" (Lk 23:34). Jeered and tormented, *He implored mercy for His torturers.* In this way His wide-open arms and pierced

side became the universal sacrament of the fatherly tenderness of God who offers forgiveness and reconciliation to all.

When He appeared to His disciples on the day of the Resurrection, the Lord greeted them with these words: "*Peace be with you*," and showed them His hands and His side with the marks of the passion. Eight days later, as we read in today's Gospel, Jesus once again came and stood among them in the Upper room, and once again said to them: "*Peace be with you*" (cf. Jn 20:19-26).

Peace results from Christ's victory

2. *Peace is the gift par excellence of the crucified and risen Christ*, the result of the victory of His love over sin and death. In offering Himself as an immaculate victim of expiation on the altar of the Cross, He poured out on humanity the beneficial flow of Divine Mercy.

Jesus, therefore, is our peace, because He *is the perfect manifestation of Divine Mercy*. In the human heart, which is an abyss always exposed to the temptation of evil, He infuses God's merciful love.

Divine Mercy linked to Penance

3. Today, the Second Sunday of Easter, we are celebrating *Divine Mercy Sunday*. The Lord is also sending us out to bring everyone His peace, which is founded on pardon and the forgiveness of sins. This is an extraordinary gift, which He desired to link with the sacrament of Penance and Reconciliation. How deeply humanity needs to experience the effectiveness of God's mercy in these times marked by growing uncertainty and violent conflicts!

May Mary, Mother of Christ our peace, who received His testament of love on Calvary, help us to be witnesses and apostles of His infinite mercy.

I now address a special greeting to the pilgrims from various nations who have gathered here on the occasion of Divine Mercy Sunday. Dear friends, I ask you to be witnesses of God's merciful love, after the example of St. Faustina Kowalska.

I wish everyone a good Sunday!

CHAPTER 3
DIVINE MERCY IN VARIOUS WRITINGS

✝ *Redeemer of Man* (*Redemptor Hominis*), March 4, 1979
In the opening line of his first encyclical, John Paul II proclaims:

The Redeemer of Man, Jesus Christ, is the center of the universe and of history (1).

... Through the Incarnation God gave human life the dimension that He intended man to have from his first beginning; He has granted that dimension definitively — in the way that is peculiar to Him alone, in keeping with *His eternal love and mercy* (1).

Then in the chapter on the *Mystery* of the *Redemption*, John Paul II describes the great gift of love that is also described as *mercy*, which is a person, *Jesus Christ*:

Therefore "for our sake (God) made Him (the Son) to be sin who knew no sin." If He "made to be sin" Him who was without any sin whatever, it was to reveal the love that is always greater than the whole of creation, the love that is He, Himself, since "God is love." Above all, love is greater than sin, than weakness, than the "futility of creation"; it is stronger than death; it is a love always ready to raise up and forgive, always ready to go to meet the prodigal son; always looking for "the revealing of the sons of God," who are called to the glory that is to be revealed. *This revelation of love is also described as mercy; and in man's history this revelation of love and mercy has taken a form and a name: that of Jesus Christ* (emphasis added, 9).

This revelation of mercy is further developed in John Paul II's second encyclical *Rich in Mercy as Mercy Incarnate:* Jesus Christ. He uses as a repeated theme: Mercy, love's second name, is more powerful than evil, more powerful than sin and death.

In *Redeemer of Man*, John Paul II first develops the mystic sense of the "new Advent," the exhortation "Do not be afraid!" and the need of imploring God's mercy.

✝ *Lord and Giver of Life* (*Dominum et Vivificatem*) Encyclical on the Holy Spirit in the Life of the Church and world, Pentecost, May 18, 1986

In the third encyclical of the trilogy, John Paul II opens with a description of the Holy Spirit in terms of the "Law of the Gift":

The Church professes her faith in the Holy Spirit as "the Lord, the giver of life."

In section 39, John Paul II describes the Holy Spirit as Spirit-Love who transforms suffering into salvific love — mercy personified:

The Holy Spirit, who is the love of the Father and the Son ... is the source of every divine giving of gifts to creatures. Precisely in Him we can picture as person-ified and actualized in a transcendent way that mercy which the Patristic and theological tradition, following the line of the Old and New Testaments, attributes to God. In man, mercy includes sorrow and compassion for the misfortunes of one's neighbor. In God, the Spirit-Love expresses the consideration of human sin in a fresh outpouring of salvific love (39).

The Holy Spirit is not only the Giver of Life, Spirit-Love, He is also mercy personified! He is salvific love.

✟ *Mission of the Redeemer* (*Redemptoris Missio*) December 7, 1990

The theme of this encyclical is the urgency of missionary activity based on the mission of the Holy Trinity (see 1). The one purpose of renewed missionary commitment is to serve man by revealing to him the love of God manifest in Jesus Christ (2). Christ is the revelation and incarnation of the Father's mercy (12). Christ makes the kingdom of God present and inaugurates the kingdom of the Father's love and compassion. All are invited to repent and believe in God's merciful love (13).

✟ *Gospel of Life* (*Evangelium Vitae*), March 25, 1995

In his encyclical *Evangelium Vitae*, John Paul II begins with a statement on the Gospel of mercy. He states that Jesus, Mercy Incarnate, reveals the Good News that God's love is life-giving:

The Gospel of life is at the heart of Jesus' message (1).

In dealing with the culture of death — with birth control, abortion, euthanasia, suicide — He proclaims the Gospel of life — Jesus!:

> Jesus is the only Gospel. To proclaim Jesus is itself to proclaim life. ... This Gospel exceeds every human expectation and reveals the sublime heights to which the dignity of the human person is raised by grace (80).

The Gospel of life is *mercy*: life-giving love and love-giving life:

As part of the spiritual worship acceptable to God (cf. Rom 12:1), the Gospel of life is to be celebrated above all in daily living, which should be filled with self-giving love for others. In this way, our lives will become a genuine and responsible acceptance of the gift of life and a heartfelt song of praise and gratitude to God, who has given us this gift. This is already happening in the many different acts of selfless generosity, often humble and hidden, carried out by men and women, children and adults, the young and the old, the healthy and the sick.

It is in this context, so humanly rich and filled with love, that *heroic actions* too are born. These are the most solemn celebration of the Gospel of life, for they proclaim it by the total gift of self. They are the radiant manifestation of the highest degree of love, which is *to give one's life for the person loved* (cf. Jn 15:13). They are a sharing in the mystery of the cross, in which Jesus reveals *the value of every person and how life attains its fullness in the sincere gift of self* (86).

The Gospel of life is not for believers alone: It is for everyone (101).

It is precisely in the *flesh* of every person that Christ continues to reveal Himself and to enter into fellowship with us, so that the rejection of human life, in whatever form that rejection takes, is really a rejection of Christ (104).

Life is a gift of God's mercy, John Paul II teaches to all. A rejection of life is a rejection of God Himself.

✝ *Gift and Mystery: on the Fiftieth Anniversary of My Priestly Ordination*, November 1, 1946-1996
Pope John Paul II writes in his memoirs:

I recall these things above all in order to thank the Lord. "I will sing of the mercies of the Lord forever"

(Ps 89:2). I offer this to priests and to the people of God as a testimony of love [Introduction].

The priest is a minister of mercy ... the witness and instrument of Divine Mercy. ... It is in the confessional that every priest becomes a witness of the great miracles Divine Mercy works in souls which receive the grace of conversion (p. 86).

✝ *The Day of the Lord* (*Dies Domini*), Apostolic Letter, May 31, 1998
John Paul II described the weekly Sunday celebration of the Holy Eucharist as the "weekly Easter" and the "weekly Pentecost." Now that he has declared the Second Sunday of Easter as "Divine Mercy Sunday," the prime eighth day becomes a "weekly Divine Mercy celebration." The Gospel of the Easter night appearance is used on both Mercy Sunday and Pentecost.

✝ *Encyclical Letter, The Church of the Eucharist* (*Eccelsia de Eucharisti*), Holy Thursday, April 17, 2003
The Encyclical is also the Holy Thursday Letter to Priests, 2003.
In the first chapter of his encyclical on the Eucharist entitled "The Mystery of Faith," John Paul II made a powerful statement about the Eucharist and mercy:

> The Church's Magisterium has constantly reaffirmed through faith [in the Holy Eucharist] with joyful gratitude for this inestimable gift. I wish once more to recall this truth and to join you, my dear brothers and sisters, in adoration before this mystery: *a great mystery, a mystery of faith, a mystery of mercy.* What more could Jesus have done for us? Truly, in the Eucharist He shares a love which goes "to the end" (Jn 13:1), a love which knows no measure (11, emphasis added).

What a powerful description of the Eucharist: "A mystery of mercy!" In his second encyclical *Rich in Mercy*, John Paul II calls mercy the second name of love:

For mercy is an indispensible dimension of love; it is as it were love's second name and, at the same time, the specific manner in which love is revealed and effected … (*Rich in Mercy*, 7).

Then he describes the Eucharist in terms of love:

The Eucharist brings us ever nearer to that love which is more powerful than death (*Rich in Mercy*, 13, emphasis in the text).

In his first encyclical *Redeemer of Man*, John Paul II describes the magnitude and dimensions of the Eucharist:

… It is not permissible for us, in thought, life or action, to take away from this truly most holy Sacrament its full magnitude and its essential meaning. It is at one and the same time a *Sacrifice*-Sacrament, a *Communion*-Sacrament, and a *Presence*-Sacrament (*Redeemer of Man* 20, emphasis added).

The Eucharist truly is "a great mystery, a mystery of faith, a mystery of mercy."

✝ *Rise, Let Us Be on Our Way* (2004) is John Paul II's second-to-last book reflecting on his twenty years as a bishop and then Archbishop of Krakow and how it influenced his then twenty-five years as Pope. He writes to his fellow bishops in the Introduction:

I offer this book as a sign of love to my brother bishops and to all the people of God. May it help all who wish to learn about the greatness of the episcopal ministry, the difficulty associated with it, but also about the joy that daily accompanies its fulfillment. (Introduction, viii)

In writing of the Saints of Krakow, John Paul II describes how he came to know of The Divine Mercy devotion and the marvelous response of Fr. Rozycki to his (Archbishop Wojtyla's) request that Fr. Rozycki, who was a professor, review the *Diary of St. Faustina Kowalska*:

> During the Second World War, I worked as a laborer in the solvay factory, near the monastery of Lagiewniki. I often visited the grave of Sister Faustina, who at that time was not yet beatified. Everything about her was extraordinary, impossible to foresee in such a simple girl. How could I have imagined that one day I would beatify her and canonize her? She entered the convent in Warsaw, and was later sent to Vilnius, and finally to Krakow. A few years before the war, she had a great vision of the merciful Jesus, who called her to be the apostle of the devotion to The Divine Mercy, later to spread throughout the Church. Sister Faustina died in 1938. Devotion to The Divine Mercy began in Krakow, and from there took on a worldwide dimension. When I became Archbishop of Krakow, I asked Professor Father Ignacy Rozycki to examine her writings. At first he didn't want to, but later he agreed, and went on to make a thorough study of the available documents. Finally he said, "She's a wonderful mystic" (*Rise, Let Us Be on Our Way*, p. 194).

In the final paragraph of his book, John Paul II encourages his brother bishops to trust in Jesus:

> Echoing the words of our Lord and Master. I too say to each one of you, dear brothers in the episcopate: "Rise, let us be on our way!" Let us go forth full of trust in Christ! He will accompany us as we journey toward the goal that He alone knows (*Rise, Let Us Be on Our Way*, pp. 215-216).

✝ ***Memory and Identity: Conversations at the Dawn of a Millennium*, 2005.**

In this last book of John Paul II, he reflects on the evil in the world as he experienced it under Nazi and Soviet Communism in Poland. He especially deals with what sets a limit on evil, namely Divine Mercy. He credits St. Faustina as a uniquely enlightened interpreter of the truth of Divine Mercy (p. 5). John Paul II continues to stress:

> It is significant that Sister Faustina saw Jesus as the Merciful God, yet contemplated Him not so much on the Cross, but rather in His subsequent state of risen · glory [She saw the radiant image of Jesus]. She thus linked her mystical sense of mercy with the Mystery of Easter, in which Christ appears triumphant over sin and death (cf. Jn 20:19-23). ... St. Faustina's *Diary* appears as a particular [unique] Gospel of Divine Mercy. ... It is as if Christ had wanted to reveal that the limit imposed upon evil ... is ultimately Divine Mercy. ... God can always draw good from evil, He wills that all should be saved and come to the knowledge of the truth (cf. 1 Tim 2:4): God is Love (cf. 1 Jn 4:8) Christ, crucified and risen [as in the image of The Divine Mercy], just as He appeared to Sister Faustina, is the supreme revelation of this truth (pp. 54-55, Chapter titled "The Mystery of Mercy").

Here in this final book John Paul II echoes the repeated theme of his second encyclical, *Rich in Mercy* (*Dives in Misericordia*): Mercy is the second name of love ... that love which is more powerful than evil: more powerful than sin and death (see *Rich in Mercy*, 15).

Pope John Paul II continues his commentary on St. Faustina and her amazing message of Divine Mercy:

> I should like to return to what I said about the experience of the Church in Poland during the period of resistance to communism. It seems to me to have a universal value. I think that the same applies to Sister Faustina and her witness to the mystery of Divine Mercy. The patrimony of her spirituality was of great importance, as we know from experience, for the

resistance against the evil and inhuman systems of the time. The lesson to be drawn from all this is important not only for the Poles, but also in every part of the world where the Church is present. This became clear during the beatification and canonization of Sister Faustina. It was as if Christ had wanted to say through her: "Evil does not have the last word!" The Paschal Mystery confirms that good is ultimately victorious, that life conquers death and that love triumphs over hate (Chapter titled "The Mystery of Mercy," p. 55).

PART III
MODEL OF MERCY

John Paul II not only taught about
mercy, he put his teaching into practice:
by praying for mercy; by forgiving and
asking for forgiveness; by radiating
mercy; by his presence; by his ministry
to the sick, the suffering, and the poor.

CHAPTER 1
PRAYER FOR MERCY

On November 11, 1986, I had the privilege of concelebrating Holy Mass with the Holy Father in his private chapel. We entered the chapel at 6:45 a.m. for the 7:00 Mass. John Paul was deep in prayer, kneeling with his face in his hands. I was seated a yard from him. For that quarter of an hour, I wondered what he was praying. What came to me was that he was praying: "Jesus, mercy!"

It was years later that he said at the Shrine of The Divine Mercy in Poland, June 7, 1997, "I pray unceasingly that God will have 'mercy on us and on the whole world'" (quoting from the Chaplet of Divine Mercy).

John Paul II shared his call for prayer for mercy at the conclusion of his encyclical on Divine Mercy:

THE CHURCH APPEALS TO THE MERCY OF GOD (See note at the end of this chapter about the English translation of this text.)

The Church proclaims the truth about God's mercy which is made known in the crucified and risen Christ, and she makes it known in various ways. The Church also tries to be merciful to people through people because she considers this to be an indispensable condition for a better, "more human" world, today and tomorrow.

And yet at no time and in no period of history — especially at a turning point like ours — can the Church forget about *prayer, which is a cry for the mercy of God* in the midst of the many forms of evil that weigh upon mankind and threaten it. This imploring of mercy is precisely the fundamental right and at the same time the duty of the Church in Christ Jesus. It is the right and duty of the Church toward God and at the same time toward humanity.

The more the human conscience succumbs to secularization and loses its sense of the very meaning of the word "mercy," the more it moves away from God and the mystery of mercy. Therefore the *Church has all the more the right and the duty* to appeal to God's mercy with "loud cries" (Heb 5:7). Such "loud cries" ought to be the cry of the Church of our times to God for mercy as she announces and proclaims the certainty of that mercy in the crucified and risen Christ, that is, the Paschal Mystery. This mystery carries within itself the fullest revelation of mercy, namely, that love is more powerful than death, more powerful than sin and every evil, that love lifts man from his deepest falls and frees him from his greatest threats.

Modern man feels these threats. What has been said on this point is only a beginning. Modern man often asks about the solutions of these terrible tensions which have built up in the world between peoples. And if at times he *lacks the courage to utter this word "mercy,"* or if his conscience is empty of religious content and he does not find the equivalent, so much greater is the necessity *for the Church to utter this word*, not only in her own name but also in the name of all people of our time.

It is necessary that everything that I have said in this present letter on mercy be *continuously changed and transformed into an ardent prayer:* into a cry for mercy on the people of the modern world with all their needs and threats. *May this cry be filled with that truth about mercy* which has found such rich expression in the Sacred Scriptures, in Tradition, and in the authentic life of faith of countless generations of the People of God. Like the sacred writers, let us cry out to God who cannot despise anything that He has made (cf. Gen 1:31; Ps 145:9; Wis 11:24), to Him who is faithful to Himself, His fatherhood and His love. And like the prophets, let us appeal to that love which has maternal characteristics — and, like a mother, goes after each of her children, after each lost sheep, even if the lost are in the millions, even if the evil in the world outweighs honesty, even if mankind deserves, because of its sins, a kind of modern "flood," as did the generation of Noah.

Let us then appeal also to that kind of fatherly love revealed to us by Christ in His messianic mission, which reached its ultimate expression in His cross, in His death and in His resurrection! Let us appeal to God through Christ, mindful of the words of Mary's *Magnificat* which proclaims "mercy from age to age." Let us cry out for God's own mercy for this present generation! May the Church which, like Mary, continues to be the spiritual mother of humankind, express in this prayer her total maternal concern, as well as that trusting love from which is born the most burning need for prayer.

Let us cry out, guided by that faith, hope, and love that Christ grafted in our hearts. This cry for mercy is at the same time an expression of our *love of God*, from whom modern man has distanced himself and made of Him a stranger, proclaiming in various ways that he doesn't "need" God. This then is mercy, the love of God whose insult — rejection by modern man — we feel deeply and are ready to cry out with Christ on the cross, "Father, forgive them, for they do not know what they do" (Lk 23:34 RSV).

This cry for mercy is at the same time love for all of mankind. Mercy is love for all peoples without exception or division: without difference of race, culture, language, or worldview, without distinction between friends and enemies. This cry for mercy is love for all people. Mercy desires every true good for each individual and for every human community, for every family, for every nation, for every social group, for youth, adults, parents, and for the elderly and the sick. It is love for everyone, without exception or division. This cry for mercy is love for all people, the care which ensures for everyone all true good, and removes and drives away every sort of evil.

And if any of our contemporaries do not share the faith and hope which bid me, as servant of the mysteries of God (cf. 1 Cor 1:1), to implore the mercy of God Himself for mankind in this hour of history, *then may they understand the reason for my concern. It is dictated by love* for mankind, for all that is human and which, according to the intuitions of many of our contemporaries, is threatened by an immense danger.

The same mystery of Christ, which reveals to us the great vocation of mankind, which obliged me to proclaim in the encyclical *Redemptor Hominis* mankind's incomparable dignity, also obliges me to announce mercy as God's merciful love revealed in that same mystery of Christ. This mystery of Christ also obliges me to appeal to this mercy and implore this mercy on these difficult and critical times of the Church and of the world as we approach the end of the second millennium.

In the name of Jesus Christ crucified and risen from the dead, in the spirit of His messianic mission, which endures in the works of mankind, *we lift up our voice and plead:* that the love which is in the Father, may once again be revealed at this stage of history; and that, through the work of the Son and the Holy Spirit, this love which is in the Father, may once again be shown to be present in our modern world as more powerful than evil and more powerful than sin and death. We plead this through the intercession of Mary, who does not cease to proclaim "mercy ... from generation to generation," and also through the intercession of the saints in whom have been completely fulfilled the words of the Sermon on the Mount: "Blessed are the merciful, for they shall obtain mercy" (Mt 5:7).

It is not permissible for the Church, for any reason, to withdraw into herself as she continues the great task of implementing the Second Vatican Council. In this implementing we can rightly see a new phase of the self-realization of the Church — in keeping with the age in which it has been our destiny to live. *The reason for her existence* is, in fact, to reveal God, that Father who allows us to "see" Himself in Christ (cf. Jn 14:9). No matter how strong the resistance of human history may be, no matter how estranged the civilization of the world, no matter how great the denial of God in the human world, so much the greater must be our closeness to that mystery which, hidden for centuries in God, was then truly shared with man, in time, through Jesus Christ.

Note on this translation:

This is from a new translation of my own of the encyclical *Rich in Mercy.* The original Polish text, written in longhand by Pope John Paul II in his native tongue flows ever so smoothly, using words that are delicately and specifically chosen. The Latin and English translations, which had to be done quickly and immediately for the Vatican Polyglot Press, do not convey the full strength and beauty of the original text.

The intention of this translation, using the original Polish as well as the English and Latin Vatican Polyglot Press translations as a basis, is to convey the spiritual power of the message. There are a number of factors that would need to be combined to do this with the greatest force: a knowledge of Polish, an ease with the existential philosophical mode of thinking of John Paul II, a thorough grasp of his message of mercy and the origins of his concern about mercy, and a knowledge of the English language. I cannot claim expertise in all of the above needed factors, but I am very much aware of the urgency of the message of mercy and the origins of the concern of Pope John Paul II. May my inadequacy in Polish and English, and my weakness in existential philosophy be overcome by my burning desire to convey the Holy Father's message of mercy.

I tried to bring out the force of the Pope's message by using the English phrases and words that seemed to be as strong as his words. The changes made most often involved an addition of the phrase or word referred to in a reflective pronoun. Often, the sentences or paragraphs in the official English translation were so long that the "it" became ambiguous and the sentence lost its force. This repeating of the subject makes the sentences clear and strong. Some sentences were divided in order to convey the full impact of the message.

CHAPTER 2
FORGIVING AND ASKING
FOR FORGIVENESS

Forgiveness is the first act of mercy. *The Catechism of the Catholic Church* teaches the centrality of forgiveness when it tells us God will "forgive us our trespasses as we forgive those who trespass against us" (CCC, 2838 to 2845). This section is one of the most extraordinary teachings in the *Catechism*.

Sacred Scripture teaches us that "our redemption is the forgiveness of sins" (Col 1:14). And in St. Paul's letter to Titus we read:

When the kindness and love of God our Savior appeared, He saved us; not because of any righteous deeds we have done, but because of His mercy (3:5).

John Paul II in his encyclical, *Rich in Mercy* points out the source of the mercy we need in order to be merciful and forgive; namely, Christ crucified:

Christ's messianic program, the program of mercy, becomes the program of His people, the program of the Church. At its very center there is always the cross, for it is in the cross that the revelation of merciful love attains its culmination (8).

And further he points to the Heart of Jesus as the center:

The Church seems in a special way to profess the mercy of God and to venerate it when she directs herself to the Heart of Christ. In fact, it is precisely this drawing close to Christ in the mystery of His Heart which enables us to dwell on this point ... of the revelation which constituted the central content of the messianic mission of the Son of Man (13).

John Paul II in sections 12 and 14 develops the relationship of mercy, forgiveness, and justice. As we shall point out, forgiveness is a major *modus operandi* for him in the present world condition. After developing the lack of peace and the threat of destruction which is linked with the very existence of humanity (11), he asks the question: "Is justice enough?" "Justice alone is not enough" (12). Mercy, "that deeper power, which is love, must shape human life in its various dimensions — otherwise the highest justice is the greatest injury" (cf. 12).

In section 14, John Paul II points out that the "Church must acknowledge as her principal duty — at every stage of history and especially in our modern age — *to proclaim and to introduce into life* the mystery of mercy. ... It is precisely in the name of this mystery that Christ teaches us to forgive always."

It is important, John Paul II points out, that:

Forgiveness does not cancel out the objective require-
ments of justice. ... Properly understood, justice
constitutes the goal of forgiveness. ... Mercy has the
power to confer on justice a new content, which is
expressed most simply in forgiveness (14).

Then he summarizes the mission of the Church in terms
of forgiveness:

The Church rightly considers it her duty and purpose
of her mission to guard the authenticity of forgiveness
... by guarding its *source* which is the mystery of the
mercy of God Himself as revealed in Jesus Christ. ...
The basis of the Church's mission is none other than
"drawing from the wells of the Savior" (Is 12:3) (14).

✝ THE POPE ASKS FORGIVENESS

One of the characteristics of the Mercy Pope was to express
the mission of the Church in concrete terms by asking for
forgiveness.

In *Tertio Millennium Adveniente* (November 10, 1994)
John Paul II prays that unity among all Christians will increase
until they reach full communion — as soon as possible (16).
The jubilee preparation was to make the Church more fully
conscious of our sinfulness, especially of scandal and counter-
witness (33). We must repent of sins against unity. We must
make amends and teach forgiveness. We should invoke the
Holy Spirit with greater insistence for the grace of Christian
unity (34). The Church must express profound regret for
intolerance and violence in the service of truth (35).

John Paul II did this in his meetings with Protestant
groups, for example, with the Protestants in the Czech Republic.
In *Orientale Lumen* (May 2, 1995) he says that we must
ceaselessly implore Divine Mercy and a new heart for a shared
conversion (21).

In his encyclical *Ut Unum Sint* (May 25, 1995), he writes
that what is needed is "a vision enlivened by Divine Mercy" to
break down walls of division and distrust:

The commitment to ecumenism must be based upon conversion of hearts and upon prayer, which will lead to the necessary purification of past memories. With the grace of the Holy Spirit, the Lord's disciples, inspired by love, by the power of the truth and a sincere desire for mutual forgiveness and reconciliation are called to *re-examine together their painful past. ... What is needed is* ... a vision enlivened by Divine Mercy (2).

John Paul II writes strongly of his ministry as Bishop of Rome as a ministry of mercy, even as Peter received mercy to, in turn, minister mercy to his brethren (cf. Jn 22:32):

The Bishop of Rome exercises a ministry originating in the manifold mercy of God. This mercy converts hearts ... and is completely at the service of God's merciful plan (92) ... [He] knows that he must be a sign of mercy. His is a ministry of mercy, born of an act of Christ's own mercy. ... God in His mercy can convert hearts to unity and enable them to enter into communion with Him (93). This service of unity, rooted in the action of Divine Mercy, is entrusted within the College of Bishops. ... This task can require the offering of one's own life (cf. Jn 10: 11-18) (94).

In addition to his encyclicals, John Paul II expressed mercy by asking forgiveness from various groups for the lack of mercy they have experienced from the Catholic Church over the course of history. In addition to the Eastern Churches and various Protestant groups, he asked forgiveness of those who experienced injustice and lack of understanding in the Inquisition. He also asked forgiveness of Jewish groups for the persecution they experienced, and from scientists because of the condemnation of Galileo. In a moving encounter, he forgave Ali Agca, the man who shot him and caused him months of pain. (See *When a Pope Asks Forgiveness, The Mea Culpas of John Paul II*, by Luigi Accattoli, Pauline Books and Media, 1998.) In June, 2000, Pope John Paul II expressed his pleasure with the Italian government's decision to grant clemency to his would-be assassin.

In *Incarnationis Mysterium*, November 29, 1998, John Paul II officially proclaimed the Jubilee of the Year 2000. In a beautiful way he described the Year of Jubilee as the "Year of Mercy." He asked the Church to exercise the mercy she had received from the Lord by kneeling before God and imploring forgiveness for the past and present sins of her sons and daughters (11). He prayed that the year would be "*an especially deep experience of grace and Divine Mercy*" (6). Once again he wrote of the mercy of God as a sign of the charity that is needed to reduce or even forgive the debt of the poorer nations, presented earlier in *Tertio Millenio Adveniente* (51):

> Some nations, especially the poorer ones, are oppressed by a debt so high that repayment is impossible. ... The abuses of power which result in some dominating others must stop: Such abuses are sinful and unjust (12).

In one of the highlights of the Jubilee Year of Mercy Incarnate, on March 12, 2000, Pope John Paul II, along with seven cardinals who were heads of Vatican Congregations, solemnly asked God for forgiveness for a number of past and present actions of the sons and daughters of the Church. They prayed in turn a confession of sins, asking for forgiveness (see *Appendixes*, p. 231, for the full text):

I.   Sins in general.

II.   Sins committed in the service of truth.

III.   Sins which have harmed the unity of the Body of Christ.

IV.   Sins against the people of Israel.

V.   Sins committed in actions against love, peace, the rights of peoples, and respect for cultures and religions.

VI.   Confession of sins against the dignity of women
and the unity of the human race.

VII. Sins in relation to the fundamental rights
of persons.

✝ *ANGELUS* MESSAGE FOLLOWING MASS, "Meditation on the *Miserere*" (Psalm 51), October 24, 2001

> As we ask for forgiveness, we forgive. This is what we
> say every day when we pray the prayer Christ taught
> us: "Our Father ... forgive us our trespasses as we
> forgive those who trespass against us" (Full text in the
> *Appendixes*, p. 247.)

Divine Mercy is Stronger than our Misery

"Divine Mercy is stronger than our misery," the Pope says
in reflecting on the *Miserere*, a hymn of sin and forgiveness,
Vatican City, Oct. 24, 2001 (Zenit.org). — At today's General
Audience, John Paul II meditated on the *Miserere*, Psalm 50
[51], that speaks of the darkness of sin and the unique
experience of God's forgiveness.

"Even if our sins were as black as night, Divine Mercy is
stronger than our misery," the Pope said, echoing Sister
Faustina Kowalska, one of his favorite saints.

"Only one thing is necessary: that the sinner at least leave
the door of his heart ajar, the rest will be done by God. Everything begins and ends in Your mercy," the Pope added, as he
commented on Psalm 50 [51] to thousands of pilgrims gathered
in St. Peter's Square.

The Holy Father was continuing a yearlong series of
meditations on the Psalms.

Psalm 50 [51] is a poetic composition attributed to David's
adultery with Bathsheba and the killing of her husband, Uriah.

The *Miserere*, as it is also known, begins by showing the
malice of sin ("Against You alone have I sinned; I have done
such evil in Your sight"), which distances man from God and

his brothers. The Psalm also shows how when "man confesses his sin, God's salvific justice is ready to purify him radically," the Holy Father said.

"In fact, through confession of faults, for the man of prayer a horizon of light opens, where God is at work," the Pope explained. "The Lord does not just act negatively, eliminating sin, but re-creates sinful humanity through His vivifying Spirit: He infuses a new and pure heart in man, namely, a renewed conscience, and opens the possibility of a limpid faith and worship that is pleasing to God."

Recognition of one's own sin, conversion, and God's forgiveness are "fundamental components of a spirituality that should reverberate in the daily life of the faithful," John Paul II concluded.

✝ WORLD DAY OF PEACE, "No Peace Without Justice, No Justice Without Forgiveness," January 1, 2002

L'Osservatore Romano introduces the World Day of Peace Message of John Paul II:

"The shattered order cannot be fully restored except by a response that combines justice with forgiveness," Pope John Paul II says in his message for the January 1, 2002 World Day of Peace, released at the Vatican on December 11. This year's World Day of Peace "offers all humanity and particularly the leaders of nations, the opportunity to reflect upon the demands of justice and the call to forgiveness in the face of grave problems which continue to afflict the world, not the least of which is the new level of violence introduced by organized terrorism," the Pope writes. "Terrorism," he says, "is often the outcome of that fanatic fundamentalism which springs from the conviction that one's own vision of the truth must be forced upon everyone else." Terrorism exploits both people and God, the Pope says. "It ends by making [God] an idol to be used for one's own purposes." The Pope believes "terrorism is built on contempt for human life. For this reason, not only does it commit intolerable crimes, but because it resorts to terror as a political and military means it is itself a true crime against humanity." There is "a right to defend oneself against terrorism," says the Pope. At the same time, he says "the recruitment of terrorists in fact is easier in situations where rights are trampled upon and injustices tolerated over a long period of time." The Pope calls for an international "commitment to relieving situations of oppression and marginalization." While adding that injustices "in the world can never be used to excuse acts of terrorism," he urges world religions to "work together to eliminate the social and cultural causes of terrorism," and to "take the lead in publicly condemning terrorism and in denying terrorists any form of religious or moral legitimacy." He adds, "The help that religions can give to peace and against terrorism consists precisely in their teaching forgiveness." Forgiveness "is the opposite of resentment and revenge, not of justice," he says. Forgiveness does not mean overlooking "the need to right the wrong done." But, the Pope writes: "What sufferings are inflicted on humanity because of the failure to reconcile!" (The Vatican's English text of the message is found in the *Appendixes*, p. 249.)

✝ *LETTER TO PRIESTS* FROM JOHN PAUL II, Holy Thursday March 17, 2002, on the Sacrament of Reconciliation

The focus is on the call of priests to be "ministers of mercy." The ministry of Jesus to Zacchaeus is used to illustrate the power of forgiveness (see Lk 19:1-10) and resembles the Sacrament of Reconciliation. Some 18 times in the letter, the Pope refers to God's mercy expressed in the story of Zacchaeus and the Sacrament of Reconciliation:

> *With joy and trust let us rediscover this sacrament.* Let us experience it above all for ourselves, as a deeply-felt need and as a grace which we constantly look for in order to restore vigour and enthusiasm to our journey of holiness and to our ministry.

> At the same time, let us make every effort to be *true ministers of mercy.* We know that in this sacrament, as in others, we are called to be agents of a grace which

comes not from us but from on high and works by its own inner power. In other words "and this is a great responsibility," God counts on us, on our availability and fidelity, in order to work His wonders in human hearts. In the celebration of this sacrament, perhaps even more than in the others, it is *important that the faithful have an intense experience of the face of Christ the Good shepherd.*

Allow me therefore to speak to you on this theme, imagining as it were all the places "cathedrals, parishes, shrines, or elsewhere" in which you are daily engaged in administering this sacrament. Our minds turn to the pages of the Gospel which reveal most directly the *merciful face of God.* How can we fail to think of the moving meeting between the prodigal son and his forgiving father? Or the image of the sheep which was lost and then found, and which the shepherd joyfully lifts onto his shoulders? The father's embrace and the good shepherd's joy must be visible in each one of us, dear brothers, whenever a penitent asks us to become ministers of forgiveness.

In order to bring out certain specific aspects of the unique saving dialogue that is sacramental confession, I would like to use the "biblical icon" of the meeting between Jesus and *Zacchaeus* (cf. Lk 19: 1-10). To me it seems that what takes place between Jesus and the "chief tax collector" of Jericho resembles in a number of ways the celebration of the *Sacrament of Mercy.* As we follow this brief but powerful story, we try to capture in Christ's demeanour and in His voice all those nuances of wisdom, both human and supernatural, which we too must strive to communicate if the sacrament is to be celebrated in the best possible way.

CHAPTER 3
RADIATING PRESENCE: HOLINESS

J ohn Paul II radiated God's presence. He electrified people when he greeted them individually or in massive crowds. People were converted by his very presence.

Saint Faustina recorded the words of our Lord about the radiation of His mercy:

> "I am Love and Mercy itself. When a soul approaches Me with trust, I fill it with such an abundance of graces that it cannot contain them within itself, *but radiates them to other souls*" (*Diary*, 1074).

Saint Faustina prayed for this radiation of mercy:

> I want to be completely transformed into Your mercy and to be Your living reflection, O Lord. May the greatest of all divine attributes, that of Your unfathomable mercy, pass through my heart and soul to my neighbor (*Diary*, 163).

John Paul II was a holy man who entrusted his pontificate to The Divine Mercy: "Jesus, I trust in You!" and Divine Mercy "form[ed] the image of [his] pontificate" (Shrine of The Divine Mercy, Poland, June 7, 1997). He was totally abandoned to the truth of the living Word of God (see *Mother of the Redeemer*, 14), and, like Mary, totally entrusted to the will of God: "*Totus Tuus.*" In short, John Paul II was a holy man, a man of God, a man who prayed.

We can understand John Paul II better from the answer Father Adam Boniecki, MIC (past editor of the Polish edition of *L'Osservatore Romano* and personal friend of John Paul), gave to a question about the personal life of John Paul II: "Why don't you write about the personal life of the Pope? For example, what does he like for breakfast? What does he do to relax?"

Father Boniecki answered, "I did write an article about the Pope's daily life, which the Pope okayed. But he lives the life of a Carmelite. He is either working or praying!"

John Paul II's dedication to prayer and to the work of the Lord was so evident that mercy radiated out from him.

✠ JOHN PAUL II Entrusts His 25-Year Pontificate to Divine Mercy, October 16, 2003

During a Mass celebrated at the same hour he was elected Pope exactly 25 years ago, John Paul II placed his life in God's hands and requested the help of believers worldwide.

The Holy Father sang some of the songs and not only presided at, but also celebrated the Mass in a packed St Peter's Square.

In the homily, John Paul II recalled those moments when the College of Cardinals elected him at age 58 as St. Peter's 264th Successor.

As news of his election in 1978 went out, church bells pealed throughout his native Poland.

"Humanly speaking, how could I not tremble?" the Pope asked. "How could I not feel the weight of such a great responsibility?"

"It was necessary to take *recourse to Divine Mercy* so that when asked the question 'Do you accept?' I could answer with confidence: 'In obedience of the faith, before Christ my Lord, commending myself to the Mother of Christ and of the Church, conscious of the great difficulties, I accept,' " he recalled.

This entrustment echoes John Paul II's statement of June 7, 1997 during his visit to the Shrine of Divine Mercy, Lagiewniki-Krakow Poland:

> On the threshold of the third millennium I come to entrust to Him once more my Petrine ministry —
> "Jesus, I trust in You!"

CHAPTER 4
MINISTRY TO THE SICK AND THE POOR

John Paul II responded with mercy to the sick. He established a yearly celebration, *The World Day of the Sick* (February 11, the Feast of Our Lady of Lourdes).

On February 11, 1989, I personally saw his compassion for the sick as he laid hands of blessing upon each of the hundreds of sick in wheelchairs and stretchers assembled in St. Peter's Basilica.

In the encyclical *Gospel of Life*, May 13, 1993, John Paul II wrote:

> Pain and suffering have meaning and value when they are experienced in close connection with love received and given. In this regard I have called for the yearly celebration of the World Day of the Sick, [February 11], emphasizing the salvific nature of offering up of suffering which, experienced in communion with Christ, belongs to the very essence of the redemption (94).

In the apostolic letter *On the Christian Meaning of Human Suffering* (*Salvifici Dolores*), February 11, 1984, John Paul II describes how Jesus Christ transforms suffering into salvific love. Moreover, He has opened His salvific suffering to man. He lives in the one He has loved by suffering and dying (20). "At one and the same time Christ has taught man *to do good by his suffering and to do good to those who suffer*. He has completely revealed the meaning of suffering" (30).

In his conclusion, John Paul II prayed that all peoples of all times might find in the Redeemer, the Man of Sorrows who has taken on all our physical and moral sufferings, the love that gives salvific meaning to their sorrows. He asked all who suffer to support him. "May your suffering in union with the cross of Christ be victorious!" (31).

In his pilgrimages around the world, John Paul II visited the ghettoes, the poorest of the poor, and the native peoples. His very presence was a sign of hope and encouragement.

The progressively increasing infirmity of John Paul II was a model of offering suffering and pain as a powerful means of intercession, united with Jesus at the Throne of the Father, for mercy on the whole world. He was a living homily that became stronger than words, especially when he lay dying in the papal apartment in late March and early April of 2005.

✝ **DURING THE PILGRIMAGE OF HIS HOLINESS JOHN PAUL II TO LOURDES on the Occasion of the 150th Anniversary of the Promulgation of the Dogma of the Immaculate Conception**

On August 14, 2004, at Lourdes, with the infirmity of his advancing age he was like a living homily, identifying himself with the suffering of the sick:

> Here at this Grotto of Massabielle, I wish first of all to greet the sick who come in ever greater numbers to this Shrine, those who have accompanied them, their caregivers and their families.
>
> I am here with you, dear brothers and sisters, as a pilgrim to Our Lady. I make my own your prayers and your hopes. With you I share a time of life marked by physical suffering, yet not for that reason any less fruitful in God's wondrous plan. With you I pray for all those who trust in your prayers.
>
> In carrying out my apostolic ministry I have always trusted greatly in the offerings, prayers, and sacrifices of the suffering. During this pilgrimage I ask you to join me in offering to God, through the intercession of the Virgin Mary, all the intentions of the Church and of the world.
>
> Dear brothers and sisters who are sick, how I would like to embrace each and every one of you with affec-

tion, to tell you how close I am to you and how much I support you. I now do so in spirit, entrusting you to the maternal love of the Mother of the Lord and entreating her to obtain for all of us the blessings and consolations of Jesus, her Son.

✝ **IN HIS BOOK,** *Rise Let Us Be on Our Way* **(2004), John Paul II gives his very personal testimony about visiting the sick during his pastoral visits in Krakow:**

I have always been very conscious of the fundamental importance of what the suffering contribute to the life of the Church. I remember that at the beginning the sick intimidated me. I needed a lot of courage to stand before a sick person and enter, so to speak, into his physical and spiritual pain, not to betray discomfort, and to show at least a little loving compassion. Only later did I begin to grasp the profound meaning of the mystery of human suffering. In a sense, the sick provoke mercy. Through their prayers and sacrifices, they not only ask for mercy but create a "space for mercy," or better, open up spaces for mercy. By their illness and suffering they call forth acts of mercy and create the possibility for accomplishing them. I would entrust the needs of the Church to the prayers of the sick, and the results were always positive.

CHAPTER 5
THE INFLUENCE OF JOHN PAUL II

✝ THE INFLUENCE ON THE VATICAN STAFF

May 13, 2001, from Diario Cardinal Castrillon Hoyos, prefect of the Congregation of the Clergy.

> "Priests of God, You embody the Mystery of Mercy: Reflection and Prayers on the Priesthood and the Mercy of God in Light of the Letter of the Holy Father John Paul II to Priests," Holy Thursday 2001.

> In six pages of *L'Osservatore Romano*, August 8/15, 2001 Cardinal Castrillon Hoyos gives a summary of The Divine Mercy message and devotion to all the priests of the world!

✝ DAYS OF PRAYER FOR THE SANCTIFICATION OF PRIESTS HELD

Vatican City, June 4, 2002

Mindful of the sexual abuses involving priests, the Catholic Church observed a World Day of Prayer for the Sanctification of Priests.

The majority of dioceses observed it on June 4, the feast of the Sacred Heart.

Cardinal Dario Castrillon Hoyos, prefect of the Vatican Congregation for the Clergy, wrote a letter to the world's more than 400,000 priests, proposing the renewal of the *experience of God's mercy* in their lives in order to rediscover their priestly identity.

Specifically, he suggested two indispensable means: frequent recourse to the Sacraments of Reconciliation and the Eucharist.

"If, absurdly, we do not do this, we will find ourselves increasingly submerged in the night, in a confused ethical darkness, in spiritual impotence in face of a wave of evil that would run the risk of drowning us," the Colombian Cardinal explained.

Cardinal Castrillon's letter, signed May 8, proposed to all priests to transform their lives by experiencing Divine Mercy, the devotion promoted by now St. Faustina Kowalska.

"If we make Jesus' call to have 'confidence in His Divine Mercy' penetrate our being, which the Pope has relaunched in the present time, we will realize that it is precisely priests who are personally called to allow themselves to be imbued by the Spirit given to us by the risen Christ, which makes us a sign of God's forgiveness for all," the letter continues.

"Without forgiveness, the fruit of mercy, peace would be a pure utopia, and vengeance and reprisal would inevitably take its place." the cardinal stressed.

Given the present situation, the prefect concluded: "Although at times our discouragement may be intense in face of the indifference of the world, which can even become hostility against the Church, we must not forget that our society thirsts for the forgiveness and peace that the risen Christ has come to bring, and that has its origin only in Him."

✝ JUNE 29, 2002: Indulgences attached to Divine Mercy Devotion

On June 29, the Apostolic Penitentiary published the Decree in which the Holy Father attached a plenary and a partial indulgence to the devout observance of the Second Sunday of Easter or Divine Mercy Sunday. In an audience given to the Pro-Penitentiary Major and the Regent of the Apostolic Penitentiary on June 13, the Holy Father approved the content of the Decree. The Decree was published in the press on August 3 and announced by the Holy Father at the Sunday *Angelus* on August 4.

The Decree gives the reason and conditions for the plenary and partial indulgence. A summary of The Divine Mercy devotion explains the Image, the Feast, the Chaplet, and the Hour of Mercy.

The Decree concludes with the duty of priests:

Priests who exercise pastoral ministry, especially parish priests, should inform the faithful in the most suitable way of the Church's salutary provision. they should promptly and generously be willing to hear their confessions. On Divine Mercy Sunday, after celebrating Mass or Vespers, or during devotions in honor of Divine Mercy, with the dignity that is in accord with the rite, they should lead the recitation of the prayers that have been given above. Finally, since "Blessed are the merciful, for they shall obtain mercy" (Mt 5:7), when they instruct their people, priests should gently encourage the faithful to practice works of charity or mercy as often as they can, following the example of, and in obeying the commandment of Jesus Christ, as is listed for the second general concession of indulgence in the *Enchiridion Indulgentiarum.*

✝ **THE INFLUENCE OF JOHN PAUL II on the Knights of Columbus**

The Knights of Columbus provide parishes with The Divine Mercy Hour of Prayer and Divine Mercy Images for Mercy Sunday.

In July of 2002, John Paul II inspired the Knights of Columbus by telling them:"Now is the time for a great catch." Alluding to the words that Jesus spoke to Peter, the Pope urged the Knights to "cast out their nets out into the deep" (Lk 5-4). In an article by Felix Carroll appearing in *Marian Helper* magazine (Spring 2004), "Divine Mercy far and wide" describes how the Knights are helping parishes to discover the message of Divine Mercy by providing a Divine Mercy Hour of Prayer. Then Felix Carroll gives the inside story of a great promoter of Divine Mercy, Bob Allard, who provides Divine Mercy Images to parishes:

When I heard this [being said to the Knights of Columbus by the Pope] said Robert Allard, a Knight from Port St. Lucie, Florida, "My eyes were just wide open." I thought, "Wow, Divine Mercy is written all over the Pope's urgings."

The April 2004 issue of *Columbia*, the official magazine of the Knights of Columbus, carried four articles on the Knights and The Divine Mercy:

• "A Father Rich in Mercy" by Supreme Knight Carl A. Anderson. He concludes with:

> The Knights of Columbus has many programs to strengthen family life. One of the most important is our current Divine Mercy Hour of Prayer. This devotion has a special place in the Holy Father's heart. It can have a special place as well in each of our families, councils, and parishes. and it can — and will — strengthen the bond of brother Knights committed to the principles of Charity, Unity, and Fraternity.

• "What the World Needs Now: The Message of Divine Mercy Transmitted by St. Faustina Kowalska and Being Furthered by the Knights Is a Very Contemporary One," by Ludmila Grygiel. She concludes with:

> We must never despair or allow ourselves to be passive observers of the chaos around us. Instead, what we see must convince us of the world's desperate need for Divine Mercy.

> In the 1930s, Christ spoke to Sister Faustina words that are just as true now at the start of the 21st century: "Tell acking mankind to snuggle close to My merciful Heart and I will fill it with peace" (*Diary*, 1074). It would not be incorrect then, that while we work for justice and peace we must work above all for mercy.

Ludmila Grygiel writes from Rome. She is the author of a spiritual biography of St. Faustina in Polish.

• "Mercy Messengers: A Devotion Close to the Holy Father's Heart Is Being Popularized by the Knights of Columbus," by Brian Caulfield, the managing editor of *Columbia*. He concludes his article by saying:

"We were the first council in D.C. to receive the [Divine Mercy] image, so we thought it was appropriate to hold the prayer service on the Pope's anniversary. Divine Mercy in my life was a stimulus for my own vocation, and I think it has meaning for all Knights." said Father Kalisch, who was ordained last spring. "It underlines the role of charity in our lives, the role of forgiveness and small acts of goodness. These are things we can all practice."

• "The Secretary and Priest of Divine Mercy: St. Faustina Kowalska and Fr. Michael Sopocko," by Fr. Robert Barnhill. In this article, Fr. Barnhill describes St. Faustina's call by the Lord and the spiritual direction that Fr. Sopocko gave her. Saint Faustina was the first saint of the Great Jubilee Year to be canonized by Pope John Paul II, April 30, 2000, She was also hailed by the Pope John Paul II as "the great Apostle of Divine Mercy in our time" (Divine Mercy Sunday, April 13, 1994).

PART IV
MERCY THEMES

Repeated themes in the writings and teachings of John Paul II, like repeated themes in a symphony, express his compassion and love for God and for all human beings.

CHAPTER 1
THE VALUE AND DIGNITY
OF EACH PERSON

Throughout his teachings and writings, we hear the repeated theme of the dignity, the meaning and the value of each person, stressing the right to freedom of every human being. This repeated theme is an expression of his existential phenomenology, a philosophy that focuses on the subjective response to objective reality. It is a form of personalism that stresses the fact that we are created in the image and likeness of God (see Gen 1:26-27). This text of Genesis is the foundation of his moral ethic: Since we are created in the image of God, we are to behave like God.

John Paul II repeated often the text of the Vatican II document on the Church and the modern world (*Gaudium et spes*, 22) that:

> Christ, the new Adam, in the very revelation of the mystery of the Father and His love, *fully reveals man to himself and brings to light his most high calling* (quoted in *Redeemer of Man*, 8).

In the same encyclical he deals with the Church's mission and human freedom, quoting the Vatican II document on Human Freedom:

> The missionary attitude always begins with a feeling of deep esteem for "what is in man" (Declaration *Nostra Aetate*, 1-2).

This theme of human dignity, developed more fully in the second encyclical of John Paul II, *Rich in Mercy*, is found in the parable of the prodigal son (see 5-6):

The inheritance that the son has received from his father was a quantity of material goods, but more important than the goods was *his dignity as a son in his father's house* (5). ... The father's fidelity to himself is totally concentrated upon the humanity of the lost son, upon his dignity (6). ... The relationship of mercy is based on the common experience of the dignity that is proper to him (6). ... Mercy is manifested in its true and proper aspect when it restores to value, promotes, and draws good from all the forms of evil existing in the world and in man (6).

The *Catechism of the Catholic Church* develops the theme of the "Dignity of the Human Person" (1700-1876) in an extensive way, quoting Sacred Scripture, the Church Fathers, the Vatican II document on the Church and the Modern World (*Gaudium et Spes*), and the writings of John Paul II. This theme of the dignity of man is also developed in the sections on creation (355-421), on the sixth commandment (2331-2400), and the Sacrament of Marriage (400-414).

The theme of the dignity, freedom, and equality of man is strongly developed in John Paul II's *Theology of the Body* (Wednesday elocutions from 1979 to 1984), pointing out his teaching on sexuality, marriage, and celibacy as an expression of the "Law of the Gift." Christopher West beautifully summarizes John Paul II's *Theology of the Body* (*Inside the Vatican*, November 1998, p.42 ff.).

CHAPTER 2
BE NOT AFRAID

J ohn Paul II began his papacy with the cry: "Be not afraid!"

> When, on October 22, 1978, I said the words "Be not afraid!" in St. Peter's Square, I could not fully know how far they would take me and the entire Church. Their meaning came more from the Holy Spirit, the Consoler, promised by the Lord Jesus to His disciples, than from the man who spoke them. Nevertheless, with the passing of the years, I have recalled these words on many occasions. ... Why should we have no fear? Because man has been redeemed by God. ... The power of Christ's Cross and Resurrection is greater than any evil which man could or should fear (*Threshold of Hope*, 1994).

On one special occasion he recalled these words, "Be not afraid" while at the Shrine of The Divine Mercy in Poland, June 7, 1997. He related them to the abandonment of self-giving that is the "Law of the Gift" in the message of Divine Mercy:

> And it is a *message that is clear and understandable for everyone*. Anyone can come here, look at this image of the merciful Jesus, His Heart radiating grace, and hear in the depths of his own soul what Blessed Faustina heard: "*Fear nothing. I am with you always*" (*Diary*, 586).

> And if this person responds with a sincere heart: "*Jesus, I trust in You*," he will find comfort in all his *anxieties* and fears. In this "dialogue of abandonment," there is established between man and Christ a *special bond that sets love free*. And "there is no fear in love, but perfect love casts out fear" (1 Jn 4:18).

John Paul II relates his "Be not afraid" theme to *trust in Jesus.* He then goes on to renew once more his entrustment of his Petrine pontificate to the merciful Lord by praying: "Jesus, I trust in You!"

At the canonization of St. Faustina, John Paul II again related the prayer "Jesus, I trust in You!" to his theme of "Be not afraid:"

> This simple act of abandonment to Jesus dispels the thickest of clouds and lets a ray of light penetrate every life. *"Jezu, ufam Tobie"* (8).

And addressing Faustina, he prayed as a conclusion to his homily:

> Fixing our gaze with you on the face of the risen Christ, let us make our own your prayer of trusting abandonment and say with firm hope: Christ "Jesus, I trust in you!" *"Jezu, ufam Tobie!"*

✝ **"SINGING OF THE MERCIES OF THE LORD FOREVER"** (Ps 89:2) is another way John Paul II expresses his trust and hope that overcomes fear. He has repeated this "singing of the mercies of the Lord forever" at the significant moments of his pontificate:

> *At Fatima,* May 13, 1982, a year after the attempted assassination, he came to give thanks to the Mother of Divine Mercy by "singing of the mercies of the Lord" (Ps 89). In his parting address he said:

>> I began this pilgrimage with the canticle of God's mercy in my heart; and, on my departure, I want to tell you that my soul is still vibrating with this canticle; and "I will sing the mercies of the Lord" (Ps 89) in the choir of the present generation of the Church, which has as first soloist the Mother of Divine Mercy.

On his 75th birthday, May 18, 1995, he thanked God for the graces of his parents, his ordination as priest and bishop, saying he is "singing the mercies of God forever!"

On his 50th anniversary of ordination, November 1, 1996, he published his memoirs as priest recalling all these things as "singing of the mercies of the Lord forever!"

On coming to the Shrine of The Divine Mercy in Poland, June 7, 1997, he began his address with "'I will sing of the mercies of the Lord forever!' — and join the unending hymn in honor of Divine Mercy."

Then at the canonization of St. Faustina, April 30, 2000, he began with Psalm 118:1, "Give thanks to the Lord for He is good; His mercy endures forever." In his text, he quoted Psalm 89 and stated that Sr. Faustina had made her life a hymn to mercy. Then again he said:

> "The mercies of the Lord I will sing forever" (Ps 89:2). Let us too, the pilgrim Church, join our voice to the voice of Mary most holy, "Mother of Mercy," and to the voice of the new saint [St. Faustina] who sings of mercy with all God's friends in the heavenly Jerusalem.

CHAPTER 3

THE CALL TO HOLINESS, EVANGELIZATION, AND ECUMENISM

✝ JOHN PAUL II REACHED OUT TO ORTHODOX CHRISTIANS AND MUSLIMS, MAY 2001

In Damascus, Syria, and them in Athens, Greece, the Pope met with Archbishop Christodoulos of the Greek Orthodox Church. They prayed together the Lord's Prayer, breaking an Orthodox taboo against joint prayer with Catholics. At the end of the visit, Christodoulos declared it "the beginning of a new era."

John Paul II focused on three areas of the Second Vatican Council and made them into themes of his pontificate: the universal call to holiness, a new evangelization, and ecumenism that will lead to Church unity.

✝ UNIVERSAL CALL TO HOLINESS

In Chapter Five of the Dogmatic Constitution (*Lumen Gentium*) of Vatican II entitled: "The Call of the Whole Church to Holiness," we read:

> In the Church, everyone belonging to the hierarchy, or being cared for by it, is called to holiness, according to the saying of the Apostle: "For this is the will of God, your sanctification" (1 Thes 4:3; Eph 1:4).

Pope John Paul II very actively encouraged us to sanctity, to union with Jesus Christ. From the beginning of his pontificate he challenged us to "open our hearts to the Redeemer!"

Moreover, John Paul II gave us many models of holiness during his more than 26 years as Pope. He beatified over 800 men and women, most of them martyrs for their faith in the Lord. Saint Faustina was the 197th saint he canonized — there have been only 593 saints canonized in the last 500 years! John

Paul II certainly made it loud and clear that he wanted us to follow their example. This world needs millions of saints to call down God's mercy!

✝ NEW EVANGELIZATION

In the encyclical *Mission of the Redeemer* (*Redemptoris Missio*), 1990, John Paul II presents the third millennium as a time to reach out with the Good News of Jesus Christ to the nations and to those who need re-evangelization:

> As the third millennium of redemption draws near, God is preparing a *great springtime for Christianity.* ... For each believer as for the entire Church, the missionary task must remain foremost, for it concerns the eternal destiny of humanity and corresponds to God's mysterious and merciful plan (18).

Everyone is called to evangelize — to tell others of *God's mysteries and merciful plan!*

And the first form of evangelization is witness (see 42) of our own lives. The first proclamation of Christ is to proclaim His salvation in our own lives and the offering of salvation to all people "as a gift of God's grace and mercy."

St. Augustine loved to say that we must evangelize and, if necessary, use words!

✝ ECUMENISM: COMMITMENT TO CHURCH UNITY

"Promoting the restoration of unity among all Christians is one of the chief concerns of the Second Vatican Council." The Decree on Ecumenism opens with this statement that John Paul II carried out as a major thrust of his pontificate and his encyclical *That They Be One* (*Ut Unum Sint*), with the subtitle "On Commitment to Ecumenism."

John Paul II reached out to Protestant and Orthodox groups around the world, calling for prayer, dialogue of our gifts (not just a dialogue of ideas), mutual forgiveness, and conversion.

John Paul II set his heart on the unity of the Church. How can the world believe our witness if those who confess the name of Christ are divided?

CHAPTER 4
MARY, MOTHER OF MERCY

Mary was a central figure of John Paul II's pontificate. This is evident in his motto *"Totus Tuus"* — "I am all yours, Mary" — and his repeated consecrations to Mary at various shrines around the world. He concluded each of his encyclicals with a prayer to Mary.

✝ **RICH IN MERCY** (*Dives in Misericordia*, Nov., 1980), has a special section on Mary, Mother of Mercy (9): (See the *Appendixes* for the full text.)

> Mary proclaimed on the threshold of her kinswoman's house: "His mercy is ... from generation to generation" (Lk 1:50). Mary is also the one who experienced mercy in a particular and exceptional way, as no other person has. At the same time, still in an exceptional way, she made possible with the sacrifice of her heart her own sharing in revealing God's mercy. This sacrifice is intimately linked with the Cross of her Son, at the foot of which she was to stand on Calvary. Her sacrifice is a unique sharing in the revelation of mercy.

✝ **MOTHER OF THE REDEEMER** (*Redemptoris Mater*), Encyclical on the Blessed Virgin Mary in the Life of the Pilgrim Church, March 25, 1987.

John Paul II describes the faith of Mary and how she abandoned herself to the truth of the word of the living God (see 14).

Mary shares in the great mystery of mercy:

> Through this faith Mary is perfectly united with Christ in His self-emptying [the Law of the Gift in our redemption] ... At the foot of the Cross, Mary shares through faith in the shocking mystery of this self-emptying. This is perhaps the deepest "*kenosis*" of faith in human history (18).

> As Virgin and Mother she was singularly united in His first coming, so through her continued collaboration with Him she will also be united with Him in the expectation of the second; ... she also has that specifically maternal role of mediatrix of mercy at His final coming (41, emphasis added).

✝ **GOSPEL OF LIFE** (*Evangelium Vitae*) March 25, 1995 John Paul II concludes his encyclical by entrusting the unborn babies to Mary with a prayer to proclaim the Gospel of Life:

> O Mary,
> bright dawn
> of the new world,
> Mother of the living,
> to you do we entrust
> the cause of life:
> Look down, O Mother,
> upon the vast numbers
> of babies not allowed
> to be born,
> of the poor whose lives
> are made difficult,
> of men and women who are
> victims of brutal violence,

of the elderly
and the sick killed
by indifference
or out of misguided mercy.
Grant that all who
believe in your Son may
proclaim the Gospel of Life
with honesty and love
to the people of our time.
Obtain for them the grace
to accept that Gospel
as a gift ever new,
the joy of celebrating it
with gratitude throughout
their lives and the courage
to bear witness to it
resolutely, in order
to build, together with
all people of good will,
the civilization of
truth and love,
to the praise and glory
of God, the Creator
and lover of life.

✝ **MERCY SUNDAY,** *April 10, 1994*

John Paul II ends his *Regina Caeli* address with a prayer for trust to the Mother of Mercy:

> O Mary, Mother of Mercy! You know the heart of your divine Son better than anyone. Instill in us the filial trust in Jesus practiced by the saints, the trust that animated Blessed Faustina Kowalska, the great apostle of Divine Mercy in our time.
>
> Look lovingly upon our misery: O Mother, draw us away from the contrary temptations of self-sufficiency and despair, and obtain for us an abundance of saving mercy.

✝ VICTORY STRATEGY in VERITATIS SPLENDOR

In his tenth encyclical, *Veritatis Splendor* (*Splendor of the Truth*), August 6, 1993, John Paul II revealed his "victory strategy" for overcoming the greatest moral problems of our times. In the conclusion of *Veritatis Splendor* he turns to the same "victory strategy" that he invoked in the defeat of Soviet atheistic communism.

It is commonly accepted that Pope John Paul II had a significant role in the dissolution of the U.S.S.R. It is even acknowledged by Mikhail Gorbachev and *Time magazine*. But John Paul II attributed the victory not to himself, but to the Virgin Mother of God.

The "victory strategy" of John Paul II was to entrust all to Mary, the Mother of God.

This was the victory strategy of the Primate of Poland, Stefan Cardinal Wyszynski who, while imprisoned by the communist Polish government, entrusted himself to Mary for the sake of the Church and the nation. He then arranged for a national renewal of vows to Mary on the 400th anniversary of the vows of King Kazimierz in thanksgiving to Mary for the victory over the Swedes at Jasna Gora. Over a million people gathered with the Polish bishops on May 3, 1956, at Jasna Gora to entrust the Church and the Polish nation to Mary. The next ten years were a novena in preparation for the solemn consecration of the nation marking the millennium of Christianity (May 3, 1966). Archbishop Karol Wojtyla preached the homily. Later, when he returned to Poland as Pope, he said:

> It seems to me that we have done something great, something that first demands faith and that later will bring forth great fruit for the Holy Church in Poland and the world (June 4, 1979).

As the newly elected Pope, John Paul II dedicated his pontificate to Mary, using as his motto: *Totus Tuus*. On his first visit to Poland as Pope, he returned to Jasna Gora (June 4, 1979) and renewed his solemn consecration to Mary:

I entrust to you, Mother of the Church, all the work-
ings of the Church, all its missions and all its service in
perspective of the second thousand years of Christianity
that are now ending on earth.

Both the Primate and the Pope believed in the mediation
of Mary for the freedom of the Church around the world, and
they wanted to entrust everything to her. Truly they believed
that victory in the universal Church, when it comes, will be her
victory (*Cardinal Wyszynski: A Biography*, Andrzej Micewski,
Harcourt Brace, 1984).

Pope John Paul II continued this "victory strategy" in his
pilgrimages around the world, entrusting each nation and the
Church at the various national shrines to Our Lady. His
"victory strategy" reached a pinnacle of power as he knelt
before the original Fatima statue of Mary on the square of St.
Peter's Basilica on the feast of the Annunciation, March 25,
1984, and entrusted all the nations of the world to the Mother
of God, together with the bishops around the world. The
bishops were asked to join in this collegial consecration in their
local dioceses.

From that moment, a cascade of events started: Mikhail
Gorbachev came into power and initiated *peristroika* and
glasnost; solidarity came into power and one Eastern European
country after another shook off atheistic communism, beginning with Poland; the Berlin wall was torn down and the Soviet
Union and communism in Eastern Europe dissolved.

John Paul II's "victory strategy" was entrustment to Mary
—give all to Mary, the woman of victory, in imitation of our
heavenly Father who gave the promise of victory to the woman
(see Gen 3:15), and in imitation of Jesus, who gave all to His
mother (see Jn 19:26) in giving her His Church.

In his tenth and greatest encyclical, *Veritatis Splendor*, John
Paul II applies his "victory strategy" to the great problems of our
day — practical atheism and moral relativism. Practical atheism is
a form of life without God and without truth. Moral relativism is
a life separated from absolute truth — truth separated from

God's laws, separated from laws of nature, separated from conscience and freedom — separated from the power of the Cross.

John Paul II concluded this encyclical by using his
"victory strategy": He entrusts all people of good will and the
research of moralists specifically to Mary, the Mother of God
and Mother of Mercy: (see full text of his entrustment to Mary
in the *Appendixes.*)

> At the end of these considerations, let us entrust our-
> selves, the sufferings and the joys of our life, the moral
> life of believers and people of good will, and the
> research of moralists, to Mary, Mother of God and
> Mother of Mercy (118).

He then goes on to point out that Mary is Mother of
Mercy because she is mother of her Son, Jesus, who revealed
the mercy of the Father. He revealed the fullness of God's
mercy by His Passion, death, and Resurrection, sending the
Holy Spirit to give us new life and making it possible for us to
do good and live the new life of "following Jesus Christ."

Mary is also Mother of Mercy because Jesus entrusted His
Church and all of humanity to her. In her perfect docility to
the Holy Spirit, she "obtains for us Divine Mercy."

Mary is the model of the moral life, John Paul II continues. "She lived and exercised her freedom precisely by giving
herself to God ... and entered fully into the plan of God who
gave Himself to the world." She truly is the "Seat of Wisdom."

Mary is compassionate and understands and loves sinful
man as a mother. She is on the side of truth and shares the burden of the Church in calling all to the demands of morality and
to the power of the Cross.

During his pilgrimage of thanksgiving to Fatima in 1982
after his recovery from the assassination attempt, John Paul II
described consecration of the world to mercy as returning to
the Cross of Christ. Later the next week at the Vatican in his
Regina Caeli message, he developed this theme of consecration
as allowing Mary to bring us to the Cross of Jesus, to the
source of all mercy:

Consecrating the world to the Immaculate Heart of the Mother means returning beneath the Cross of the Son. It means consecrating this world to the pierced Heart of the Savior, bringing it back to the very source of its Redemption. Redemption is always greater than man's sin and the "sin of the world." The power of the Redemption is infinitely superior to the whole range of evil in man and in the world (Homily, May 13, 1982).

In the conclusion of *Veritatis Splendor*, John Paul II writes of God's mercy:

No human sin can erase the mercy of God, or prevent Him from unleashing all His triumphant power, if we only call upon Him. Indeed, sin itself makes even more radiant the love of the Father who, in order to ransom a slave, sacrificed His Son.

Pope John Paul II, aware of the "victory strategy" of entrusting all to the Mother of Mercy prays in conclusion:

O Mary,
Mother of Mercy,
watch over all people,
that the Cross of Christ
may not be emptied of its power,
that man may not stray
from the path of the good
or become blind to sin,
but may put his hope ever more fully in God
who is "rich in mercy" (Eph 2:4).
May he carry out the good works
prepared by God beforehand (cf Eph 2:10)
and so live completely
"for the praise of His glory" (Eph 1:12).

(See the *Appendixes*, p. 207, for a fuller text of the conclusion of the encyclical *Veritatis Splendor*, August 1993.)

CHAPTER 5
THE GREAT JUBILEE YEAR 2000

Pope John Paul II announced the Jubilee Year of 2000 in his encyclical on the Holy Spirit in the Life of the Church and the World, Pentecost 1986. He gives a description of the role of the Jubilee Year. (For a fuller explanation see the next chapter and the *Appendixes*, p. 199, under *Dominum et Vivificantem*, 1986.)

On the solemnity of the Assumption of Our Lady (Aug 15, 1999) John Paul II said in his homily that "the spirit of the Magnificat is the spirit of the Jubilee":

> "My soul magnifies the Lord!" (Lk 1:26). In this perspective, the Virgin of the *Magnificat* helps us to understand better the value and meaning of the Great Jubilee now at our door, a favorable time when the universal Church will join in her canticle to praise the wonder of the Incarnation.

The spirit of the *Magnificat* is the spirit of the Jubilee.

At John Paul II's election as Pope in 1978, Stephan Cardinal Wyszynski, the Primate of Poland told Pope John Paul II that "the Lord has called you [to be Pope]. You are to lead the Church into the third millennium." The Pope took this word as prophetic. In fact, so much so, that understanding the meaning of the Jubilee year as entering into the third millennium is key to understanding John Paul II's pontificate.

In his first encyclical, *Redeemer of Man*, he took up this task and then in *Tertio Millennio Adveniente*, November 10, 1994 (*As the Third Millennium Draws Near*), he laid out a plan of preparation for and celebration of the Jubilee Year 2000. The first phase (1995-1996) was to be a time of preparation, purification, and prayer that introduced the second phase of three years. The year 1997 was devoted to Jesus Christ; the year 1998, to the Holy Spirit; and the year 1999, to the Father.

The Jubilee Year of 2000 was to be celebrated in Rome and in churches throughout the world: a year that presented the goal and fulfillment of Christian life — intensely Eucharistic — with the theme of "Jesus Christ is the same, yesterday, today, and forever" (see Heb 13:8).

John Paul II gave a strong and clear challenge to the Church:

> One thing is certain: Everyone is asked to do as much as possible to ensure that the great challenge of the Year 2000 is not overlooked, for this challenge certainly involves a special grace of the Lord for the Church and for the whole of humanity (*TMA*, 55).

In the official declaration of the Jubilee Year of 2000, *Incarnationis Mysterium* (*The Mystery of the Incarnation*), he called the Jubilee Year a "year of mercy" (41) and "an especially deep experience of mercy" (6).

The celebration of the Jubilee Year for John Paul was the summit of his life, with celebrations of mercy by forgiveness, pilgrimages to Egypt and Mount Sinai, and then to the Holy Land. He called the celebration of Corpus Christi "the heart of the Jubilee Year."

Truly a high point of the Jubilee Year for the Holy Father, and a day of special joy, was the canonization of Saint Faustina:

> Today my joy is truly great in presenting the life and witness of Sr. Faustina Kowalska to the whole Church as a gift of God for our time (Homily, April 30, 2000). ... Sr. Faustina's canonization has a particular eloquence: by this act, I intend to pass this message on to the new millennium. I pass it on to all people, so that they will learn to know even better the true face of God and the true face of their brethren (5, ibid).

The Jubilee Year was certainly a triumph of John Paul II's vision, planning, and determination. Millions of pilgrims swarmed to the heart of the Church for a deeper encounter with the Lord.

CHAPTER 6

THE JUBILEE YEAR, THE NEW ADVENT, THE THIRD MILLENNIUM, AND THE COMING OF THE LORD

The Jubilee Year of 2000 was the "year of mercy," the year of the door leading us into the new Advent and the opening up of the third millennium.

John Paul II writes of the "new Advent" in what can be called a mystical, or even prophetic sense. He wants and expects the Church to encounter the Lord in a new and deeper way. We need to allow the Holy Spirit to act as in a "new Pentecost."

A. THE ENCYCLICALS THAT DESCRIBE THE JUBILEE YEAR

John Paul II writes of a "new Advent" in each of the three encyclicals of the triad on the Holy Trinity in relationship to the new millennium:

✝ **Redeemer of Man** (*Redemptor Hominis*), his first encyclical, March 4, 1979:

We are in a certain way in a season of a new Advent, a season of expectation (1).

What should we do, in order that this new Advent of the Church connected with the approaching end of the second millennium may bring us closer to Him whom Sacred Scripture calls the "Everlasting Father" (Is. 9:6; *RH*, 7)?

It is certain that the Church of the new Advent, the Church that is continually preparing for the new coming of the Lord, must be the Church of the Eucharist and of Penance (20).

As I end this meditation with a warm and humble call to prayer, I wish the Church to devote herself to this prayer, together with Mary, the Mother of Jesus (cf. Acts 1:14), as the Apostles and disciples of the Lord did in the Upper Room in Jerusalem after His Ascension. Above all, I implore Mary, the heavenly Mother of the Church, to be so good as to devote herself to this prayer of humanity's new Advent, together with us who make up the Church, that is to say the Mystical Body of her Only Son. I hope that through this prayer we shall be able to receive the Holy Spirit coming upon us and thus be witnesses "to the end of the earth" (Acts 1:8), like those who went forth from the Upper Room in Jerusalem on the day of Pentecost (22).

✝ **Rich in Mercy** (*Dives in Misericordia*) First Sunday of Advent, 1980:

The same mystery of Christ, which reveals to us the great vocation of man and which led me to emphasize in the encyclical *Redemptor Hominis* His incomparable dignity, also obliges me to proclaim mercy as God's merciful love revealed in that same mystery of Christ. [This mystery of Christ] likewise obliges me to have recourse to that mercy and to beg for it at this difficult, critical phase of the history of the Church and of the world as we approach the end of the second millennium (15).

✝ **Lord and Giver of Life** (*Dominum et Vivificantem*), on the Holy Spirit in the life of the Church and World, Pentecost Sunday, 1986.

In the third encyclical of the trilogy on the Holy Trinity, John Paul II gives a thorough description of the Jubilee Year and its transition to the third millennium. Eighteen times he refers to this transition. A few highlights will illustrate the importance he placed on the Great Jubilee:

The Great Jubilee will mark the passage from the second to the third Christian millennium (2).

In Part II of the encyclical, John Paul II dedicates two sections to the "Reason for the Jubilee of the Year 2000:"

1. Christ, who was conceived of the Holy Spirit (49).

    The Church cannot prepare for the Jubilee in another way than in the Holy Spirit (51).

2. Grace has been made manifest (52)

    In the mystery of the Incarnation, the work of the Spirit "who gives life," reaches its highest point (52).

John Paul ends his reflections on the Holy Spirit and the Great Jubilee by imploring the Holy Spirit for the peace and joy that are the fruit of love in the transition from the second to the third Christian millennium (see 67).

B. THE MESSAGE OF DIVINE MERCY IS THE MESSAGE OF THE THIRD MILLENNIUM

On Mercy Sunday, April 30, 2000, in the homily for the canonization of St. Faustina, John Paul II stressed the message of Divine Mercy as *the* message for the third millennium:

> Jesus told Sr. Faustina: "Mankind will not find peace until it turns with trust to My mercy" (*Diary*, 300). Through the work of [this] Polish religious, this message has been linked forever to the 20th century, the last of the second millennium and the bridge to the third. ... The light of Divine Mercy, which the Lord in a way wished to return to the world through Sr. Faustina's charism, will illumine the way for men and women of the third millennium. ...

> Sister Faustina's canonization has a particular eloquence: by this act I intend today to pass this message on to the new millennium. I pass it on to all people (2, 3, 5).

C. TWO PROPHETIC STREAMS ABOUT THE THIRD MILLENNIUM

In the March 1999 issue of the *Renewal Ministries* newsletter, Ralph Martin described two prophetic streams about the future: John Paul II's prophetic announcement of a "new springtime" and Mary's urgent call to conversion.

The two streams may appear to be contradictory, but rather, they are complementary. The Scripture text that brings these two streams into a unity is Luke 7:31-35:

> "What comparison can I use for the men of today? What are they like? They are like children squatting in the city squares and calling to their playmates,
>
> > 'We piped you a tune but you did not dance, we sang you a dirge but you did not wail.'
>
> "I mean that John the Baptist came neither eating bread nor drinking wine, and you say, 'He is mad!' The Son of Man came and He both ate and drank, and you say, 'Here is a glutton and a drunkard, a friend of tax collectors and sinners!' God's wisdom is vindicated by all who accept it."

Ralph Martin comments on the two different approaches of John Paul II and Mary:

> *Pope John Paul II* is piping a tune of "new springtime," of "new Pentecost," of a "Great Jubilee" — and there are many refusing to dance, to undergo the preparation "in the Holy Spirit" to become "docile to the Holy Spirit" which are preconditions for the coming of the new springtime.
>
> *Mary* is weeping, is singing a dirge, weeping for her children who are in danger of being swept away by the immense and proximate danger, the closeness of the chastisement and judgment, the danger of eternal

death, of hell. And there are many who are refusing to have their hearts broken by her tears; there are many who are refusing to respond to the profound simplicity of her repeated calls to conversion. ...

John Paul is calling us to a dance of preparation for the "greatest Jubilee the Church has ever celebrated."

Mary is weeping for those in danger of missing the visitation and has unveiled a personal plan of preparation for what is coming that involves prayer, fasting, repentance and Reconciliation, daily Eucharist, rosary, conversion and faith.

These messages are complementary, they are two sides of one coin, two edges of one sword. It is urgent that we respond.

D. AT THE BEGINNING OF THE NEW MILLENNIUM

✝ *NOVO MILLENNIUM INUENTE,* Apostolic Letter of Pope John Paul II, January 6, 2001, the Solemnity of the Epiphany

In this letter, John Paul II reflects on and makes a general assessment of the Jubilee Year 2000, setting before the Church the challenge to "put out into the deep" (*Duc in Altum,* Lk 5:6) as we enter into the third millennium.

He gives "thanks to the Lord for He is good, for His mercy endures forever" (Ps 118:1), and he "sings of the mercies of the Lord forever" (Ps 89:2):

This Jubilee Year has been an experience of the three essential aspects [true hope, reconciliation, one unceasing hymn of praise of the Trinity], reaching moments of intensity which have made us as it were *touch with our hands the merciful presence of God ...* (4, emphasis added).

John Paul II challenges us "to contemplate the face of Christ" and "put out into the deep" (15) — by a life of faith based on prayer and contemplation — allowing grace to take us by the hand. He calls us to the experience of silence and prayer, which is the setting for development of faith (20). Yes, he calls us to contemplate Christ's face of sorrow and of resurrection (28). He calls us to "start afresh from Christ" (29).

The Holy Father makes it clear that:

> all pastoral initiations [in setting out into the deep] must be set in relationship to holiness (30), prayer (32), the Sunday Eucharist (35), and the Sacrament of Reconciliation (36).

In all of this planning we must observe the principle: "the primacy of grace" (38). Throughout he calls us to mercy, to forgiveness, to compassion.

John Paul then reflects on the challenges of the third millennium: the need for the witness of love (42), a spirituality of communion (43), ecumenism (48), the works of charity and mercy (49), as well as the challenges of the present: an ecological crisis, problems of peace, and fundamental human rights (51).

He concludes with the challenge of *Duc in Altum*! Put out into the deep:

> Let us go forward in hope! A new millennium is opening before the Church like a vast ocean upon which we shall venture, relying on the help of Christ ... (58).

> We need to imitate the zeal of St. Paul: "straining forward to what lies ahead, and pressing on towards the goal for the prize of the upward call in Christ Jesus" (Phil 3:13-14) (58).

✝ LETTER OF JOHN PAUL II TO PRIESTS: Holy Thursday 2001

Pope John Paul II challenges the priests of the world to rediscover their vocation as a "mystery of mercy":

So, as we gaze upon Christ at the Last Supper, as He becomes for us the "bread that is broken," as He stoops down in humble service at the feet of the Apostles, how can we not experience, together with Peter, the same feeling of unworthiness in the face of the greatness of the gift received? "You shall never wash my feet" (Jn 13:8). Peter was wrong to reject Christ's gesture. But he was right to feel unworthy of it. It is important, on this day of love par excellence, that we should feel the grace of the priesthood as a super-abundance of mercy.

Mercy is the absolutely free initiative by which God has chosen us: "You did not choose Me but I chose you" (Jn 15:16).

Mercy is His deigning to call us to act as His representatives, though He knows that we are sinners.

Mercy is forgiveness which He never refuses us, as He did not refuse it to Peter after his betrayal. The avowal that "there will be more joy in heaven over one sinner who repents than over ninety-nine righteous persons who need no repentance" (Lk 15:7) also holds true for us.

Let us then rediscover our vocation as a "mystery of mercy." In the Gospel we find that Peter receives his special ministry with precisely this spiritual attitude. His experience is indicative for all those who have received the apostolic task in the different grades of the Sacrament of Orders.

PART V
THE LEGACY OF JOHN PAUL II

Discover why Divine Mercy — as the message John Paul II singled out for the third millennium — is the Great Mercy Pope's "exceptional" legacy. Learn of John Paul II's strong and lasting influence on his successor, Pope Benedict XVI, whom we can consider the guarantor of the Great Mercy Pope's enduring legacy.

CHAPTER 1
THE LEGACY OF DIVINE MERCY

John Paul II taught us how to live in God's mercy by his entrustment of his life to The Divine Mercy: "Jesus, I TRUST in you" (Lagiewniki-Krakow, June 7, 1997). He taught us how to live in God's Mercy by *TRUST*, by his words, his deeds, and his prayer — and by his repeated exhortation: "Do not be afraid!" He lived out the teaching of Jesus: "Fear is useless, what is needed is trust" (Mk 5:36). He tried to treat every person with mercy and dignity as a precious, unique creation of God.

John Paul II taught us how to die in God's mercy. As his infirmity increased, he united his sufferings with Jesus for the salvation of souls. By accepting God's Providence, he accepted God's providential manner of his death. In embracing his suffering, he was an even more eloquent witness than with his words. He lived out the teaching of St. Paul:

> Now I rejoice in my sufferings for your sake, and in my flesh I am filling up what is lacking in the afflictions of Christ on behalf of His body, which is the Church ... (Col. 1:24).

John Paul II quoted this text on how St. Paul found joy in his sufferings — because he found meaning in suffering (see *Salvifici Doloris* [*The Christian Meaning of Suffering*], 1984).

John Paul II also cooperated with God's providential timing of his death on the vigil of Divine Mercy Sunday. He died saying "AMEN" — his final word of trust, of yes, of so be it!

John Paul II's life and death proclaimed the legacy of Divine Mercy. In his first public appearance after recuperation from the attempted assassination (May 13, 1981), he spoke in November 1981 at the Shrine of Merciful Love, marking the first anniversary of his second encyclical (*Dives in Misericordia,* Nov. 1980) and spoke of his commitment to the message of Divine Mercy:

Right from the beginning of my ministry in St. Peter's See in Rome, I considered this message [of Divine Mercy] my special task. Providence has assigned it to me in the present situation of man, the Church and the world. It could be said that precisely this situation assigned that message to me as my task before God (November 22, 1981, Shrine of Merciful Love in Collevalenza, Italy).

Then at the Shrine of Divine Mercy in Krakow-Lagiewniki he again described his pontificate in terms of Divine Mercy:

On the threshold of the third millennium, I come to entrust to Him once more my Petrine ministry — "Jesus, I trust in You!" ... I took with me [the message of Divine Mercy] to the See of Peter and which in a sense forms the image of this pontificate (Shrine of The Divine Mercy, Krakow-Lagiewniki, Poland, June 7, 1997).

John Paul II's legacy of Divine Mercy is capsulized in the celebration of Divine Mercy Sunday, the Second Sunday of Easter (*Dominca in Albis*). And in turn Divine Mercy Sunday capsulizes The Divine Mercy message and devotion. The role of John Paul II in proclaiming Divine Mercy Sunday as his legacy can be summarized in the following points:

- His classmate in the clandestine seminary at Krakow, who became Cardinal Deskur, introduced Karol Wojtyla to the message of the mystic Sister Faustina Kowalska (early 1940s).

- Karol Wojtyla as a pilgrim regularly visited the grave of Sister Faustina on the way home from work at the Solvay plant wearing wooden shoes (early 1940s).

- He initiated and completed the cause of St. Faustina.

- He wrote the encyclical *Dives in Misericordia* (Nov. 1980, *Rich in Mercy*) and told George Weigel that he felt spiritually "very near" to Sr. Faustina, and had been "thinking about her for a long time when he began writing *Dives in Misericordia*" (George Weigel, *Witness to Hope*, 1999).

- From 1993 through 2005 (posthumously in 2005) he delivered an annual Divine Mercy Sunday Message at the noontime *Regina Caeli*.

- He founded the Shrine of The Divine Mercy in Rome at Holy Spirit Church in Rome, where he celebrated Divine Mercy Sunday, April 25, 1995.

- He proclaimed Divine Mercy in very significant homilies at the beatification of Sr. Faustina (1993), her canonization (2000), the dedication of the Basilica of Divine Mercy, and the entrustment of the world to The Divine Mercy (2002).

- He shared a very personal witness of over a half-century of involvement in the message and devotion of Divine Mercy (Lagiewniki-Krakow, June 7, 1997).

(Note: for the various texts referred to please see the *Appendixes* under the respective dates.)

- Pope John Paul II the Great Mercy Pope died April 2, 2005, on the vigil of Divine Mercy Sunday.

The significance of Divine Mercy Sunday as the capsulization of John Paul II's legacy of Divine Mercy can be more clearly appreciated as summarized in the following facts:

- Pope John Paul II died shortly after Archbishop Stanislaus Dziwisz offered the Mass of Divine Mercy Sunday at 8:00 p.m. at his bedside and gave him *Viaticum* (The spiritual food for the spiritual journey);

- Then John Paul II pronounced with great effort the word "AMEN" to the prayers of the Rosary outside his window and died at 9:37 p.m. (reported by the Vatican Archbishop J. Michael Miller, CSB);

- When John Paul II died on the Vigil of Divine Mercy Sunday, it was already Mercy Sunday for most of the world in the East;

- He had prepared a written message for Divine Mercy Sunday 2005 as his posthumous final annual message on Divine Mercy Sunday that had started in 1993. He wrote in his posthumous message:

  Lord, who with [Your] Death and Resurrection reveal the love of the Father, we believe in You and with confidence repeat to You today: Jesus, I trust in You, have mercy on us and on the whole world (Mercy Sunday, April 3, 2005).

- At the canonization of St. Faustina on Divine Mercy Sunday, he declared Divine Mercy Sunday as a feast for the universal Church (April 30, 2000).

- In the homily of the canonization of St. Faustina he said: "Sister Faustina's canonization has a particular eloquence; by this act, I intend to pass this message on to the third millennium" (Homily April 30, 2000).

- Joseph Cardinal Ratzinger, now Pope Benedict XVI, spoke powerfully in his homily at John Paul II's funeral Mass before some four million people gathered for the funeral, and uncounted millions watching on TV, cable, and the Internet around the world. He concluded his homily by underscoring John Paul II's legacy of Divine Mercy:

[John Paul II] interpreted for us the paschal mystery as a mystery of Divine Mercy. In his last book, he wrote: The limit imposed upon evil "is ultimately Divine Mercy" (*Memory and Identity*. pp. 54-55). And reflecting on the assassination attempt, he said: "In sacrificing Himself for us all, Christ gave a new meaning to suffering, opening up a new dimension, a new order, the order of love. ... It is this suffering which burns and consumes evil with the flame of love and draws forth even from sin a great flowering of good" (p. 167). Impelled by this vision, the Pope suffered and loved in communion with Christ, and that is why the message of his suffering and his silence proved so eloquent and so faithful.

Divine Mercy: the Holy Father found the purest reflection of God's mercy in the Mother of God. He, who at an early age had lost his own mother, loved his divine mother all the more. He heard the words of the crucified Lord as addressed personally to him: "Behold your mother." and so he did as the beloved disciple did: "He took her into his own home" (Jn 19:27) — "*Totus tuus.*" And from the mother he learned to conform himself to Christ (April 8, 2005).

✝ WHY IS DIVINE MERCY SUNDAY SO IMPORTANT?

Why is Divine Mercy Sunday so significant in the life and death of John Paul II? According to the words of our Lord recorded in the *Diary of St. Faustina*, it is to prepare for the coming of the Lord:

"Souls perish in spite of My bitter Passion. I am giving then the last hope of Salvation; that is the Feast of My Mercy. If they will not adore My Mercy, they will perish for all eternity. Secretary of My Mercy, write, tell souls about this great mercy of Mine, because the awful day, the day of My justice is near" (*Diary*, 965 and see also *Diary*, 998).

The Blessed Mother also told St. Faustina to speak to the world about the Lord's great mercy and prepare the world for His coming (see *Diary*, 635 and *Diary*, 625). Other texts also carry this urgency to prepare for the coming of the Lord (see *Diary*, 155, 1588, and 1782).

Pope John Paul II referred to the significance of Divine Mercy Sunday and his establishment of the feast in Poland while at the Shrine of The Divine Mercy in Lagiewniki-Krakow:

> I give thanks to Divine Providence that I have been enabled to contribute personally to the fulfillment of Christ's will, through the institution of the Feast of Divine Mercy [in Poland]. Here, near relics of Blessed Faustina Kowalska, I give thanks also for the gift of her beatification. I pray unceasingly that God will have "mercy on us and on the whole world" (From The Chaplet of Divine Mercy, *Diary*, 476) (June 7, 1997).

Then on Divine Mercy Sunday, April 30, 2000, he canonized St. Faustina and during the homily he instituted the universal Feast of Divine Mercy and so in a sense he "canonized" The Divine Mercy message:

> It is important then that we accept the whole message that comes to us from the Word of God on this Second Sunday of Easter, *which from now on throughout the Church will be called "Divine Mercy Sunday"* (April 30, 3000, homily, emphasis added).

After the canonization of St. Faustina and the Mass of Divine Mercy Sunday at a buffet breakfast for the principal guests, Pope John Paul II said:

"This is the happiest day of my life" (the Pope's words to Dr. Valentin Fuster — the cardiologist who investigated the miraculous healing of the heart of Fr. Ron Pytel through the intercession of St. Faustina).

Then, in his homily at the consecration of the Basilica of Divine Mercy at Lagiewniki-Krakow, he solemnly entrusted the world to The Divine Mercy as a fulfillment of the Lord's words about the "spark" to come from Poland to prepare for Jesus' final coming:

Today, therefore, in this Shrine, I will solemnly to entrust the world to Divine Mercy. I do so with the burning desire that the message of God's merciful love, proclaimed here through Saint Faustina, may be made known to all the peoples of the earth and fill their hearts with hope. May this message radiate from this place to our beloved homeland and throughout the world. May the binding promise of the Lord Jesus be fulfilled: from here there must go forth "the spark which will prepare the world for [Jesus'] final coming" (*Diary*, 1732).

This spark needs to be lighted by the grace of God. *This fire of mercy needs to be passed on to the world. In the mercy of God the world will find peace and mankind will find happiness!* I entrust this task to you, dear brothers and sisters, to the Church in Krakow and Poland, and to all the devotees of Divine Mercy who will come here from Poland and from throughout the world. May you be witnesses to mercy! (Aug. 17, 2002).

For the complete text of this significant homily, which describes the world condition and the need of God's mercy now, see the *Appendixes* under August 17, 2002.

Finally, the death of Pope John Paul II, after the Mass of Divine Mercy Sunday on the vigil of Divine Mercy Sunday is celebrated in his presence, and then his posthumous *Regina*

Caeli message, all proclaimed the significance and urgency of celebrating Divine Mercy Sunday.

The message of Divine Mercy was proclaimed by his life and death as the message for the third millennium.

He concluded his message of Divine Mercy with his great "AMEN!" at 9:37 p.m. April 2, 2005.

CHAPTER 2

DIVINE MERCY, THE EXCEPTIONAL LEGACY OF BLESSED JOHN PAUL II

Among the many legacies of Blessed John Paul II, his legacy of Divine Mercy stands out as exceptional. Among the two dozen marvelous legacies of John Paul II, which I have read about, only in the legacies of Divine Mercy and that of the apostolic letter *At the Beginning of the New Millennium* (January 6, 2001) where he gives the prayer "contemplate the face of Jesus with Mary" does he specifically say that he is passing them on to the whole world as the message and prayer for the Third Millennium:

At the canonization of St. Faustina, John Paul II said in his homily:

> Sister Faustina's canonization has a particular eloquence. By this act I intend today to pass this message on to the new millennium. I pass it on to all people, so that they will learn to know even better the true face of God and the true face of their brethren (Homily of Canonization, Divine Mercy Sunday, April 20, 2000).

A year later another expression of John Paul II's legacy of Divine Mercy was given at his *Regina Caeli* message, following the Mass of Divine Mercy Sunday (April 22, 2001), honoring the anniversary of the canonization of St. Faustina. Again, he passes on this message of hope to the third millennium:

Filled with joy we present ourselves before the Risen One today and say with faith: "Jesus, I trust in You!" May this confession full of love strengthen everyone on the path of daily life and encourage them to undertake works of mercy for their brothers and sisters. May this be a message of hope for the entire new millennium.

The Pope then challenges us to collaborate with the plan of Divine Mercy for the whole world:

Now, with the recitation of the antiphon *Regina Caeli*, we ask Mary to enable us to experience the deep joy of the Resurrection and to collaborate with dedication in the universal plan of Divine Mercy (ibid).

At the departure ceremony of his visit to Krakow for the dedication of the Basilica of The Divine Mercy (August 19, 2002), John Paul II again repeated his unique legacy of Divine Mercy to the third millennium:

"God, rich in mercy." These are the words that sum up this visit. We have heard them as a call to the Church and to Poland in the new millennium. I pray that my compatriots will welcome with open hearts this message of mercy and will succeed in carrying it to wherever men and women are in need of the light of hope. … I repeat before the merciful Jesus; "Jesus, I trust in You! May these heartfelt words bring comfort to future generations in the new millennium. May God who is rich in mercy bless you!

In his last book *Memory and Identity*, John Paul II ends his chapter on the mystery of mercy with a strong statement on the power of this mystery. He states that the lesson of Divine Mercy is not only for the Polish people but also for every part of the world where the Church is present:

Here I should like to return to what I said about the experience of the Church in Poland during the period of resistance to communism. It seems to me to have a universal value. *I think that the same applies to Sister Faustina and her witness to the mystery of Divine Mercy.* The *patrimony of her spirituality* was of great importance, as we know from experience, for the resistance against the evil and inhuman systems of the time. *The lesson to be drawn from all this is important not only for the Poles, but also in every part of the world where the Church is present.* This became clear during the beatification and canonization of Sister Faustina. It was as if Christ had wanted to say through her: "Evil does not have the last word!" The Paschal Mystery confirms that good is ultimately victorious, that life conquers death, and that love triumphs over hate (The Mystery of Mercy, in *Memory and Identity*, John Paul II, p. 55, emphasis added).

✝ POPE JOHN PAUL II'S FINAL MESSAGE

In his final Divine Mercy Sunday message, read posthumously, John Paul summarized his message of Divine Mercy and passed it on to us as a legacy:

"Jesus, I trust in You! Have Mercy on us and on the whole world! Amen!" (Divine Mercy Sunday, April 3, 2005).

These are the closing and final words of Pope John Paul II written prior to his death, and read by Archbishop Leonardo Sandri, substitute of the Vatican Secretariat of State, following the Mass for the eternal repose of John Paul II (Vatican City, April 3, 2005, Zenit.org).

This was the final annual Divine Mercy Sunday message begun in 1993, and the summary of John Paul's message of Divine Mercy. These final words capsulized two major points of his life's legacy of Divine Mercy:

1. *"Jesus, I Trust in You"* was first expressed at the Shrine of Divine Mercy in Krakow-Lagiewniki, Poland, June 7, 1997, where he shared his half-century of involvement with The Divine Mercy message and devotion. In his talk, he said:

> I come here to commend the concerns of the Church and of humanity to the merciful Christ. On the threshold of the third millennium *I come to entrust to Him once more my Petrine ministry* — "*Jesus, I trust in You!*" (emphasis in the text).

It is significant that he said "*once more*" I entrust my Petrine ministry to the merciful Christ. This was his way of entrusting himself, to the merciful Christ, like a parallel to his motto of entrustment to Mary: "Totus Tuus."

2. "… have mercy on us and on the whole world." in the same talk (June 7, 1997) he expressed his constant prayer:

> I pray unceasingly that God will have "mercy on us and on the whole world." (From the Chaplet of Divine Mercy, *Diary*, 476).

After prayerful reflection on John Paul's final and closing words, I consider that these words "Jesus, I trust in You! Have mercy on us and on the whole world" are John Paul's personal expression of the "Jesus Prayer" so much a part of the spirituality of the Eastern Church.

> "Lord Jesus Christ, Son of the Living God, have mercy on me a sinner."

With the added dimension "and on the whole world," I have begun to pray the "Jesus Prayer" by including the phrase "… and on the whole world" and find it a powerful extension of the already powerful prayer. It is also an expression of the beatitude: "Blessed are the merciful, for they shall obtain mercy" (Mt 5:7), quoted by John Paul II in the talk at the International Shrine of The Divine Mercy in Poland and quoted five times as a repeated theme of his encyclical *Rich in Mercy* (*Dives in Misericordia*, 1980).

These final words of John Paul II also confirm a personal experience I had while watching the Pope pray, in preparation for his celebrating Mass. While I have shared it twice earlier, it bears repeating here. It was the occasion of filming a presentation to the Holy Father for the film *Divine Mercy — No Escape*. The guests and camera crew were ushered into the private chapel of the Pope at 6:45 a.m. for a 7:00 a.m. Mass with the Holy Father. Msgr. Stanislaus Dziwisz assigned my place next to the Pope. For the next 15 minutes, I watched him praying, kneeling with his hands holding his head. But I was distracted! One question stayed in my head:"What is he praying?" The words that kept coming to me were: "Have mercy on us and on the whole world" (November 13, 1986).

Then, it was on reading the text of John Paul II's talk at the International Shrine of The Divine Mercy in Poland (June 7, 1997) that he himself confirmed my sense of what he was praying: "I pray inceasingly, that 'God will have mercy on us and on the whole world' " (from the Chaplet of Divine Mercy, *Diary*, 476).

In conclusion, on Divine Mercy Sunday 2005, the Pope's posthumous message was read:

> Jesus, I trust in You! Have mercy on us and on the whole world! (April 3, 2005).

CHAPTER 3
THE INFLUENCE ON
POPE BENEDICT XVI

After the death of John Paul II, the first to take up the challenge to be an apostle of Divine Mercy was Cardinal Joseph Ratzinger. Let us look to the example of Cardinal Joseph Ratzinger, now Pope Benedict XVI, and how he declared himself as an apostle of Divine Mercy.

✝ CARDINAL JOSEPH RATZINGER AT THE FUNERAL OF JOHN PAUL II, APRIL 8, 2005

As the Dean of the College of Cardinals, he presided over the funeral of Pope John Paul II. In his homily at the funeral Mass (April 8, 2005) before some four million people gathered for the funeral, and uncounted millions watching on TV, cable, and the Internet around the world, he concluded his powerful homily by describing John Paul II's legacy of Divine Mercy:

> [John Paul II] interpreted for us the paschal mystery as a mystery of Divine Mercy. In his last book, he wrote: The limit imposed upon evil "is ultimately Divine Mercy" (*Memory and Identity*, p. 55). And reflecting on the assassination attempt, he said: "In sacrificing Himself for us all, Christ gave a new meaning to suffering, opening up a new dimension, a new order: the order of love. ... It is this suffering which burns and consumes evil with the flame of love and draws forth even from sin a great flowering of good." Impelled by this vision, the Pope suffered and loved in communion with Christ and that is why the message of his suffering and his silence proved so eloquent and so fruitful.

Divine Mercy: The Holy Father found the purest reflection of God's mercy in the Mother of God. He, who at an early age had lost his own mother, loved his divine mother all the more. He heard the words of the crucified Lord as addressed personally to him: "Behold, your mother." And from the mother, he learned to conform himself to Christ (emphasis added).

✝ POPE BENEDICT XVI IN HIS FIRST ADDRESS AS POPE, APRIL 20, 2005

Then, in his first address as Pope Benedict XVI in the morning after his election (April 20, 2005), he spoke to the Cardinals who elected him. He began his address by stressing John Paul II's legacy of Divine Mercy to himself as his successor:

May grace and peace be multiplied to all of you (cf. Pet 1:2)! In these hours, two contrasting sentiments coexist in my spirit. On one hand, a sense *of inadequacy* and of human anxiety before the universal Church, because of the responsibility that was entrusted to me yesterday as successor of the apostle Peter in this See of Rome. On the other hand, I feel very intensely in myself a profound *gratitude* to God who — as we sing in the liturgy — does not abandon His flock, but leads it through the times, under the guidance of those whom He Himself has chosen as vicars of His Son and has constituted pastors (cf. Preface of the Apostles, 1).

Beloved, this profound *gratitude for a gift of Divine Mercy* prevails in my heart despite everything. And I consider it in fact as a special grace obtained for me by my venerable Predecessor, John Paul II. I seem to feel his strong hand gripping mine; I seem to see his smiling eyes and to hear his words, addressed at this moment particularly to me, "Be not afraid!" (emphasis added).

✞ POPE BENEDICT XVI INTERVIEWED ON POLISH TV, OCTOBER 16, 2005

On the occasion of the Polish Parliment in 2005 establishing October 16th (the day Cardinal Karol Wojtyla of Krakow was elected Pope) as Pope John Paul II Day in Poland, a Polish television station interviewed Pope Benedict XVI about his predecessor's legacy (Zenit.org and KofC.org).

The interviewer asked several questions among them was:

In your opinion what are the most significant moments of John Paul II's pontificate?

Pope Benedict XVI responded:

We can see it from two perspectives: one ad extra — toward the world, and the other ad intra — toward the Church. ...

In the Church, he created *a new love for the Eucharist. He created a new awareness of the greatness of Divine Mercy*, and he *deepened devotion to Our Lady*. In this way he guided us toward an internalizing of the faith and, at the same time toward a greater efficiency (emphasis added).

Pope Benedict XVI responded with three very significant legacies of John Paul II. I was greatly delighted to read of this three-fold focus on strengthening the Church: A new love for the Eucharist, a new awareness of the greatness of Divine Mercy, and a deepened devotion to Our Lady!

Then the Polish TCV interviewer asked a final question that opened the heart of our new Pope to the world:

Finally, a very personal question: Do you continue to feel the presence of John Paul II, and if you do, in what way?

Pope Benedict XVI responded:

Certainly ... the Pope is always close to me through his writings: I hear him and I see him speaking, so I can keep up a continuous dialogue with him. He is always speaking to me through his writings. So I can continue my conversations with the Holy Father.

This nearness to him isn't limited to words and texts, because behind the texts I hear the Pope himself. A man who goes to the Lord doesn't disappear. I believe that someone who goes to the Lord comes even closer to us and I feel he is close to me and that I am close to the Lord.

I am near the Pope and now he helps me to be near the Lord and I try to enter this atmosphere of prayer, of love for our Lord, for Our Lady, and I entrust myself to his prayers. So there is a permanent dialogue and we're close to each other in a new way, in a very deep way.

✝ POPE BENEDICT XVI ON MARCH 26, 2006

It was nearly a year after the death of the Servant of God John Paul II on March 26, 2006, and Pope Benedict XVI was visiting the Roman parish of God the Merciful Father on the Fourth Sunday of Lent. He was speaking of the importance of "a personal encounter with the Crucified and Risen Christ," based on the Sunday readings, when he turned to the "testament" of mercy that Pope John Paul II left the Church in his last message:

In meditating on the Lord's mercy that was revealed totally and definitively in the mystery of the Cross, the text that John Paul II had prepared for his meeting with the faithful on April 3, [Divine Mercy Sunday] the Second Sunday of Easter, comes to my mind. In the divine plan it was written that he would leave us precisely on the eve of that day, Saturday, April 2 — we all remember it well — and for that reason he was unable to address his words to you. I would like to address them to you now, dear brothers and sisters, "To humanity, which sometimes seems bewildered and overwhelmed by the power of evil, selfishness, and fear, the Risen Lord offers his love that pardons, reconciles, and reopens hearts to hope. It is a love that converts hearts and gives peace."

The Pope, in this last text which is like a testament, then added: "How much the world needs to understand and accept Divine Mercy!" (*Regina Caeli* message, read by Archbishop Leonardo Sandri, Substitute of the Secretariat of State, to the faithful gathered in St. Peter's Square, April 3, 2005).

✝ POPE BENEDICT XVI ON MERCY SUNDAY 2006

Then, on April 23, 2006, Divine Mercy Sunday, in his *Regina Caeli* message, Pope Benedict XVI made some truly remarkable statements about John Paul II and his legacy of Divine Mercy, even underscoring that Divine Mercy was the center of John Paul's pontificate. Here is the complete text:

This Sunday the Gospel of John tells us that the Risen Jesus appeared to the disciples, enclosed in the Upper Room, on the evening of the "first day of the week" (Jn 20:19), and that He showed Himself to them once again in the same place "eight days later" (Jn 20:26). From the beginning, therefore, the Christian community began to live a weekly rhythm, marked by the meeting with the Risen Lord.

This is something that the Constitution on the Liturgy of the Second Vatican Council also emphasizes, saying: "By a tradition handed down from the Apostles, which took its origin from the very day of Christ's Resurrection, the Church celebrates the Paschal Mystery every eighth day, which day is appropriately called the Lord's Day" (*Sacrosanctum Concilium*, 106).

The evangelist further recalls that on the occasion of both His appearances — the day of the Resurrection and eight days later — the Lord Jesus showed the disciples the signs of the crucifixion, clearly visible and tangible even in His glorified Body (cf. Jn 20: 20, 27).

Those sacred wounds in His hands, in His feet, and in His side, are an inexhaustible source of faith, hope, and love from which each one can draw, especially the souls who thirst the most for Divine Mercy.

In consideration of this, the Servant of God John Paul II, highlighting the spiritual experience of a humble Sister, St. Faustina Kowalska, desired that the Sunday after Easter be dedicated in a special way to Divine Mercy; and Providence disposed that he would die precisely on the eve of this day in the hands of Divine Mercy.

The mystery of God's merciful love was the center of the pontificate of my venerable predecessor. Let us remember in particular his 1980 encyclical *Dives in Misericordia*, and his dedication of the new Shrine of The Divine Mercy in Krakow in 2002. The words he spoke on the latter occasion summed up, as it were, his Magisterium, pointing out that the cult of Divine Mercy is not a secondary devotion but an integral dimension of Christian faith and prayer.

May Mary Most Holy, Mother of the Church, whom we now address with the *Regina Caeli*, obtain for all Christians that they live Sunday to the full as "the Easter of the week," tasting the beauty of the encounter with the Risen Lord and drawing from the source of His merciful love to be apostles of His peace.

✝ POPE BENEDICT XVI IN 2006 AT KRAKOW-LAGIEWNIKI, POLAND

As part of his pastoral visit to Poland in 2006, Pope Benedict XVI visited the International Shrine of The Divine Mercy in Krakow-Lagiewniki on Saturday, May 27. At Lagiewniki, the Pope prayed at the tomb of St. Faustina Kowalska, where Karol Wojtyla often went as a laborer and later as an underground seminarian. Pope Benedict then went to the Basilica or Shrine, where 800 people awaited him. Here is the Vatican translation of his address to them:

> Dear Brothers and Sisters, I am very pleased to be able to meet you during my visit here to the Shrine of The Divine Mercy. I extend heartfelt greetings to all of you: to the sick, their caregivers, the priests engaged in pastoral ministry at the Shrine, to the Sisters of Our Lady of Mercy, to the members of the "Faustinum" and to all those present.
>
> On this occasion we encounter two mysteries: the mystery of human suffering and the mystery of Divine Mercy. At first sight these two mysteries seem to be opposed to one another. But when we study them more deeply in the light of faith, we find that they are placed in reciprocal harmony through the mystery of the Cross of Christ. As Pope John Paul II said in this place: "The Cross is the most profound bowing down of the Divinity towards man ... the Cross is like a touch of eternal love on the most painful wounds of humanity's earthly existence" (August 17, 2002). Dear friends who are sick, who are marked by suffering in body and soul, you are most closely united to the Cross of Christ, and at the same time, you are the most eloquent witnesses of God's mercy. Through you and through your suffering, He bows down towards humanity with love. You who say in silence: "Jesus, I trust in You" teach us that there is no faith more profound, no hope more alive,

and no love more ardent than the faith, hope, and love of a person who in the midst of suffering places himself securely in God's hands. May the human hands of those who care for you in the name of mercy be an extension of the open hands of God.

I would so willingly embrace each one of you. But since this is impossible, I draw you spiritually to my heart, and I impart my Blessing in the name of the Father and of the Son and of the Holy Spirit.

✝ POPE BENEDICT XVI DURING HIS WEDNESDAY GENERAL AUDIENCE ON MAY 31, 2006

Pope Benedict XVI reflected on his pastoral visit to Poland in May 2006 during his General Audience on May 31 in St. Peter's Square. In the following excerpts from his remarks, he made particular mention of Divine Mercy as he recalled his visit to the Shrine of The Divine Mercy in Krakow-Lagiewniki and then his meeting with young people in Krakow's Blonie Park:

My next stop, at the Shrine of The Divine Mercy in Lagiewniki, gave me the opportunity to stress that Divine Mercy alone illumines the mystery of man. It was here at the neighbouring convent that Sr. Faustina Kowalska, contemplating the shining wounds of the Risen Christ, received a message of trust for humanity which John Paul II echoed and interpreted and which really is a central message precisely for our time: Mercy as God's power, as a divine barrier against the evil of the world.

Another beautiful experience was my meeting with young people that took place in Krakow's large Blonie Park. I symbolically consigned the "Flame of Mercy" to the crowds of young people who had come, so that they might be heralds of Love and Divine Mercy in the world.

✝ POPE BENEDICT XVI ON APRIL 2, 2007

On April 2, 2007, the second anniversary of the death of the Servant of God John Paul II, Pope Benedict XVI celebrated a Mass in "suffrage for his chosen soul." Here are some excerpts from his homily in which Pope Benedict highlights the Servant of God's eloquent witness in suffering and prayer, especially as he approached death:

Two years ago, at a slightly later hour than now, beloved Pope John Paul II departed this world for the house of the Father.

With this celebration, let us first of all renew our thanksgiving to God for having given him to us for well near 27 years as a father and reliable guide in the faith, a zealous Pastor and courageous prophet of hope, a tireless witness, and passionate servant of God's love.

As we offer the Eucharistic Sacrifice in suffrage for his chosen soul, we remember the unforgettable devotion with which he celebrated the Holy Mysteries and adored the Sacrament of the Altar, the center of his life and of his untiring mission. ...

For us, gathered in prayer in memory of my Venerable Predecessor, the gesture of the anointing of Mary of Bethany [in today's Gospel] is full of spiritual echoes and suggestions. It evokes John Paul II's shining witness of love for Christ, unreserved and unstinting.

The "house," that is, the entire Church, "was filled with the fragrance" of his love (cf. Jn 12: 3).

Of course, we who were close to him benefited from it and are grateful to God, but even those who knew him from afar were able to enjoy it because Pope Wojtyla's love for Christ was so strong, so intense, we could say, that it overflowed in every region of the world.

Was not the esteem, respect, and affection expressed to him at his death by believers and non-believers alike an eloquent witness of this? ...

The fruitfulness of this witness, as we know, depended on the Cross. In Karol Wojtyla's life, the word "cross" was not merely a word. From his childhood, he was familiar with suffering and death. As priest and Bishop and especially as Supreme Pontiff, he took most seriously the Risen Christ's last call to Simon Peter on the shore of the Lake of Galilee: "Follow me. ... Follow me!" (Jn 21: 19, 22).

His whole life, particularly with the slow but implacable advance of the disease which gradually stripped him of everything, became an offering to Christ, a living proclamation of his passion in hope brimming with faith in the resurrection.

He lived his Pontificate in the sign of "prodigality," generously spending himself without reserve. What motivated him other than mystical love for Christ, for the One who, on October 16, 1978, had called him with the ceremonial words: "*Magister adest et vocat te* — the Teacher is here and is calling you?"

On April 2, 2005, the Teacher called him again, this time without intermediaries, in order to take him home to the house of the Father. And once again he promptly responded with his brave heart in a whisper: "Let me go to the Lord" (cf. S. Dziwisz, *Una vita con Karol*, p. 223).

He had been preparing for a long time for this last encounter with Jesus, as the various drafts of his Testament reveal.

During the long periods he spent in his private chapel, he spoke to Jesus, abandoning himself totally to his will, and entrusted himself to Mary, repeating the *Totus tuus.* Like his Divine Teacher, he lived his agony in prayer. On the last day of his life, on the eve of Divine Mercy Sunday, he asked that the Gospel of John be read to him.

With the help of those who were nursing him, he wanted to take part in all the daily prayers and in the Liturgy of the Hours, he wanted to do adoration and meditation. He died while he was praying. He truly fell asleep in the Lord.

"And the house was filled with the fragrance of the ointment" (Jn 12:3).

✝ POPE BENEDICT XVI ON DIVINE MERCY SUNDAY 2007

On Divine Mercy Sunday, April 15, 2007, a little more than two years after the Servant of God John Paul II's death, Pope Benedict XVI remembered his predecessor, saying that he has "entered the light of Divine Mercy" and "speaks to us in a new way. Have faith, he tells us, in Divine Mercy!" Here are some excerpts from his homily:

Two years ago now, after the First Vespers of this Feast, John Paul II ended his earthly life. In dying, he entered the light of Divine Mercy, of which, beyond death and starting from God, he now speaks to us in a new way.

Have faith, he tells us, in Divine Mercy! Become day after day men and women of God's mercy. Mercy is the garment of light which the Lord has given to us in Baptism. We must not allow this light to be extinguished; on the contrary, it must grow within us every day and thus bring to the world God's glad tidings.

✝ POPE BENEDICT XVI ON SEPTEMBER 16, 2007

It's interesting that Pope Benedict XVI chose to highlight the Divine Mercy legacy of John Paul II not only on special occasions but during his ordinary teaching office as Pope. In his September 16, 2007, *Angelus* message, for instance, he spoke about "the three parables of mercy" in that Sunday's Gospel reading from Luke 15. Then he pointed to the significance in our time of the Servant of God's John Paul II's "strong proclamation and witness of God's mercy":

> In our time, humanity needs a strong proclamation and witness of God's mercy. Beloved John Paul II, a great apostle of Divine Mercy, prophetically intuited this urgent pastoral need. He dedicated his second Encyclical to it and throughout his Pontificate made himself the missionary of God's love to all peoples.

> After the tragic events of September 11, 2001, which darkened the dawn of the third millennium, he invited Christians and people of good will to believe that God's mercy is stronger than all evil, and that only in the Cross of Christ is the world's salvation found.

✝ POPE BENEDICT XVI ON DIVINE MERCY SUNDAY 2008

On March 30, 2008, Divine Mercy Sunday, in his *Regina Caeli* message, Pope Benedict XVI linked both the Servant of God John Paul II and St. Faustina as apostles of Divine Mercy. He spoke as well of John Paul's legacy that he "bequeathed to us which we joyfully welcome and make our own":

> Like Sr. Faustina, John Paul II in his turn made himself an apostle of Divine Mercy. In the evening of the unforgettable Saturday, April 2, 2005, when he closed his eyes on this world, it was precisely the eve of the Second Sunday of Easter and many people noted the

rare coincidence that combined the Marian dimension — the first Saturday of the month — and the dimension of Divine Mercy. This was in fact the core of John Paul II's long and multi-faceted Pontificate. The whole of his mission at the service of the truth about God and man and of peace in the world is summed up in this declaration, as he himself said in Krakow-Lagiewniki in 2002 when he inaugurated the large Shrine of Divine Mercy: "Apart from the mercy of God there is no source of hope for mankind." John Paul II's message, like St. Faustina's, thus leads back to the Face of Christ, a supreme revelation of God's mercy. Constant contemplation of this Face is the legacy he bequeathed to us which we joyfully welcome and make our own.

In this *Regina Caeli* message, Pope Benedict also produced a masterful summary of how mercy is central to the Gospel, reveals the very face of God to us, and is at the heart of the Church's life and mission:

Indeed, mercy is the central nucleus of the Gospel message; it is the very name of God, the Face with which he revealed himself in the Old Covenant and fully in Jesus Christ, the incarnation of creative and redemptive Love. May this merciful love also shine on the face of the Church and show itself through the sacraments, in particular that of Reconciliation, and in works of charity, both communitarian and individual. May all that the Church says and does manifest the mercy God feels for man, and therefore for us. When the Church has to recall an unrecognized truth or a betrayed good, she always does so impelled by merciful love, so that men and women may have life and have it abundantly (cf. Jn 10:10). From Divine Mercy, which brings peace to hearts, genuine peace flows into the world, peace between different peoples, cultures and religions.

Further in this *Regina Caeli* message, Pope Benedict sets the table for the first World Apostolic Congress on Mercy, which he will inaugurate in the coming days:

> In the coming days, on the occasion of the first World Apostolic Congress on Divine Mercy, there will be a special reflection on Divine Mercy. It will be held in Rome and will begin with Holy Mass at which, please God, I shall preside on Wednesday morning, April 2, the third anniversary of the pious death of the Servant of God John Paul II. Let us place the Congress under the heavenly protection of Mary Most Holy, *Mater Misericordiae.*

✟ POPE BENEDICT XVI ON APRIL 2, 2008, OPENING THE FIRST WORLD APOSTOLIC CONGRESS ON MERCY

Pope Benedict XVI opened the first World Apostolic Congress on Mercy in St. Peter's Square on April 2, 2008, with Mass to mark the third anniversary of the death of the Servant of God John Paul II. Although more than 40,000 people were gathered in the square, Pope Benedict in his homily singled out the nearly 4,000 delegates who were present for the opening of the World Mercy Congress:

> I address a special thought to the participants of the first World Congress on Divine Mercy, which is opening this very day and which intends to deepen [John Paul II's] rich Magisterium on the subject. God's mercy, as he himself said, is a privileged key to the interpretation of his Pontificate. He wanted the message of God's merciful love to be made known to all and urged the faithful to witness to it (cf. Homily at Krakow-Lagiewniki, August 17, 2002).

✝ POPE BENEDICT XVI ON APRIL 6, 2008, AT THE CLOSE OF THE FIRST WORLD APOSTOLIC CONGRESS ON MERCY

It was on April 6, 2008, after the closing Mass for the World Apostolic Congress on Mercy that Pope Benedict XVI gave his Divine Mercy "mandate" in his *Regina Caeli* message. In forceful language, his "mandate" called on the participants of the first World Mercy Congress to "go forth and be witnesses of God's mercy, a source of hope for every person and for the whole world":

> Yes, dear friends, the first World Congress on Divine Mercy ended this morning with the Eucharistic Celebration in St. Peter's Basilica. I thank the organizers, especially the Vicariate of Rome, and to all the participants I address my cordial greeting which now becomes a mandate: go forth and be witnesses of God's mercy, a source of hope for every person and for the whole world. May the Risen Lord be with you always! (*Regina Caeli* message, April 6, 2008).

✝ POPE BENEDICT XVI ON DIVINE MERCY SUNDAY 2009

On April 19, 2009, Divine Mercy Sunday, in his *Regina Caeli* message, Pope Benedict XVI spoke of how the Servant of God John Paul II's deep conviction regarding the Risen Christ's message of forgiveness and inner renewal had inspired him to call the Second Sunday of Easter Divine Mercy Sunday. He also highlighted how John Paul accepted the message of Divine Mercy that the Lord gave to St. Faustina, a message summed up in the words "Jesus, I trust in You":

> Risen, Jesus gave his disciples a new unity, stronger than before, invincible because it was founded not on human resources but on Divine Mercy, which made them all feel loved and forgiven by him. It is therefore

God's merciful love that firmly unites the Church, today as in the past, and makes humanity a single family; divine love which through the Crucified and Risen Jesus forgives us our sins and renews us from within. Inspired by this deep conviction, my beloved Predecessor, John Paul II, desired to call this Sunday, the Second Sunday of Easter, Divine Mercy Sunday, and indicated to all the Risen Christ as the source of trust and hope, accepting the spiritual message transmitted by the Lord to St. Faustina Kowalska, summed up in the invocation "Jesus, I trust in you!"

✝ POPE BENEDICT XVI ON DIVINE MERCY SUNDAY 2010

On April 11, 2010, Divine Mercy Sunday, Pope Benedict XVI in his *Regina Caeli* message said that the Venerable Servant of God John Paul II entitled the Octave Day of Easter or Sunday *in albis* Divine Mercy Sunday. Pope Benedict further highlighted that the Venerable John Paul II had named this Sunday Divine Mercy Sunday when he canonized Sr. Maria Faustina Kowalska:

This Sunday concludes the Octave of Easter. It is a unique day "made by the Lord," distinguished by the outstanding event of the Resurrection and the joy of the disciples at seeing Jesus. Since antiquity this Sunday has been called *in albis* from the Latin name, *alba*, which was given to the white vestments the neophytes put on for their Baptism on Easter night and took off eight days later, that is, today. Venerable John Paul II entitled this same Sunday "Divine Mercy Sunday" on the occasion of the canonization of Sr. Mary Faustina Kowalska on April 30, 2000.

✝ POPE BENEDICT XVI ON JANUARY 16, 2011

After the January 14th announcement concerning May 1, 2011, Divine Mercy Sunday, being chosen as the date for the Venerable Servant of God John Paul II's beatification, Pope Benedict XVI said on January 16, 2011, of the news:

> On May 1, I'll have the joy of beatifying Venerable Pope John Paul II, my beloved predecessor. The date that has been chosen is very significant: It will be the Second Sunday of Easter, which he himself entitled "Divine Mercy." ... Those who knew him, those who esteemed and loved him, cannot but rejoice with the Church for this event. We are happy!

✝ POPE BENEDICT XVI ON DIVINE MERCY SUNDAY 2011, AT THE BEATIFICATION OF THE VENERABLE SERVANT OF GOD JOHN PAUL II

On May 1, 2011, Divine Mercy Sunday, Pope Benedict XVI beatified his predecessor, the Venerable Servant of God John Paul II in St. Peter's Square. An overflow crowd, estimated at more than 1.5 million people, attended the beatification in Rome in 2011, which came in record-breaking time, only six years after John Paul's death in 2005. In fact, it was the largest crowd Rome had seen since John Paul II's funeral. Further, it is significant that Blessed John Paul II was being beatified on the day he had entitled Divine Mercy Sunday, which Pope Benedict highlighted at the beatification in his homily. Also, in his homily, Pope Benedict spoke personally of his longtime collaboration as then-Cardinal Joseph Ratzinger with Pope John Paul II, and how the late Pope's spiritual life and example had inspired him. Here are excerpts from the homily focused on these highlights:

> Today is the Second Sunday of Easter, which Blessed John Paul II entitled Divine Mercy Sunday. The date was chosen for today's celebration because, in God's

providence, my predecessor died on the vigil of this feast. ...

Finally, on a more personal note, I would like to thank God for the gift of having worked for many years with Blessed Pope John Paul II. I had known him earlier and had esteemed him, but for twenty-three years, beginning in 1982 after he called me to Rome to be Prefect of the Congregation for the Doctrine of the Faith, I was at his side and came to revere him all the more. My own service was sustained by his spiritual depth and by the richness of his insights. His example of prayer continually impressed and edified me: he remained deeply united to God even amid the many demands of his ministry. Then too, there was his witness in suffering: the Lord gradually stripped him of everything, yet he remained ever a "rock," as Christ desired. His profound humility, grounded in close union with Christ, enabled him to continue to lead the Church and to give to the world a message which became all the more eloquent as his physical strength declined. In this way he lived out in an extraordinary way the vocation of every priest and bishop to become completely one with Jesus, whom he daily receives and offers in the Church.

✝ POPE BENEDICT XVI ON OCTOBER 2, 2011, SENDING A MESSAGE TO THE SECOND WORLD APOSTOLIC CONGRESS ON MERCY

On October 2, 2011, at the second World Apostolic Congress on Mercy, which was celebrated at the Basilica of Divine Mercy in Krakow-Lagiewniki, Poland, the participants received a message from Pope Benedict XVI. The Pope was in St. Peter's Square, and he gave his message to the congress after praying the *Angelus*. Here is the official translation of his remarks in English to the participants at the congress. We also provide an English translation of his remarks in Polish:

In English:

> ... In particular, I extend cordial greetings to the participants in the Second International Congress on Divine Mercy in Krakow, and to the students from Iona College, Australia. The Gospel of today's liturgy spurs us to pray for all who work in the Lord's vineyard, especially where they face violence and threats because of their faith. May God grant them, and all of us, strength in our service to him and to one another. God bless all of you!

The Translation from Polish:

> With a special greeting, I turn to the organizers and participants of the Second World Congress on Divine Mercy, which these days takes place in Krakow-Lagiewniki. Beloved, through common reflection and prayer, strengthen your trust in the Lord, so that you may effectively bring to the world the joyful news that "Mercy is a source of hope." May God bless you.

✝ CONCLUSION

In summary, it's clear that Blessed John Paul II's Divine Mercy legacy has had a profound and lasting influence on his successor, Pope Benedict XVI. It starts with the gift of Divine Mercy that Benedict says he received at his election as Pope through the intercession of John Paul. We then see this influence at work throughout Benedict's papacy as he celebrates Divine Mercy Sunday each year, marks the annual anniversary of John Paul's death, inaugurates the first World Apostolic Congress on Mercy, and beatifies John Paul on Divine Mercy Sunday.

We can even consider Pope Benedict XVI as the guarantor of the Great Mercy Pope's legacy. As John Paul II's successor, he is ensuring that this important legacy remains front and center in the life of the Church. Here, it's worth recalling Benedict's words about joyfully welcoming and making this legacy our own. They came on March 30, 2008, Divine Mercy Sunday:

> Like Sr. Faustina, John Paul II in his turn made himself an apostle of Divine Mercy. In the evening of the unforgettable Saturday, April 2, 2005, when he closed his eyes on this world, it was precisely the eve of the Second Sunday of Easter and many people noted the rare coincidence that combined the Marian dimension — the first Saturday of the month — and the dimension of Divine Mercy. This was in fact the core of John Paul II's long and multi-faceted Pontificate. The whole of his mission at the service of the truth about God and man and of peace in the world is summed up in this declaration, as he himself said in Krakow-Lagiewniki in 2002 when he inaugurated the large Shrine of Divine Mercy: "Apart from the mercy of God there is no source of hope for mankind." John Paul II's message, like St. Faustina's, thus leads back to the Face of Christ, a supreme revelation of God's mercy. Constant contemplation of this Face is the legacy he bequeathed to us which we joyfully welcome and make our own.

APPENDIXES

✝ *DIVES IN MISERICORDIA*. "MOTHER OF MERCY" (NO. 9), November 1980 (From a translation by Rev. George W. Kosicki, CSB; see Chapter 1 of Part II)

These words of the Church at Easter: "I will sing of the mercies of the Lord forever," re-echo the full prophetic content of the words Mary uttered during her visit to Elizabeth, the wife of Zechariah: "His mercy is ... from generation to generation." At the very moment of the Incarnation, these words opened up a new perspective of salvation history. After the Resurrection of Christ, this perspective is new on both the historical and final (eschatological) level. From that time onwards, there is a succession of new generations of individuals in the immense human family, in ever-increasing size; there is also a succession of new generations of the People of God, marked with the sign of the Cross and of the Resurrection and "sealed" (cf. 2 Cor 1:21-22) with the sign of the Paschal Mystery of Christ, the radical revelation of the mercy that Mary proclaimed on the threshold of her kinswoman's house: "His mercy is ... from generation to generation" (Lk 1:50).

Mary is also the one who experienced mercy in a remarkable and exceptional way, as no other person has. At the same time, still in an exceptional way, she paid for her share in revealing God's mercy by the sacrifice of her heart. This sacrifice is intimately linked with the Cross of her Son at the foot of which she was to stand on Calvary. Her sacrifice is a unique sharing in the revelation of mercy, that is, a sharing in the absolute fidelity of God to His own love, to the covenant that He willed from eternity and that He entered into in time with man, with the people, with humanity; it is a sharing in that revelation that was decisively fulfilled through the Cross. *No one has experienced to the same degree as the Mother of the Crucified One* the mystery of the Cross, the overwhelming encounter of divine transcendent justice with love: that "kiss" given by mercy to justice (cf. Ps 85:11). No one as much as Mary has accepted into their heart that mystery, that truly divine dimension of the Redemption accomplished on Calvary by means of the death of her Son, together with the sacrifice of her maternal heart and with her final "fiat."

Mary, then, is also the one who knows to the fullest the mystery of God's mercy. She knows its price, she knows how great it is. In this sense we call her the *Mother of Mercy*, God's Mother (*Theotokos*) of Mercy or the Mother of the God of Mercy. Each one of these titles contains its own deep theological meaning. Each of them expresses the special preparation of her soul, of her whole personality, so that she was able to see through the complex events, first of Israel, then of every individual and the whole of humanity, that mercy "from generation to generation" (Lk 1:50) in which people share, according to the eternal design of the most Holy Trinity.

The above titles which we attribute to the God-bearer speak of her above all, however, as the Mother of the Crucified and Risen One; as *the one* who experienced mercy *in an exceptional way*, and in an equally exceptional way "merits" that mercy throughout her earthly life and particularly at the foot of the Cross of her Son. Finally, these titles speak of her as the one who, through her hidden and at the same time incomparable sharing in the messianic mission of her Son, was called in a special way to bring close to people that love which He had come to reveal. That love finds its most concrete expression in all of the suffering, the poor, those deprived of their own freedom, the blind, the oppressed and sinners; just as Christ spoke of Isaiah, first in the synagogue at Nazareth (cf. Lk 4:18) and then in response to the question of the messengers of John the Baptist (cf. Lk 7:22).

Mary shared precisely in this "merciful" love, which proves itself above all in contact with moral and physical evil. She shared singularly and exceptionally by her heart as the Mother of the Crucified and Risen One. This "merciful" love does not cease to be revealed in her and through her in the history of the Church and all mankind. This revelation is especially fruitful, because it is based on the remarkable docility of the maternal heart of the God-bearer, on her unique sensitivity and fitness to reach all who accept this merciful love most easily from a mother's side. This is one of the great life-giving mysteries of Christianity, a mystery intimately connected with the mystery of the Incarnation.

"The motherhood of Mary in the order of grace," as the Second Vatican Council explains, "lasts without interruption from the consent she faithfully gave at the Annunciation and which she sustained without hesitation under the Cross, until the eternal fulfillment of all the elect. In fact, being assumed into heaven she has not laid aside this office of salvation, but by her manifold intercession she continues to obtain for us graces of eternal salvation. By her maternal charity, she takes care of the brethren of her Son who still journey on earth, surrounded by dangers and difficulties, until they are led into their blessed home" (*Lumen Gentium*, 62).

✝ THE JUBILEE YEAR IN *LORD AND GIVER OF LIFE* (*Dominum et Vivificantem*) — on the Holy Spirit in the Life of the Church and World, Pentecost Sunday, 1986

John Paul II gives a thorough description of the role of the Jubilee Year of 2000:

- The Church feels herself called to this mission of pro-claiming the Spirit, while together with the human family she approaches *the end of the second Millennium after Christ* (2).

- The great Jubilee will mark the passage from the second to the third Christian millennium (2).

- In our own century, when humanity is already close to the end of the second millennium after Christ, this era of the Church expressed itself in a special way through the Second Vatican Council. As the Council of our century. … We can say that in its rich variety of teaching the Second Vatican Council contains precisely all that "the Spirit says to the Churches" (Rev 2:29; 3:6,13, 22) with regard to the present phase of the history of salvation (26).

In Part III of the encyclical "The Spirit who Gives Life," John Paul II gives first the "Reason for the Jubilee of the Year 2000: Christ who was conceived of the Holy Spirit":

- *The Church's mind and heart turn to the Holy Spirit as this twentieth century draws to a close and the third millennium* since the coming of Jesus Christ into the world approaches, and as we look towards the *Great Jubilee* with which the Church will celebrate the event (49).

- The *Great Jubilee* at the close of the second millennium, for which the Church is already preparing, has a directly *Christological aspect*: for it is a celebration of the birth of Jesus Christ. At the same time it has a *pneumatological aspect*, since the mystery of the Incarnation was accomplished "by the power of the Holy Spirit" (50).

- The conception and birth of Jesus Christ are in fact the greatest work accomplished by the Holy Spirit in the history of creation and salvation: the supreme grace — "the grace of union," source of every other grace, as St. Thomas explains (cf. St. Thomas Aquinas, *Summa Theologica*, IIIa, q.2, aa. 10-12; q.6, a.6; q.7, a. 13) *The Great Jubilee* refers to this work and also — if we penetrate its depths — to the author of this work, *to the person of the Holy Spirit* (50).

- All this is accomplished by the power of the Holy Spirit, and so is part of the great Jubilee. The Church cannot prepare for the Jubilee in any other way than in *the Holy Spirit* (51).

John Paul II develops a second "reason for the Jubilee": *grace has been made manifest*:

- In the mystery of the Incarnation the w*ork of the Spirit "who gives life"* reaches its highest point (52).

All the graces of creation, adoption as children of God, our redemption and sanctification:

- *All this* may be said to fall within the scope of the Great Jubilee (53).

- The Great Jubilee to be celebrated at the end of this millennium and at the beginning of the next ought to constitute a powerful call to all those who "worship God in Spirit and truth" (54).

- The Church's entire life, as will appear in the Great Jubilee, means going to meet the invisible God, the hidden God: a meeting with the Spirit "who gives life" (54).

John Paul II states a prophetic sense about the new Advent and the third millennium:

- Against this background [of anti-religious materialism] so characteristic of our time, in preparing for the Great Jubilee we must emphasize the "desires of the Spirit," as exhortations echoing in the night of a new time of Advent, at the end of which, like two thousand years ago, "every man will see the salvation of God" (Lk 3:6; cf. Is 40:5) (56).

The Jubilee calls for a gift of self:

- *As the year 2000* since the birth of Christ draws near, it is a question of ensuring that an ever greater number of people "may fully find themselves ... through a sincere gift of self" (59).

- The Great Jubilee of the year 2000 thus contains a message of liberation by the power of the Spirit (60).

As the end of the second millennium approaches, we recall the coming of the Lord:

- The most complete sacramental expression of the "departure" of Christ through the Mystery of the Cross and Resurrection is the *Eucharist*. In every celebration of the Eucharist His coming, His salvific presence, is sacramentally realized: in the Sacrifice and in Communion (62).

- In the time leading up to the third millennium after Christ, while "the Spirit and the bride say to the Lord Jesus: Come!" this prayer of theirs is filled, as always, with an eschatological significance, which is also destined to give fullness of meaning to the celebration of the great Jubilee (66).

- The Church wishes to *prepare* for this Jubilee *in the Holy Spirit*, just as the Virgin of Nazareth in whom the Word was made flesh was prepared by the Holy Spirit. (66).

✝ **"THE EASTER MESSAGE OF THE MERCIFUL CHRIST,"** General Audience, April 10, 1991

(*L'Osservatore Romano*, April 15, 1991)

This is the 53rd talk in the "Jasna Gora Cycle," a series of meditations which the Holy Father used to prepare for his forthcoming trip to Poland. He gave it at the General Audience on April 10, 1991:

1. In the name of Jesus Christ crucified and risen, in the spirit of His messianic mission, enduring in the history of humanity, we raise our voices and pray that the love which is in the Father may once again *be revealed at this stage of history* and that, through the work of the Son and Holy Spirit, it may be shown to be present in our modern world and to be more powerful than evil: more powerful than sin and death.

We pray for this through the intercession of her who does not cease to proclaim 'mercy ... from generation to generation,' and also through the intercession of those for whom there have been completely fulfilled the words of the Sermon on the Mount: 'Blessed are the merciful, for they shall obtain mercy'" (Mt 5:7) (*Dives in Misericordia*, 15).

2. Our Lady of Jasna Gora! *The words of the encyclical on Divine Mercy* (*Dives in Misericordia*) are particularly close to us. They recall the figure of the Servant of God, Sister Faustina Kowalska. This simple woman religious particularly brought the *Easter message of the merciful Christ* closer to Poland and the whole world.

This happened before the Second World War and all its cruelty. In the face of all the organized contempt for the human person, the message of Christ who was tormented and rose again became for many people in Poland and beyond its borders, and even on other continents, a source of the hope and strength necessary for survival.

3. And today? Is it perhaps not necessary also "in the contemporary world" in our homeland, in society, among the people who have entered into a new phase of our history, *for love to reveal that it is stronger than hatred and selfishness*? Is it perhaps not necessary to translate into the language of today's generations the words of the Gospel, "Blessed are the merciful, for they shall obtain mercy" (Mt 5:7)?

O Mother, who announces Divine Mercy "from generation to generation" (Lk 1:50), help our generation *to rise from the moral crisis*. May Christ's new commandment, "love one another" (Jn 13:34) be established ever more fully among us.

The significant points in regard to St. Faustina and the message of Divine Mercy are:

- That St. Faustina is mentioned in print in *L'Osservatore Romano* — a breakthrough.

- That St. Faustina is related to the encyclical *Dives in Misericordia*.

- That St. Faustina illustrates the need for mercy — before World War II and now!

- The message is called the "*Easter* message of the merciful Christ" – it ties in with the Feast of Divine Mercy being part of the Easter message.

- A preparation for John Paul II's visit to Poland where he will bless the new Shrine at Plock where St. Faustina had the vision of The Divine Mercy "Image" (February 22, 1931).

✝ BEATIFICATION OF SR. FAUSTINA, HOMILY, DIVINE MERCY SUNDAY, APRIL 18, 1993

(*L'Osservatore Romano*, April 21, 1993)

On Sunday, April 18, Sister Faustina was beatified by Pope John Paul II in St. Peter's Square in Vatican City during a Mass celebrated with over 100,000 pilgrims from all over the world. During the Mass, the Pope preached the homily in Italian, Spanish, Polish, and English, based on the readings for the Second Sunday of Easter. The following excerpts are taken from that homily:

> "Give thanks to the Lord for He is good, for His mercy endures forever" (Ps 118 [117]: 1).

> Like a band of light this psalm of thanksgiving passes through the Octave of Easter. It is the choral "thank

You" of the Church which adores God for the gift of Christ's resurrection: for the gift of new and eternal life revealed in the risen Lord. With one heart the Church adores and thanks Him for the infinite love which has been communicated to every person and to the whole universe in Him. ...

I salute you, Sister Faustina. Beginning today the Church calls you Blessed, especially the Church in Poland and Lithuania. O Faustina, how extraordinary your life is! Precisely you, the poor and simple daughter of Mazovia, of the Polish people, were chosen by Christ to remind people of this great mystery of Divine Mercy! You bore this mystery within yourself, leaving this world after a short life, filled with suffering. However, at the same time, this mystery has become a prophetic reminder to the world, to Europe. Your message of Divine Mercy was born almost on the eve of World War II. Certainly you would have been amazed if you could have experienced upon this earth what this message meant for the suffering people during that hour of torment, and how it spread throughout the world. Today, we truly believe, you contemplate in God the fruits of your mission on earth. Today you experience it at its very source, which is your Christ, *"dives in misericordia."*

"I clearly feel that my mission does not end with death, but begins," Sister Faustina wrote in her diary. And it truly did! Her mission continues and is yielding astonishing fruit. It is truly marvelous how her devotion to the merciful Jesus is spreading in our contemporary world and gaining so many human hearts! This is doubtlessly *a sign of the times — a sign of our 20th century.* The balance of this century which is now ending, in addition to the advances which have often surpassed those of preceding eras, presents a deep restlessness and fear of the future. Where, if not in The Divine Mercy, can the world find refuge and the light of hope? Believers understand that perfectly.

"Give thanks to the Lord, for He is good. Give thanks to the Lord, for He is merciful."

Today, on the day of the Beatification of Sister Faustina, we praise the Lord for the great things He has done in her soul, we praise and thank Him for the great things He has done and always continues to do in the souls who through Sister Faustina's witness and message discover the infinite depths of The Divine Mercy.

✝ GENERAL AUDIENCE, April 19, 1993

(*L'Osservatore Romano*, Monday-Tuesday, April 19-20, 1993)

"[May] the example of the newly Beatified accompany you on your daily Christian walk." This is the wish expressed by John Paul II to the thousands of pilgrims gathered in Rome to participate in the solemn rite of beatification of Sunday, the 18th, and received in audience on the morning of Monday, the 19th. During the meeting, that took place in St. Peter's Square, the Pope pronounced the following discourse:

1. I greet all of you, dearest brothers and sisters, who have come to Rome to render homage to the newly beatified.

Our encounter today represents a joyous prolongation of the solemn celebration that took place yesterday in this very square. With you I praise the Lord for such an extraordinary spiritual experience, and I wish everyone to give faithful witness to the Gospel, imitating the luminous examples of these Servants of God, elevated to the honors of the altar. [...]

2. Words of greeting I direct, next, to the Sisters of the Congregation of Our Lady of Mercy and to the

numerous devotees of The Divine Mercy, gathered in Rome from many regions of Italy for the Beatification of Sister Faustina Kowalska. Yesterday has been a great day for all of you.

Dearly beloved, be apostles, by your word and your works, of the divine merciful love revealed to the highest degree in Jesus Christ. We are speaking of a mystery that, in a certain sense, is for all people the fountain of a life different from that which human beings are in a position to build with their own strength (cf. *Dives in Misericordia*, 14).

May this mystery be for every one of you the inspiration and the strength to carry out Divine Mercy in actual life. In the name of this mystery, Christ teaches us to pardon always and to love one another reciprocally as He Himself has loved us.

"God, rich in mercy"(cf. Eph 2:4) bless you and make fruitful your apostolic commitment.

6. Since we came back to Sr. Faustina, one more wish, that these simple words "Jesus, I trust in You!" that I see here on so many images, continually be for human hearts also in the future, near the end of this century and this millennium, and the next, a clear indicator of the way. "Jesus, I trust in You." There is no such darkness in which man would need to lose himself. If only he will put his trust in Jesus, he will always find himself in the light. Praised be Jesus Christ!

✝ *VERITATIS SPLENDOR,* August 1993

Conclusion of Encyclical

Mary, Mother of Mercy

118. At the end of these considerations, let us entrust ourselves, the sufferings and the joys of our life, the moral life

of believers and people of good will, and the research of moralists, to Mary, Mother of God and Mother of Mercy.

Mary is Mother of Mercy because her Son, Jesus Christ, was sent by the Father as the revelation of God's mercy (cf. Jn 3:16-18). Christ came not to condemn but to forgive, to show mercy (cf. Mt 9:13). And the greatest mercy of all is found in His being in our midst and calling us to meet Him and to confess, with Peter, that He is "the Son of the living God" (Mt 16:16). No human sin can erase the mercy of God, or prevent Him from unleashing all His triumphant power, if we only call upon Him. Indeed, sin itself makes even more radiant the love of the Father who, in order to ransom a slave, sacrificed His Son: His mercy towards us is Redemption. This mercy reaches its fullness in the gift of the Spirit who bestows new life and demands that it be lived. No matter how many and great the obstacles put in His way by human frailty and sin, the Spirit, who renews the face of the earth (cf. Ps 104:30), makes possible the miracle of the perfect accomplishment of the good. This renewal, which gives the ability to do what is good, noble, beautiful, pleasing to God and in conformity with His will, is in some way the flowering of the gift of mercy, which offers liberation from the slavery of evil and gives the strength to sin no more. Through the gift of new life, Jesus makes us sharers in His love and leads us to the Father in the Spirit.

119. Such is the consoling certainty of Christian faith, the source of its profound humanity and extraordinary simplicity. At times, in the discussions about new and complex moral problems, it can seem that Christian morality is in itself too demanding, difficult to understand and almost impossible to practice. This is untrue, since Christian morality consists, in the simplicity of the Gospel, in *following Jesus Christ*, in abandoning oneself to Him, in letting oneself be transformed by His grace and renewed by His mercy, gifts which come to us in the living communion of His Church. Saint Augustine reminds us that "he who would live has a place to live, and has everything needed to live. Let him draw near, let him believe, let him

become part of the body, that he may have life. Let him not shrink from the unity of the members" (In *Iohannis Evangelium Tractatus*, 26, 13: CCL, 36, 266). By the light of the Holy Spirit, the living essence of Christian morality can be understood by everyone, even the least learned, but particularly those who are able to preserve an "undivided heart" (Ps 86:11). On the other hand, this evangelical simplicity does not exempt one from facing reality in its complexity; rather it can lead to a more genuine understanding of reality, inasmuch as following Christ will gradually bring out the distinctive character of authentic Christian morality, while providing the vital energy needed to carry it out. It is the task of the Church's Magisterium to see that the dynamic process of following Christ develops in an organic manner, without the falsification or obscuring of its moral demands, with all their consequences. The one who loves Christ keeps His commandments (cf. Jn 14:15).

120. Mary is also Mother of Mercy because it is to her that Jesus entrusts His Church and all humanity. At the foot of the Cross, when she accepts John as her son, when she asks, together with Christ, forgiveness from the Father for those who do not know what they do (cf. Lk 23:34), Mary experiences, in perfect docility to the Spirit, the richness and the universality of God's love, which opens her heart and enables it to embrace the entire human race. Thus Mary becomes Mother of each and every one of us, the Mother who obtains for us Divine Mercy.

Mary is the radiant sign and inviting model of the moral life. As St. Ambrose put it, "The life of this one person can serve as a model for everyone" (*De Virginibus*, Bk. II, Chap .II, 15: PL 16, 222), and while speaking specifically to virgins but within a context open to all, he affirmed: "The first stimulus to learning is the nobility of the teacher. Who can be more noble than the Mother of God? Who can be more glorious than the one chosen by Glory Itself?" (De Virginibus, Bk. II, Chap. II, 7: PL 16, 220.) Mary lived and exercised her freedom precisely by giving herself to God and accepting God's gift within herself. Until the time of His birth, she sheltered in her womb the Son of God who became man; she raised Him and enabled Him to grow, and she accompanied Him in that supreme act of freedom which is the complete sacrifice of His own life. By the gift of herself, Mary entered fully into the plan of God who gives Himself to the world. By accepting and pondering in her heart events which she did not always understand (cf. Lk 2:19), she became the model of all those who hear the word of God and keep it (cf. Lk 11:28), and merited the title of "Seat of Wisdom." This Wisdom is Jesus Christ Himself, the Eternal Word of God, who perfectly reveals and accomplishes the will of the Father (cf. Heb 10:5-10). Mary invites everyone to accept this Wisdom. To us too, she addresses the command she gave to the servants at Cana in Galilee during the marriage feast: "Do whatever He tells you" (Jn 2:5).

Mary shares our human condition, but in complete openness to the grace of God. Not having known sin, she is able to have compassion on every kind of weakness. She understands sinful man and loves him with a mother's love. Precisely for this reason she is on the side of truth and shares the Church's burden in recalling always and to everyone the demands of morality. Nor does she permit sinful man to be deceived by those who claim to love him by justifying his sin, for she knows that the sacrifice of Christ her Son would thus be emptied of its power. No absolution offered by beguiling doctrines, even in the areas of philosophy and theology, can make man truly happy: only the Cross and the glory of the Risen Christ can grant peace to his conscience and salvation to his life.

> O Mary,
> Mother of Mercy,
> watch over all people,
> that the Cross of Christ
> may not be emptied of its power,
> that man may not stray
> from the path of the good
> or become blind to sin,
> but may put his hope ever more fully in God

who is "rich in mercy" (Eph 2:4).
May he carry out the good works prepared
by God beforehand (cf. Eph 2:10)
and so live completely
"for the praise of His glory" (Eph 1:12).

Given in Rome, at St. Peter's, on August 6, Feast of the
Transfiguration of the Lord, in the year 1993, the fifthteenth
of my Pontificate.

✝ "CHRIST'S PEACE IS THE TRIUMPH OF DIVINE MERCY," *Regina Caeli,* Divine Mercy Sunday, April 10, 1994

(*L'Osservatore Romano*, April 13, 1994)

On Sunday, April 10, before praying the *Regina Caeli*,
the Holy Father reflected on the peace Christ brought by
His resurrection and the triumph of Divine Mercy. Here are
his remarks:

1. "*Peace be with you!*" This is the greeting of the Risen
Christ, which has been echoed several times in our
biblical readings during this Octave of Easter and in
particular, in the Gospel of today's liturgy. On Jesus'
lips this greeting goes far beyond the perspective of
and desire for external peace, although this is so
necessary. The peace brought by Jesus is the *fullness
of the Easter gift.*

Christ Himself is our peace (cf. Eph 2:14). Appearing
to the Apostles after the resurrection, He, the Lamb of
God who takes away the sin of the world (cf. Jn 1:29),
inaugurates *the time of great mercy offered to mankind
through the gift of the Spirit and the sacraments of
the Church: "Whose sins you forgive are forgiven them"*
(Jn 20:23).

(Unofficial translation from the original Latin document by
Archbishop George Pearce, SM)

2. The peace brought by the Risen One is consequently the *triumph of Divine Mercy*. What is mercy if not the boundless love of God, who, confronted with human sin, restrains the sentiment of severe justice and, allowing Himself to be moved by the wretchedness of His creatures, spurs Himself to the total gift of self, in the Son's cross? "O happy fault ... which gained for us so great a Redeemer!" (Easter Proclamation).

To understand the depth of this mystery, we should take Jesus' disconcerting revelation seriously: "... there will be more joy in heaven over one sinner who repents than over ninety-nine righteous people who have no need of repentance" (Lk 15:7). God is truly the Shepherd who leaves ninety-nine sheep to go in search of the one that has strayed (cf. Lk 15:4-6); He is the Father who is always ready to welcome a lost son (cf. Lk 15:11-31). Who can say he is free from sin and does not need God's mercy?

As people of this restless time of ours, wavering between the emptiness of self-exaltation and the humiliation of despair, we have a *greater need than ever for a regenerating experience of mercy* (emphasis added). We should learn to say repeatedly to God with the faith and simplicity of children: "Great is our sin, but even greater is your love!" (Vespers hymn during the season of Lent).

Opening ourselves to mercy, we must not be content with mediocrity and sin, but on the contrary, we must be revived by resolutions to lead a new life.

3. O Mary, Mother of Mercy! You know the heart of your divine Son better than anyone. Instill in us the filial trust in Jesus practiced by the saints, the trust that animated Blessed Faustina Kowalska, the great apostle of Divine Mercy in our time.

Look lovingly upon our misery: O Mother, draw us away from the contrary temptations of self-sufficiency and despair, and obtain for us an abundance of saving mercy.

✝ DIVINE MERCY SUNDAY APPROVED FOR POLAND

Congregatio De Cultu Divino Et Disciplina Sacramentorum
Prot. 822/93/L, January 23, 1995

For Poland:

In recent times, the clergy and faithful of Poland, have come to a deeper understanding of — and hence devotion to — "The Mercy of God," that is, "The Merciful Jesus." This has been evidenced by a greatly renewed sacramental life, as well as by widespread and greatly increased works of charity.

Indeed, this specific type of devotion leads by its very nature to the Lord and God who is to be glorified as "rich in mercy," above all in the celebration of the Paschal Mystery, in which the Mercy of God for all men shines forth most brilliantly.

In view of these facts, and also taking into consideration the request made by their Eminences the Cardinals, and their Excellencies the Archbishops and Bishops of Poland, set out in their letter of March 23, 1993, the Supreme Pontiff John Paul II graciously grants that, hereafter in the dioceses of Poland, to the title, "The Second Sunday of Easter," there be added this specification, "namely, Divine Mercy Sunday," prescribing also that, in the liturgical celebration of the aforementioned Sunday, the texts for that day found in the Roman Missal and in the Liturgy of the Hours be always adhered to.

We are communicating these directives of the Supreme Pontiff to the concerned parties, in order that they be duly carried out.

Anything whatsoever to the contrary notwithstanding.

Given at the Office of the Congregation for Divine

Worship and the Discipline of the Sacraments, on this 23rd day of January, 1995.

(Antonius M. Card. Javierre)
Prefect

(+ Gerardus M. Agnelo)
Archbishop Secretary

✟ "BE APOSTLES OF DIVINE MERCY"

Homily at the Church of the Holy Spirit (Shrine of The Divine Mercy for Rome), Divine Mercy Sunday, April 23, 1995

(*L'Osservatore Romano*, May 3, 1995)

"The mystical experience of Blessed Faustina Kowalska and her cry to the merciful Christ belong to the harsh context of our century's history," the Holy Father said on Divine Mercy Sunday, April 23, as he celebrated Mass in the Roman Church of the Holy Spirit "in Sassia." Here is Pope John Paul II's homily:

1. "*Peace be with you!*" (Jn 20:19).

The Risen Jesus said these words twice on appearing to the Eleven in the Upper Room, on the evening of the very day when He rose from the dead. The Lord, as the Evangelist John testifies, showed them His hands and His side, to *confirm* in their presence *the identity of His body*, as if to say: this is the same body that two days ago was nailed to the cross and then laid in the tomb; the body that bears the wounds of the crucifixion and the stab of the lance. It is the direct proof that I have risen and am alive.

From the human point of view, this observation was difficult to accept as *Thomas's reaction shows.* On the evening of the first appearance in the Upper Room, Thomas was absent. And when the other Apostles told him they had seen the Lord, *he firmly refused to believe them:* "Unless I see the mark of the nails in His hands and put my finger into the nail marks and put my hand into His side, I will not believe" (Jn 20:25). From these words it can be seen *how important Christ's physical identity was for the truth of the Resurrection.*

When the Lord Jesus, on the eighth day — like today — again entered the Upper Room, He addressed Thomas directly, as if to satisfy his request: "Put your finger here and see My hands, and bring your hand and put it into My side, and do not be unbelieving, but believe" (Jn 20:27). Faced with such proof, the Apostle not only believed but drew the ultimate conclusion of what he had seen and expressed it in the highest and briefest profession of faith: "My Lord and my God!" (Jn 20:28). *In the presence of the Risen One, the truth both of His humanity and of His divinity became clear to Thomas.* The One who had risen by His own power was the Lord: "The Lord of life does not know death" (from a Polish Easter hymn).

Thomas' confession ends the series of witnesses to Christ's Resurrection which the Church presents during the Octave of Easter. *"My Lord and my God!" Replying to these words, Jesus, in a certain sense, discloses the reality of His Resurrection to the future of all human history.* In fact, He says to Thomas: "Have you come to believe because you have seen Me? *Blessed are those who have not seen and have believed*" (Jn 20:29). He was thinking of those who would not see Him risen, nor eat and drink with Him as the Apostles had (cf. Acts 10:41), and yet would believe on the basis of eyewitnesses' accounts. They are the ones, in particular, to be called "blessed" by Christ.

I live forever that man may share in immortal life

2. *"Do not be afraid. I am the First and the Last, the One who lives"* (Rv 1:17).

There is a certain analogy between the appearance in the Upper Room — especially that of the eighth day, in Thomas' presence — and the eschatological vision St. John speaks of in the second reading from Revelation. In the Upper Room Christ shows the Apostles, and especially Thomas, the wounds in His hands, His feet and His side, to confirm the identity of His risen and glorious body with the one that was crucified and laid in the tomb. In Revelation, the Lord introduced Himself as the First and the Last, as the One from whom the history of the cosmos begins and with whom it ends, the One who is "the firstborn of all creation" (Col 1:15), "the firstborn from the dead" (Col 1:18), the beginning and the end of human history.

His identity, *which endlessly pervades the history of men,* is formulated with the words: "Once I was dead, but now I am alive for ever and ever" (Rv 1:18). It is as if He had said: In time I was dead; I accepted death to remain faithful to the very end to the Incarnation through which, remaining the Son of God consubstantial with the Father, I became true man in everything except sin (cf. Heb 4:15). The three days of My Passion and Death, necessary for the work of Redemption, remain in Me and in you. And now I live forever and, with My Resurrection, show forth the will of God who calls every man to share in My own immortal life. I have the keys of death with which I must open earthly tombs and change cemeteries from places where death reigns into vast spaces for the resurrection.

3. "Do not be afraid!" When, on the island of Patmos, Jesus addresses this exhortation to John, He reveals His victory over the many fears that accompany man in his earthly existence and especially *when he is faced with*

suffering and death. The fear of death also concerns the *great unknown which it represents*. Could it be a total annihilation of the human being? Do not the severe words: "*For you are dust, and to dust you shall return*" (cf. Gn 3:19) fully express the harsh reality of death? Thus man has serious reasons to feel afraid when he faces the mystery of death.

Contemporary civilization does all it can to *distract human attention from the inescapable reality of death* and tries to induce man *to live as though death did not exist*. And this is expressed practically in the attempt to *turn man's conscience away from God*: to make him live as through God did not exist! But the reality of death is obvious. It is impossible to silence it; it is impossible to dispel the fear associated with it.

Man fears death as he fears what comes after death. *He fears judgment and punishment, and this fear has a saving value*: it should not be eliminated in man. When Christ says: "Do not be afraid!" He wants to respond to *the deepest source of the human being's existential fear*. What He means is: Do not fear evil, since in My Resurrection good has shown itself stronger than evil. My Gospel is victorious truth. Life and death met on Calvary in a stupendous combat and life proved victorious: "*Dux vitae mortuus regnat vivus!*" "Once I was dead, but now I am alive for ever and ever" (Rv 1:18).

4. "The stone which the builders rejected has become the cornerstone" (Ps 117 [118]: 22). The verse of the responsorial psalm in today's liturgy helps us to understand the truth about Christ's Resurrection. *It also expresses the truth about Divine Mercy, revealed in the Resurrection: love gained the victory over sin, and life over death*. In a certain sense, this truth is the very essence of the Good News. Therefore Christ can say: Do not be afraid!" He repeats these words to every

man, especially to those who are suffering physically or spiritually. He can justifiably repeat them.

Sr. Faustina Kowalska heralded God's mercy

Sr. Faustina Kowalska, whom I had the joy of beatifying two years ago, especially understood this. Her mystical experiences were all focused on the *mystery of the merciful Christ* and are a remarkable commentary as it were on the word of God presented to us in this Sunday's liturgy. Sister Faustina not only recorded them, but sought an artist who could paint the image of the merciful Christ just as she saw Him. An image which, together with the figure of Blessed Faustina, is an eloquent testimony to what theologians call *"condescendentia divina."* God makes Himself understandable to His human interlocutors. Sacred Scripture, and especially the Gospel, confirm this.

Dear brothers and sisters, Sr. Faustina's message follows these lines. But was it only Sr. Faustina's, or rather, *was it not at the same time a testimony given by all those who were encouraged by this message in the cruel experiences of the Second World War, in the concentration and extermination camps, and in the bombings?* The mystical experience of Blessed Faustina Kowalska and her cry to the merciful Christ belong to the harsh context of our century's history. As people of this century which is now coming to an end, *we would like to thank the Lord for the message of Divine Mercy.*

5. Today in particular, I am pleased to be able to give thanks to God in this *Church of the Holy Spirit "in Sassia"* attached to the hospital of the same name and now a *specialized center for the pastoral care of the sick as well as for the promotion of the spirituality of Divine Mercy.* It is very significant and timely that precisely here, next to this very ancient hospital, prayers are said and work is done with constant care for the health of body and spirit.

As I express again my satisfaction to the Cardinal Vicar, I also address a grateful thought to the titular, Cardinal Fiorenzo Angelini. I greet the Bishop of the western sector, the rector and the other priests, the sisters and all of you, dear faithful, who are present here. I would also like to convey fraternal wishes to the patients of Santo Spirito Hospital, as well as to the doctors, nurses, sisters and all those who help them every day. I would like to say to all: trust in the Lord! Be apostles of Divine Mercy and, following the invitation and the example of Blessed Faustina, take care of those who suffer in body and especially in spirit. Let each one feel the merciful love of the Lord who comforts and instills joy.

May Jesus be your peace!

"Jesus Christ is the same yesterday, today and forever!" (Heb 13:8).

Contemplating Him in the mystery of the Cross and the Resurrection, let us repeat together with this Sunday's liturgy:

Give thanks to the Lord, for He is good, for His mercy endures forever!

✝ "NEW LIFE AND JOY FLOW FROM EASTER"

Regina Caeli **Address, Divine Mercy Sunday,** April 23, 1995

L'Osservatore Romano, April 26, 1995

"The spiral of hatred and violence which stains with blood the path of so many individuals and nations can only be broken by the miracle of forgiveness," the Holy Father said to the crowds gathered in St. Peter's Square on Sunday, April 23, before praying the *Regina Caeli*. Here are John Paul II's remarks:

Dear Brothers and Sisters,

1. Today ends the Octave of Easter, when the Church repeats the words of the Psalm with exultation: "This is the day the Lord has made; let us be glad and rejoice

in it" (Ps 117 [118]: 24). The whole Octave is like a single day, the new day, the day of the new creation. By conquering death, Christ has made all things new (cf. Rv 21:5). From Easter flows new life, new peace and new joy for all believers.

However, the peace and joy of Easter are not only for the Church: they are for the whole world! Joy is victory over fear, violence, and death. Peace is the antithesis of anguish. Greeting the Apostles, who were frightened and discouraged by His Passion and death, the Risen One says: "Peace be with you" (Jn 20:19). When Christ appeared to John on the island of Patmos, this was once again His invitation: "Do not be afraid. I am the First and the Last, the One who lives. Once I was dead, but now I am alive for ever and ever. I hold the keys to death and the nether world" (Rv 1:17-18).

Easter overcomes human fear because it gives the only true answer to one of man's greatest problems: death. In proclaiming Jesus' Resurrection, the Church wishes to pass on to humanity *faith in the resurrection of the dead* and in everlasting life. The Christian proclamation is essentially "the Gospel of life."

2. *Give thanks to the Lord, for He is good* (cf. Psalm 117 [118]:1). In a special way, today is the Sunday of thanksgiving for the goodness God has shown man in the whole Easter mystery. This is why it is also called *the Sunday of Divine Mercy.* Essentially, God's mercy, as the mystical experience of Blessed Faustina Kowalska, who was raised to the honors of the altar two years ago, helps us to understand, reveals precisely this truth: good triumphs over evil, life is stronger than death and God's love is more powerful than sin. All this is manifested in Christ's Paschal Mystery, in which God appears to us as He is: a tender-hearted *Father,*

who does not give up in the face of His children's ingratitude and is always ready to forgive.

3. Dear brothers and sisters, we must personally experience this mercy if, in turn, we want to be capable of mercy. *Let us learn to forgive*! The spiral of hatred and violence which stains with blood the path of so many individuals and nations can only be broken by the *miracle of forgiveness.*

May Mary obtain this gift of Divine Mercy for all humanity so that the individuals and peoples who are particularly tormented by hostility and fratricidal war may overcome hatred and build concrete attitudes of reconciliation and peace.

✝ THE PERSONAL EXPERIENCE OF THE MERCY POPE

Shrine of The Divine Mercy in Poland, June 7, 1997

"*Misericordias Domini in aeternum cantabo*" ["I will sing the mercies of the Lord forever" — Ps 89:2].

I have come here to this shrine as a pilgrim to take part in the unending hymn in honor of Divine Mercy. The psalmist of the Lord had intoned it, expressing what every generation preserved and will continue to preserve as a most precious fruit of faith.

There is nothing that man needs more than Divine Mercy — that love which is benevolent, which is compassionate, which raises man above his weakness to the infinite heights of the holiness of God.

In this place we become particularly aware of this. From here, in fact, went out the message of Divine Mercy that Christ Himself chose to pass on to our generation through Blessed Faustina.

And it is a *message that is clear and understandable for everyone.* Anyone can come here, look at this image of the merciful Jesus, His Heart radiating grace, and hear in the depths of his own soul what Blessed Faustina heard: "Fear nothing; I am always with you" (*Diary*, 586).

And if this person responds with a sincere heart: "*Jesus, I trust in You*," he will find comfort in all his *anxieties and fears*. In this "dialogue of abandonment," there is established between man and Christ a *special bond that sets love free*. And "there is no fear in love, but perfect love casts out fear" (1 Jn 4:18).

The Church rereads the message of mercy in order to bring with greater effectiveness to this generation at the end of the millennium and to future generations *the light of hope*. Unceasingly, the Church implores from God mercy for everyone.

"At no time and in no historical period — especially at a moment as critical as our own — can the Church forget t*he prayer that is a cry for the mercy of God* amid the many forms of evil which weigh upon humanity and threaten it. ...

"The more the human conscience succumbs to secularization, loses its sense of the very meaning of the word 'mercy,' moves away from God, and distances itself from the mystery of mercy, the more the *Church has the right and the duty* to appeal to the God of mercy 'with loud cries'" (*Dives in Misericordia*, 15).

Precisely for this reason, this shrine, too, has found a place on my pilgrim itinerary. I come here to commend the concerns of the Church and of humanity to the merciful Christ. On the threshold of the third millennium *I come to entrust to Him once more my Petrine ministry* — "*Jesus, I trust in You!*"

The message of Divine Mercy has always been near and dear to me. It is as if history had inscribed it in the tragic experience of the Second World War. In those difficult years it was *a particular support and an inexhaustible source of hope*, not only for the people of Krakow but for the entire nation.

This was also my personal experience, which I took with me to the See of Peter and which, in a sense, forms the image of this Pontificate.

I give thanks to Divine Providence that I have been enabled to contribute personally to the fulfillment of Christ's will, through the institution of the Feast of Divine Mercy [in

Poland in 1995]. Here, near the relics of Blessed Faustina Kowalska, I give thanks also for the gift of her beatification. I pray unceasingly that God will have "mercy on us and on the whole world" [From the Chaplet of Divine Mercy, *Diary*, 476].

"Blessed are the merciful, for they shall obtain mercy" (Mt 5:7).

Dear Sisters! An extraordinary vocation is yours. Choosing from among you, Blessed Faustina, Christ has made your congregation the guardian of this place, and at the same time He has called you to a particular apostolate, that of His mercy. I ask you: accept this responsibility!

The people of today need your *proclamation of mercy*: they need your *works of mercy* and they need your *prayer to obtain mercy* [cf. *Diary*, 742].

Do not neglect any of these dimensions of the apostolate. Fulfill it in union with the Archbishop of Krakow, to whose heart is so dear the devotion to The Divine Mercy, and in union with the whole ecclesial community over which he presides.

May this shared work bear much fruit! May The Divine Mercy transform people's hearts! May this shrine, known already in many parts of the world, become a center of worship of The Divine Mercy which shines on the whole Church! ...

I cordially bless all who are present here and all those devoted to The Divine Mercy.

✝ "ACCEPT THE GIFT OF MERCIFUL LOVE WITH AN OPEN HEART"

Regina Caeli, Divine Mercy Sunday: April 19, 1998

L'Osservatore Romano, April 22, 1998

On April 19, the Second Sunday of Easter, the Holy Father led the recitation of the *Regina Caeli*, which he introduced with a reflection on the Lord's merciful love and on the Special Synod for Asia. Here is the complete text:

Dear Brothers and Sisters,

1. In today's Gospel passage we read that Jesus appeared to the Apostles in the Upper Room and said to them: "Receive the Holy Spirit. If you forgive the sins of any, they are forgiven; if you retain the sins of any, they are retained" (Jn 20:22-23). With these words, the Risen Christ calls the Apostles to be messengers and ministers of His merciful love and from that day, from generation to generation, this proclamation of hope has resounded in the heart of the Church for every believer. Blessed are those who open their hearts to Divine Mercy! The Lord's merciful love precedes and accompanies every act of evangelization and enriches it with extraordinary fruits of conversion and spiritual renewal.

2. In every corner of the world, the way of the Christian people is marked by the constant action of Divine Mercy. This happened in the early communities and likewise in the Church's later developments on the various continents.

Today our attention is focused in particular on the signs of mercy which God worked and continues to work in Asia. In fact, this morning's solemn Eucharistic celebration in St. Peter's Basilica opened the Special Assembly for Asia of the Synod of Bishops.

The theme chosen for this Synod Assembly is "Jesus Christ the Savior and His Mission of Love and Service in Asia: 'That they may have life, and have it abundantly'" (Jn 10:10). This is a most appropriate theme for Asia, especially in view of its many religions and cultures, its variety of economic and political situations. It is an enormous land, open to the proclamation of salvation in Jesus Christ and to the witness of Christian solidarity towards peoples who are often sorely tried.

At this time, I am thinking particularly of the peoples of North Korea, exhausted by hunger and hardship: as I urge the Church's charitable organizations to take responsibility for this difficult situation, I hope that the international community will also provide the necessary assistance.

3. Let us entrust to Mary, Mother of the Church, the work of the Special Assembly for Asia of the Synod of Bishops. May she, who was at the heart of the apostolic community as a teacher of prayer and communion, obtain an abundant outpouring of the Holy Spirit on the Synod Fathers and on all the Christian communities throughout the Asian continent. May Our Lady, Mother of Divine Mercy, also enable us to accept with open hearts the gift of merciful love that the Risen Christ offers all believers, so that His mercy and His peace may mark the present and the future of all humanity.

✝ "SILENCE THE ARMS AND RESUME THE DIALOGUE"

Regina Caeli, Divine Mercy Sunday, April 11, 1999

L'Osservatore Romano, April 14, 1999

On Sunday, April 11, 1999, the Octave of Easter and Divine Mercy Sunday, the Holy Father led the recitation of the *Regina Caeli*, which he introduced with a reflection on God's merciful love, drawing attention to the glaring contrast between the suffering caused by the war in the Balkans and the Risen Christ's gift of mercy and peace. The Pope asked the faithful to intensify their prayers for an end to the war and for peaceful coexistence among all the peoples of that region. Here is Pope John Paul II's message:

Dear Brothers and Sisters,

1. At the end of the Octave of Easter, with a special thought for our Orthodox brothers and sisters who are celebrating this solemnity today, I make my own

the words of the Apostle Peter, proclaimed in the liturgy: "Blessed be the God and Father of our Lord Jesus Christ! By His great mercy we have been born anew to a living hope through the resurrection of Jesus Christ from the dead" (1 Pt 1:3). On their way to the Jubilee, the entire People of God raise a hymn of thanksgiving to God the Father who, in Christ's Paschal Mystery, revealed to the world His face and, so to speak, His heart "rich in mercy" (Eph 2:4).

This Sunday is also called Divine Mercy Sunday: in this year dedicated to God the Father, it is an excellent occasion to enter into the authentic Jubilee spirit as individuals and as the Church, in accordance with Jesus' own words: "The Spirit of the Lord is upon Me, because He has sent Me ... to announce a year of favor from the Lord" (Lk 4: 18-19). I am very pleased that many priests and faithful have gathered this morning in St. Peter's Square for a solemn Eucharist celebrated by Cardinal Fiorenzo Angelini, whom I cordially greet, and with him everyone present, as I express my pleasure with your devotion to the merciful Jesus.

I warmly encourage you to be apostles of Divine Mercy, like Blessed Faustina Kowalska, wherever you live and work.

2. How could we not note the glaring contrast between the invitation to mercy and forgiveness echoing in today's liturgy and the violence of the tragic conflicts which are soaking the Balkan region in blood? May peace prevail at last! Here I renew the appeal dictated not only by faith, but first of all by reason: may people be able to live together in harmony in their lands; may weapons be silenced and dialogue resumed!

My thoughts turn constantly to those who are suffering the harsh consequences of the war, and I pray the

Risen Lord, the Prince of Peace, to give us the gift of
His peace.

3. I would like to invite all believers to intensify their
prayer for peace, because God offers what sometimes
seems almost humanly impossible to those who
request it as a gift of His mercy.

For this reason, let us invoke the intercession of Blessed
Mary, Mother of Mercy. We pray to you to help us set
out courageously on the way of love and peace.

✝ UNIVERSAL PRAYER: CONFESSION OF SINS AND ASKING FOR FORGIVENESS, MARCH 12, 2000

Introduction

THE HOLY FATHER: Brothers and Sisters, let us turn
with trust to God our Father, who is merciful and compassionate,
slow to anger, great in love and fidelity, and ask Him to accept
the repentance of His people who humbly confess their sins, and
to grant them mercy. [All pray for a moment in silence.]

I. Confession of Sins in General

Cardinal Bernardin Gantin: Let us pray that our confession
and repentance will be inspired by the Holy Spirit, that our
sorrow will be conscious and deep, and that, humbly viewing the
sins of the past in an authentic "purification of memory," we will
be committed to the path of true conversion. [Silent prayer.]
THE HOLY FATHER: Lord God, Your pilgrim Church,
which You ever sanctify in the blood of Your Son, counts among
her children in every age members whose holiness shines brightly
forth and members whose disobedience to You contradicts the
faith we profess and the Holy Gospel. You, who remain ever
faithful, even when we are unfaithful, forgive our sins and grant
that we may bear true witness to You before all men and women.
We ask this through Christ our Lord. R. Amen. Cantor: *Kyrie,*

eleison; Kyrie, eleison; Kyrie, eleison. The assembly repeats: *Kyrie, eleison; Kyrie, eleison; Kyrie, eleison.* [A lamp is lit before the Crucifix.]

II. Confession of Sins Committed in the Service of Truth

CARDINAL JOSEPH RATZINGER: Let us pray that each one of us, looking to the Lord Jesus, meek and humble of heart, will recognize that even men of the Church, in the name of faith and morals, have sometimes used methods not in keeping with the Gospel in the solemn duty of defending the truth. [Silent prayer.] **THE HOLY FATHER:** Lord, God of all men and women, in certain periods of history Christians have, at times, given in to intolerance and have not been faithful to the great commandment of love, sullying in this way the face of the Church, Your Spouse. Have mercy on Your sinful children and accept our resolve to seek and promote truth in the gentleness of charity, in the firm knowledge that truth can prevail only in virtue of truth itself. We ask this through Christ our Lord. R. Amen. R. Kyrie, eleison; Kyrie, eleison; Kyrie, eleison. [A lamp is lit before the Crucifix.]

III. Confession of Sins Which Have Harmed the Unity of the Body of Christ

Cardinal Roger Etchegaray: Let us pray that our recognition of the sins which have rent the unity of the Body of Christ and wounded fraternal charity will facilitate the way to reconciliation and communion among all Christians. [Silent prayer.] The Holy Father: Merciful Father, on the night before His Passion, Your Son prayed for the unity of those who believe in Him: in disobedience to His will, however, believers have opposed one another, becoming divided, and have mutually condemned one another and fought against one another. We urgently implore Your forgiveness and we beseech the gift of a repentant heart, so that all Christians, reconciled with You and with one another will be able, in one body and in one spirit, to experience anew the joy of full communion. We ask this through Christ our Lord. R. Amen. R. *Kyrie, eleison; Kyrie, eleison; Kyrie, eleison.* [A lamp is lit before the Crucifix.]

IV. Confession of Sins against the People of Israel

CARDINAL EDWARD CASSIDY: Let us pray that, in recalling the sufferings endured by the people of Israel throughout history, Christians will acknowledge the sins committed by not a few of their number against the people of the Covenant and the blessings, and in this way will purify their hearts. [Silent prayer.] **THE HOLY FATHER:** God of our fathers, You chose Abraham and his descendants to bring Your Name to the Nations: we are deeply saddened by the behavior of those who in the course of history have caused these children of Yours to suffer, and asking Your forgiveness, we wish to commit ourselves to genuine brotherhood with the people of the Covenant. We ask this through Christ our Lord. R. Amen. R. *Kyrie, eleison; Kyrie, eleison; Kyrie eleison.* [A lamp is lit before the Crucifix.]

V. Confession of Sins Committed in Actions against Love, Peace, the Rights of Peoples, and Respect for Cultures and Religions

ARCHBISHOP STEPHEN FUMIO HAMAO: Let us pray that contemplating Jesus, our Lord and our Peace, Christians will be able to repent of the words and attitudes caused by pride, by hatred, by the desire to dominate others, by enmity towards members of other religions and towards the weakest groups in society, such as immigrants and itinerants. [Silent prayer.] **THE HOLY FATHER:** Lord of the world, Father of all, through Your Son You asked us to love our enemies, to do good to those who hate us and to pray for those who persecute us. Yet Christians have often denied the Gospel; yielding to a mentality of power, they have violated the rights of ethnic groups and peoples, and shown contempt for their cultures and religious traditions: be patient and merciful towards us, and grant us Your forgiveness! We ask this through Christ our Lord. R. Amen. R. *Kyrie, eleison; Kyrie, eleison; Kyrie, eleison.* [A lamp is lit before the Crucifix.]

VI. Confession of Sins against the Dignity of Women and the Unity of the Human Race

CARDINAL FRANCIS ARINZE: Let us pray for all those who have suffered offenses against their human dignity and whose rights have been trampled; let us pray for women, who are all too often humiliated and marginalized, and let us acknowledge the forms of acquiescence in these sins of which Christians too have been guilty. [Silent prayer.] **THE HOLY FATHER:** Lord God, our Father, You created the human being, man and woman, in Your image and likeness and You willed the diversity of peoples within the unity of the human family. At times, however, the equality of Your sons and daughters has not been acknowledged, and Christians have been guilty of attitudes of rejection and exclusion, consenting to acts of discrimination on the basis of racial and ethnic differences. Forgive us and grant us the grace to heal the wounds still present in Your community on account of sin, so that we will all feel ourselves to be Your sons and daughters. We ask this through Christ our Lord. R. Amen. R. *Kyrie, eleison; Kyrie, eleison; Kyrie, eleison.* [A lamp is lit before the Crucifix.]

VII. Confession of Sins in Relation to the Fundamental Rights of the Person

ARCHBISHOP FRANCOIS XAVIER NGUYEN VAN THUAN: Let us pray for all the men and women of the world, especially for minors who are victims of abuse, for the poor, the alienated, the disadvantaged; let us pray for those who are most defenseless, the unborn killed in their mother's womb or even exploited for experimental purposes by those who abuse the promise of biotechnology and distort the aims of science. [Silent prayer.] **THE HOLY FATHER:** God, our Father, You always hear the cry of the poor. How many times have Christians themselves not recognized You in the hungry, the thirsty, and the naked, in the persecuted, the imprisoned, and in those incapable of defending themselves, especially in the first stages of life. For all those who have committed acts of injustice by trusting in wealth and power and showing contempt for the "little ones" who are so dear to You, we ask Your forgiveness. Have mercy on us and accept our repentance. We ask this through Christ our Lord. R. Amen. R. *Kyrie, eleison; Kyrie, eleison; Kyrie, eleison.* [A lamp is lit before the Crucifix.]

Concluding Prayer

THE HOLY FATHER: Most merciful Father, Your Son, Jesus Christ, the judge of the living and the dead, in the humility of His first coming redeemed humanity from sin and in His glorious return He will demand an account of every sin. Grant that our forebears, our brothers and sisters, and we, Your servants, who by the grace of the Holy Spirit turn back to You in wholehearted repentance, may experience Your mercy and receive the forgiveness of our sins. We ask this through Christ our Lord. R. Amen.

[As a sign of penance and veneration the Holy Father embraces and kisses the Crucifix.]

✝ *ANGELUS*: "DAY OF PARDON," SUNDAY, MARCH 12, 2000

(This text was taken from the Vatican Website)

Dear Brothers and Sisters!

1. In the faith context of the Great Jubilee, today we are celebrating the Day of Pardon. This morning in St. Peter's Basilica, I presided at a moving and solemn penitential act. On this First Sunday of Lent, Bishops and Ecclesial Communities in various parts of the world knelt before God, in the name of the entire Christian people, to implore His forgiveness.

The Holy Year is a time of purification: the Church is holy because Christ is her Head and her Spouse; the Spirit is her life-giving soul; the Virgin Mary and the saints are her most authentic expression. However, the children of the Church know the experience of sin, whose shadows are cast over her, obscuring her beauty. For this reason the Church does not cease to implore God's forgiveness for the sins of her members.

2. This is not a judgment on the subjective responsibility of our brothers and sisters who have gone before us: judgment belongs to God alone, who — unlike us human beings — "sees the heart and the mind" (cf. Jer 20: 12). Today's act is a sincere recognition of the sins committed by the Church's children in the distant and recent past, and a humble plea for God's forgiveness. This will reawaken consciences, enabling Christians to enter the third millennium with greater openness to God and His plan of love.

As we ask forgiveness, let us also forgive. This is what we say every day when we recite the prayer Jesus taught us: "Our Father ... forgive us our trespasses as we forgive those who trespass against us" (Mt 6:12). For all believers, may the fruit of this Jubilee Day be forgiveness reciprocally given and received!

Reconciliation springs from forgiveness. This is our hope for every Ecclesial Community, for all believers in Christ and for the whole world.

3. Forgiven and ready to forgive, Christians enter the third millennium as more credible witnesses to hope. After centuries marked by violence and destruction, especially the last tragic one, the Church offers humanity, as it crosses the threshold of the third millennium, the Gospel of forgiveness and reconciliation, a prerequisite for building genuine peace.

To be witnesses to hope! This is also the theme of the Spiritual Exercises which I will begin this evening with my collaborators in the Roman Curia. For now, I thank all who wish to accompany me in prayer, and I call upon Our Lady, Mother of Divine Mercy, to help everyone to observe the Lenten season fruitfully.

✝ CANONIZATION OF SR. MARIA FAUSTINA KOWALSKA — Homily of Pope John Paul II, Divine Mercy Sunday, April 30, 2000, St. Peter's

1. "*Confitemini Domino quoniam bonus, quoniam in saeculum misericordia eius*"; "Give thanks to the Lord for He is good; His steadfast love endures forever" (Ps 118:1). So the Church sings on the Octave of Easter, as if receiving from Christ's lips these words of the Psalm; from the lips of the Risen Christ, who bears the great message of Divine Mercy and entrusts its ministry to the Apostles in the Upper Room: "Peace be with you. As the Father has sent Me, even so I send you. ... Receive the Holy Spirit. If you forgive the sins of any, they are forgiven; if you retain the sins of any, they are retained" (Jn 20:21-23).

Before speaking these words, Jesus shows His hands and His side. He points, that is, to the wounds of the Passion, especially the wound in His heart, the source from which flows the great wave of mercy poured out on humanity. From that heart, Sr. Faustina Kowalska, the blessed whom from now on we will call a saint, will see two rays of light shining from that heart and illuminating the world. "The two rays," Jesus Himself explained to her one day, "represent blood and water" (*Diary*, Libreria Editrice Vaticana Edition, p.132).

2. Blood and water! We immediately think of the testimony given by the Evangelist John, who, when a soldier on Calvary pierced Christ's side with his spear, sees blood and water flowing from it (cf. Jn 19:34). Moreover, if the blood recalls the sacrifice of the Cross and the gift of the Eucharist, the water, in Johannine symbolism, represents not only Baptism but also the gift of the Holy Spirit (cf. Jn 3:5; 4:14; 7:37-39).

Divine Mercy reaches human beings through the heart of Christ crucified. "My daughter, say that I am love and mercy personified," Jesus will ask Sr. Faustina (*Diary*, p. 374). Christ pours out this mercy on humanity through the sending of the Spirit who, in the Trinity, is the Person-Love. And is not mercy love's "second name" (cf. Dives in Misericordia, 7), understood in its deepest and most tender aspect, in its ability to take upon itself the burden of any need and, especially, in its immense capacity for forgiveness?

Today my joy is truly great in presenting the life and witness of Sr. Faustina Kowalska to the whole Church as a gift of God for our time. By divine Providence, the life of this humble daughter of Poland was completely linked with the history of the 20th century, the century we have just left behind. In fact, it was between the First and Second World Wars that Christ entrusted His message of mercy to her. Those who remember, who were witnesses and participants in the events of those years and the horrible sufferings they caused for millions of people, know well how necessary was the message of mercy.

Jesus told Sr. Faustina: "Humanity will not find peace until it turns trustfully to Divine Mercy" (*Diary*, p. 132). Through the work of the Polish religious, this message has become linked forever to the 20th century, the last of the second millennium and the bridge to the third. It is not a new message, but can be considered a gift of special enlightenment that helps us to relive the Gospel of Easter more intensely, to offer it as a ray of light to the men and women of our time.

3. What will the years ahead bring us? What will man's future on earth be like? We are not given to know. However, it is certain that, in addition to new progress, there will unfortunately be no lack of painful experiences. But the light of Divine Mercy, which the Lord in a way wished to return to the world through Sr. Faustina's charism, will illumine the way for the men and women of the third millennium.

However, as the Apostles once did, today too humanity must welcome into the upper room of history the Risen Christ, who shows the wounds of His Crucifixion and repeats "Peace be with you!" Humanity must let itself be touched and pervaded by the Spirit given to it by the Risen Christ. It is the Spirit who heals the wounds of the heart, pulls down the barriers that separate us from God and divide us from one another, and at the same time, restores the joy of the Father's love and of fraternal unity.

4. It is important then that we accept the whole message that comes to us from the Word of God on this Second Sunday of Easter, which from now on throughout the Church will be called "Divine Mercy Sunday." In the various readings, the liturgy seems to indicate the path of mercy which, while re-establishing the relationship of each person with God, also creates new relations of fraternal solidarity among human beings. Christ has taught us that "man not only receives and experiences the mercy of God, but is also called to 'practice mercy' towards others: 'Blessed are the merciful, for they shall obtain mercy' " (Mt 5:7) (*Dives in Misericordia*, 14). He also showed us the many paths of mercy, which not only forgive sins but reach out to all human needs. Jesus bent over every kind of human poverty, material and spiritual.

His message of mercy continues to reach us through His hands held out to suffering man. This is how Sr. Faustina saw Him and proclaimed Him to people on all the continents when, hidden in her convent at Lagiewniki in Krakow, she made her life a hymn to mercy; *Misericordias Domini in aeternum cantabo*.

5. Sister Faustina's canonization has a particular eloquence. By this act I intend today to pass this message on to the new millennium. I pass it on to all people, so that they will learn to know ever better the true face of God and the true face of their brethren.

In fact, love of God and love of one's brothers and sisters are inseparable, as the First Letter of John has reminded us: "By this we know that we love the children of God, when we love God and obey His commandments"(5:2). Here the Apostle reminds us of the truth of love, showing us its measure and criterion in the observance of the commandments.

It is not easy to love with a deep love, which lies in the authentic gift of self. This love can only be learned by penetrating the mystery of God's love. Looking at Him, being one with His fatherly heart, we are able to look with new eyes at our brothers and sisters, with an attitude of unselfishness and solidarity, of generosity and forgiveness. All this is mercy!

To the extent that humanity penetrates the mystery of this merciful gaze, it will seem possible to fulfill the ideal we heard in today's first reading. "The community of believers were of one heart and one mind. None of them ever claimed anything as his own; rather everything was held in common" (Acts 4:32). Here mercy gave form to human relations and community life; it constituted the basis for the sharing of goods. This led to the spiritual and corporal "works of mercy." Here mercy became a concrete way of being "neighbor" to one's neediest brothers and sisters.

6. Sister Faustina Kowalska wrote in her *Diary*: "I feel tremendous pain when I see the sufferings of my neighbors. All my neighbors' sufferings reverberate in my own heart; I carry their anguish in my heart in such a way that it even physically destroys me. I would like all their sorrows to fall upon me, in order to relieve my neighbor" (*Diary*, p. 365). This is the degree of compassion to which love leads, when it takes the love of God as its measure!

It is this love which must inspire humanity today, if it is to face the crisis of the meaning of life, the challenges of the most diverse needs and, especially, the duty to defend the dignity of every human person. Thus the message of Divine Mercy is also implicitly a message about the value of every human being. Each person is precious in God's eyes; Christ gave His life for each one; to everyone the Father gives His Spirit and offers intimacy.

7. This consoling message is addressed above all to those who, afflicted by a particularly harsh trial or crushed by the weight of the sins they committed, have lost all confidence in life and are tempted to give in to despair. To them the gentle face of Christ is offered; those rays from His heart touch them and shine upon them, warm them, show them the way and fill them with hope. How many souls have been consoled by the prayer "Jesus, I trust in You," which Providence intimated through Sr. Faustina! This simple act of abandonment to Jesus dispels the thickest clouds and lets a ray of light penetrate every life. *Jezu, ufam tobie*!

8. *Misericordias Domini in aeternum cantabo* (Ps 88 [89]:2). Let us too, the pilgrim Church, join our voice to the

voice of Mary most holy, "Mother of Mercy"; to the voice of this new saint who sings of mercy with all God's friends in the heavenly Jerusalem.

And you, Faustina, a gift of God to our time, a gift from the land of Poland to the whole Church, obtain for us an awareness of the depth of Divine Mercy. Help us to have a living experience of it and to bear witness to it among our brothers and sisters. May your message of light and hope spread throughout the world, spurring sinners to conversion, calming rivalries and hatred and opening individuals and nations to the practice of brotherhood. Today, fixing our gaze with you on the face of the Risen Christ, let us make our own your prayer of trusting abandonment and say with firm hope: Christ Jesus, I trust in You! *Jezu, ufam tobie!*

✝ CANONIZATION OF ST. FAUSTINA

Regina Caeli, Divine Mercy Sunday, April 30, 2000:

L'Osservatore Romano, May 3, 2000

Before imparting the final blessing of the Mass he celebrated on Sunday, 30 April, for the canonization of Sr. Mary Faustina Kowalska, the Holy Father led the recitation of the *Regina Caeli* prayer, which he introduced with greetings in various languages to the pilgrims in St. Peter's Square and those at the Shrine of The Divine Mercy in Krakow-Lagiewniki, Poland, who were linked by television with the celebration in Rome. Here is Pope John Paul II's message on this special occasion:

> 1. At the close of this celebration, in which our Easter joy is combined with that of Sr. Faustina Kowalska's canonization, I affectionately greet and thank all of you who have come from various parts of the world. I ardently hope that each of you can experience what Our Lady one day assured St. Faustina: "I am not only the Queen of Heaven, but also the Mother of Mercy and your Mother" (*Diary*, p. 141).

2. The message of Divine Mercy and the image of the merciful Christ of which Sr. Faustina Kowalska speaks to us today are a vivid expression of the spirit of the Great Jubilee which the whole Church is celebrating with joy and fruitfulness. Many of you have come to honor the new saint. May her intercession bring abundant gifts of repentance, forgiveness and renewed spiritual vitality to the Church in your countries. May the thought of God's loving kindness stir up in your hearts new energies for works of faith and Christian solidarity.

I cordially greet the French-speaking pilgrims, especially those who have taken part in the canonization of Sr. Faustina. Following her example, may you entrust yourselves totally to the Lord and praise Him in the power of His mercy! May the renewing strength of the Risen Christ fill your hearts!

At the same time my thoughts embrace all my compatriots and I entrust them to the intercession of the saintly Sr. Faustina. In the new millennium, may the message of the merciful love of God, who bends over all human poverty, be an endless source of hope for everyone and a call to show active love to one's brothers and sisters. I cordially bless you all.

Today we also join the Primate, Archbishop of Gniezno, and all our compatriots who have gathered in Gniezno for the solemnity of St. Adalbert.

"*Gaude Mater Poloniae* ... ." Rejoice, Mother of Poland; rejoice, Sisters of Our Lady of Mercy, because our Sister Faustina has been raised to the glory of the saints.

I cordially greet the pilgrims from Poland and all those devoted to The Divine Mercy who have gathered at the Shrine in Krakow-Lagiewniki. I am happy that on this day — so special for our country — representatives of the Government of the Republic of Poland are here with the Prime Minister, as well as representatives of Solidarity.

Divine Providence has linked Sr. Faustina's life with the cities of Warsaw, Plock, Vilnius and Krakow. Today I recall the names of these cities, of which the new saint is the patroness, entrusting to their residents a particular concern for The Divine Mercy apostolate.

3. And now let us pray to the merciful Queen of Heaven.

✝ EVENING PRAYER, DIVINE MERCY SUNDAY, APRIL 30, 2000

L'Osservatore Romano, May 3, 2000

On Sunday, 30 April, at the close of the prayer service that is held each evening of the Jubilee in St. Peter's Square, the Holy Father came to the window of his study and greeted the pilgrims gathered in front of the Basilica. He said the following:

I am pleased to extend a cordial greeting to the pilgrims attending the prayer that is celebrated each evening in St. Peter's Square during the Jubilee.

Dear brothers and sisters, on this Second Sunday of Easter, on which I had the joy of enrolling Sr. Faustina Kowalska, Apostle of Divine Mercy, among the saints, I urge you always to trust in God's merciful love revealed to us in Christ Jesus, who died and rose again for our salvation. May the personal experience of this love commit everyone to becoming, in turn, a witness of active charity towards his brothers and sisters. Make Sr. Faustina's beautiful exclamation your own: "Jesus, I trust in You!"

My Blessing to all!

[The Holy Father then said in Polish:]

I cordially greet all who have gathered on this special day in St. Peter's Square to thank God at evening prayer for the gift of Sr. Faustina's canonization. With all my heart I join you in this thanksgiving.

May you always remember the Divine Mercy Sunday of the year 2000. I pray God that this memory may increase in all hearts a firm trust in His gracious love and strengthen them on the paths of the third millennium. *Jesus, I trust in You!*

May God, rich in mercy, bless you and your loved ones.

✝ PROCLAMATION OF DIVINE MERCY SUNDAY

By virtue of a Decree issued on May 5, 2000, by the Congregation for Divine Worship and the Discipline of the Sacraments, the Holy See proclaimed the Second Sunday of Easter also as Divine Mercy Sunday. Here is the text:

DECREE

Merciful and gracious is the Lord (cf. Ps 111:4), who, out of great love with which He loved us (cf. Eph 2:4) and [out of] unspeakable goodness, gave us His Only-begotten Son as our Redeemer, so that through the Death and Resurrection of this Son He might open the way to eternal life for the human race, and that the adopted children who receive His mercy within His temple might lift up His praise to the ends of the earth.

In our times, the Christian faithful in many parts of the world wish to praise that Divine Mercy in divine worship, particularly in the celebration of the Paschal Mystery, in which God's loving kindness especially shines forth.

Acceding to these wishes, the Supreme Pontiff John Paul II has graciously determined that in the Roman Missal, after the title "Second Sunday of Easter," there shall henceforth be added the appellation "or *Divine Mercy Sunday*," and has prescribed that the texts assigned for that day in the same Missal and the Liturgy of the Hours of the Roman Rite are always to be used for the liturgical celebration of this Sunday.

The Congregation for Divine Worship and the Discipline of the Sacraments now publishes these decisions of the Supreme Pontiff so that they may take effect.

Anything to the contrary notwithstanding.

Cardinal Jorge A. Medina Esteves
Prefect
+Francesco Pio Tamburrino
Archbishop Secretary

✝ "THIS MIRACLE ... HAS CHANGED HUMANITY'S DESTINY"

Pope's Homily on Divine Mercy Sunday, April 22, 2001

VATICAN CITY, APR. 29, 2001- A year after the canonization of Sr. Faustina Kowalska, a Polish religious known as the apostle of Divine Mercy, John Paul II celebrated the Mass of Divine Mercy Sunday in St Peter's Square on April 22. Here is a translation of his homily, which was given in Italian:

1. "Fear not, I am the first and the last, and the living one; I died, and behold I am alive for evermore" (Rv1:17-18).

We heard these comforting words in the Second Reading taken from the Book of Revelation. They invite us to turn our gaze to Christ, to experience His reassuring presence. To each person, whatever his condition, even if it were the most complicated and dramatic, the Risen One repeats: "Fear not!" I died on the Cross but now "I am alive for evermore"; "I am the first and the last, and the living one."

"The first," that is, the source of every being and the first fruits of the new creation; "the last," the definitive end of history; "the living one," the inexhaustible source of life that triumphed over death for ever. In the Messiah, crucified and risen, we recognize the features of the Lamb sacrificed on Golgotha, who implores forgiveness for His torturers and opens the gates of heaven to repentant sinners; we glimpse the face of the immortal King who now has "the keys of Death and Hades" (Rv 1:18).

2. "Give thanks to the Lord, for He is good; for His mercy endures for ever!" (Ps 117: 1).

Let us make our own the Psalmist's exclamation which we sang in the Responsorial Psalm: The Lord's mercy endures for ever! In order to understand thoroughly the truth of these words, let us be led by the liturgy to the heart of the event of salvation, which unites Christ's Death and Resurrection with our lives and with the world's history. This miracle of mercy has radically changed humanity's destiny. It is a miracle in which is unfolded the fullness of the love of the Father who, for our redemption, does not even draw back before the sacrifice of His Only-begotten Son.

In the humiliated and suffering Christ, believers and non-believers can admire a surprising solidarity, which binds Him to our human condition beyond all imaginable measure. The Cross, even after the Resurrection of the Son of God, "speaks and never ceases to speak of God the Father, who is absolutely faithful to His eternal love for man.... Believing in this love means believing in mercy" (*Dives in Misericordia*, 7).

Let us thank the Lord for His love, which is stronger than death and sin. It is revealed and put into practice as mercy in our daily lives, and prompts every person in turn to have "mercy" towards the Crucified One. Is not loving God and loving one's neighbour and even one's "enemies," after Jesus' example, the program of life of every baptized person and of the whole Church?

3. With these sentiments we are celebrating the Second Sunday of Easter, which since last year, the year of the Great Jubilee, is also called "Divine Mercy Sunday." It is a great joy for me to be able to join all of you, dear pilgrims and faithful who have come from various nations to commemorate, after one year, the canonization of Sr. Faustina Kowalska, witness and messenger of the Lord's merciful love. The elevation to the honours of the altar of this humble religious, a daughter of my land, is not only a gift for Poland but for all humanity. Indeed the message she brought is the appropriate and incisive answer that God wanted to offer to the questions and expectations of human beings in our time, marked by terrible tragedies. Jesus said to Sr. Faustina one day: "Humanity will never find peace until it turns with trust to Divine Mercy" (*Diary*, Liberia Editrical Vaticana edition, p.132). Divine Mercy! This is the Easter gift that the Church receives from the risen Christ and offers to humanity at the dawn of the third millennium.

4. The Gospel, which has just been proclaimed, helps us to grasp the full sense and value of this gift. The Evangelist John makes us share in the emotion felt by the Apostles in their meeting with Christ after His Resurrection. Our attention focuses on the gesture of the Master, who transmits to the fearful, astounded

disciples the mission of being ministers of Divine Mercy. He shows them His hands and His side, which bear the marks of the Passion, and tells them: "As the Father has sent Me, even so I send you" (Jn 20: 21). Immediately afterwards "He breathed on them, and said to them, 'Receive the Holy Spirit. If you forgive the sins of any, they are forgiven; if you retain the sins of any, they are retained'" (Jn 20:22-23). Jesus entrusted to them the gift of "forgiving sins," a gift that flows from the wounds in His hands, His feet, and especially from His pierced side. From there a wave of mercy is poured out over all humanity.

Let us relive this moment with great spiritual intensity. Today the Lord also shows us His glorious wounds and His heart, an inexhaustible source of light and truth, of love and forgiveness.

5. The Heart of Christ! His "Sacred Heart" has given men everything: redemption, salvation, sanctification. St. Faustina Kowalska saw coming from this heart that was overflowing with generous love, two rays of light which illuminated the world. "The two rays," according to what Jesus Himself told her, "represent the blood and the water" (*Diary*, p. 132). The blood recalls the sacrifice of Golgotha and the mystery of the Eucharist; the water, according to the rich symbolism of the Evangelist John, makes us think of Baptism and the gift of the Holy Spirit (cf. Jn 3: 5; 4: 14).

Through the mystery of this wounded heart, the restorative tide of God's merciful love continues to spread over the men and women of our time. Here alone can those who long for true and lasting happiness find its secret.

6. "Jesus, I trust in You." This prayer, dear to so many of the devout, clearly expresses the attitude with

which we too would like to abandon ourselves trustfully into Your hands, O Lord, our only Saviour.

You are burning with the desire to be loved and those in tune with the sentiments of Your heart learn how to build the new civilization of love. A simple act of abandonment is enough to overcome the barriers of darkness and sorrow, of doubt and desperation. The rays of Your Divine Mercy restore hope, in a special way, to those who feel overwhelmed by the burden of sin. Mary, Mother of Mercy, help us always to have this trust in your Son, our Redeemer. Help us too, St. Faustina, whom we remember today with special affection. Fixing our weak gaze on the divine Saviour's face, we would like to repeat with you: "Jesus, I trust in You." Now and for ever. Amen.

[translation by *L'Osservatore Romano*]

✟ OUR LADY EXEMPLIFIES GOD'S MERCY

Regina Caeli: April 22, 2001

After celebrating Mass on Divine Mercy Sunday, April 22, almost a year after Sr. Faustina Kowalska's canonization, the Holy Father introduced the prayer of the *Regina Caeli* for the faithful in St Peter's Square with a short reflection on the spiritual motherhood of the Blessed Virgin. Here is his text:

1. As we approach the conclusion of the solemn Eucharistic celebration, let us turn our gaze to Mary Most Holy, whom we call upon today with the sweetest name of "*Mater misericordiae*." Mary is "Mother of Mercy," because she is the Mother of Jesus in whom God revealed to the world His "heart" overflowing with love.

God's compassion for man is communicated to the

world precisely through the Virgin Mary's motherhood. Mary's motherhood, which began in Nazareth through the work of the Holy Spirit, was fulfilled in the Easter mystery, when she was closely associated with the Passion, Death and Resurrection of the divine Son. At the foot of the Cross Our Lady became mother of the disciples of Christ, mother of the Church and of all humanity. "*Mater misericordiae.*"

2. I greet the pilgrims who have come here from Poland, and all who have a special devotion to God's mercy and have taken part in this Holy Mass by radio and television. In a special way I have joined in spirit the Cardinal of Krakow and the vast number of Bishops, religious and faithful who have gathered today at the Shrine of The Divine Mercy in Lagiewniki. During this celebration together with you I thanked God who almost a year ago granted me the grace to canonize Sr. Faustina Kowalska, the chosen apostle of the merciful Christ, and to proclaim the Second Sunday of Easter as the Feast of Divine Mercy for the entire Church.

Filled with joy we present ourselves before the Risen One today and say with faith: "Jesus, I trust in You!" May this confession full of love strengthen everyone on the path of daily life and encourage them to undertake works of mercy for their brothers and sisters. May this be a message of hope for the entire new millennium.

3. Now, with the recitation of the antiphon "*Regina Caeli,*" we ask Mary to enable us to experience the deep joy of the Resurrection and to collaborate with dedication in the universal plan of Divine Mercy.

✝ "MEDITATION ON THE *MISERERE*" (PSALM 51), OCTOBER 24, 2001

We have heard the *Miserere*, one of the most famous prayers of the Psalter, the most intense and repeated penitential Psalm, the hymn of sin and forgiveness, the most profound meditation on guilt and grace. The Liturgy of the Hours makes us repeat it at lauds every Friday. It has risen for centuries from the hearts of Jewish and Christian faithful as a sigh of repentance and hope addressed to the merciful God.

The Jewish tradition places the Psalm on David's lips, who was called to penance by the severe words of the prophet Nathan (cf. verses 1-2; 2 Sam 11-12), who reproached him for his adultery with Bathsheba and the killing of her husband, Uriah. However, the Psalm was enriched in subsequent centuries, with the prayer of so many other sinners, who recover the themes of the "new heart" and the "Spirit" of God infused in redeemed man, according to the teachings of the prophets Jeremiah and Ezekiel (cf. verse 12; Jer 31:31-34; Ezek 11:19; 36:24-28).

Psalm 50 [51] outlines two horizons. First there is the dark region of sin (cf. verses 3-11), in which man is situated since the beginning of his existence. "True, I was born guilty, a sinner, even as my mother conceived me" (verse 7). Although this declaration cannot be considered as an explicit formulation of the doctrine of original sin, which has been delineated by Christian theology, it undoubtedly corresponds to it. In fact, it expresses the profound dimension of the innate moral weakness of man. The first part of the Psalm is presented as an analysis of sin, made before God. There are three Hebrew words used to describe this sad reality, which stem from the evil use of human freedom.

Hattá, the first word, literally means to "miss the target." Sin is an aberration that leads us far from God, fundamental end of our relations, and, as a consequence, also from our neighbor.

The second Hebrew word is *awon*, which recalls the image of "twisting," or "curving." Sin, therefore, is a torturous deviation of the right way; it is the inversion, distortion, deformation of good and evil, in the sense expressed by Isaiah: "Woe to those who call evil good and good evil, who put darkness for light and light for darkness" (Is 5:20). Precisely because of this, the Bible describes conversion as a "return" (*"shub"* in Hebrew) to the right way, correcting one's course.

The third word with which the Psalmist speaks of sin is *"peshá."* It expresses the rebellion of the subject against the sovereign and, therefore, an open defiance of God and His plan for human history.

However, if man confesses his sin, God's salvific justice is ready to purify him radically. And thus we come to the second spiritual part of the Psalm, that of luminous grace (cf. verses 12-19). In fact, through confession of faults, for the man of prayer a horizon of light opens, where God is at work. The Lord does not just act negatively, eliminating sin, but recreates sinful humanity through His vivifying Spirit: He infuses a new and pure "heart" in man, namely, a renewed conscience, and opens the possibility of a limpid faith and worship that is pleasing to God.

In this connection, Origen speaks of a divine therapy that the Lord carries out through His word and through the healing work of Christ. "As God disposes for the body remedies of wisely combined theraopeutic herbs, so He also prepared medicines for the soul with the words He infuses, scattering them in divine Scripture. ... God gave yet another medical aid whose archetype is the Savior who says about Himself: 'It is not the healthy but the sick who are in need of a doctor.' He is the doctor par excellence, able to cure every weakness and infirmity" (*Homilies on the Psalms*, Florence 1991, pp. 247-249).

The richness of Psalm 50 [51] merits a careful exegesis throughout. It is what we will do when it resounds again at lauds on various Fridays. The overall view we have taken of this great biblical supplication reveals to us already some of the fundamental components of a spirituality that should reverberate in the daily life of the faithful. There is, first of all, a lively sense of sin, seen as a free choice of negative connotation at the moral and theological level. "Against You alone have I sinned; I have done such evil in Your sight" (verse 6).

Then there is also in the Psalm a lively sense of the possibility of conversion: The sincerely repentant sinner (cf. verse 5) comes before God in all his misery and nakedness, imploring Him not to dismiss him from His presence (cf. verse 13).

Lastly, there is in the *Miserere* a profound conviction of divine forgiveness that "cancels, washes, cleanses" the sinner (cf. verses 3-4) and finally is able to transform him into a new creature, who has a transfigured spirit, tongue, lips, and heart (cf. verses 14-19). "Even if our sins were as black as night, Divine Mercy is stronger than our misery. Only one thing is necessary: that the sinner at least leave the door of his heart ajar, the rest will be done by God. Everything begins and ends in His mercy" (M. Winowska, *L'Icona dell Amore Misericordioso. Il Messaggio di Suor Faustina*, Rome, 1981, p. 271).

✝ WORLD DAY OF PEACE, JANUARY 1, 2002

1. The World Day of Peace this year is being celebrated in the shadow of the dramatic events of last September 11. On that day a terrible crime was committed: In a few brief hours thousands of innocent people of many ethnic backgrounds were slaughtered. Since then people throughout the world have felt a profound personal vulnerability and a new fear for the future. Addressing this state of mind, the Church testifies to her hope, based on the conviction that evil, the *mysterium iniquitatis*, does not have the final word in human affairs. The history of salvation narrated in Sacred Scripture sheds clear light on the entire history of the world and shows us that human events are always accompanied by the merciful providence of God, who knows how to touch even the most hardened of hearts and bring good fruits even from what seems utterly barren soil.

This is the hope which sustains the Church at the beginning of 2002: that by the grace of God a world in which the power of evil seems once again to have taken the upper hand will in fact be transformed into a world in which the noblest aspirations of the human heart will triumph, a world in which true peace will prevail.

Peace: the Work of Justice and Love

2. Recent events, including the terrible killings just mentioned, move me to return to a theme which often stirs in the depths of my heart when I remember the events of history which have marked my life, especially my youth.

The enormous suffering of peoples and individuals even among my own friends and acquaintances caused by Nazi and communist totalitarianism has never been far from my thoughts and prayers. I have often paused to reflect on the persistent question: How do we restore the moral and social order subjected to such horrific violence? My reasoned conviction, confirmed in turn by biblical revelation, is that the shattered order cannot be fully restored except by a response that combines justice with forgiveness. The pillars of true peace are justice and that form of love which is forgiveness.

3. But in the present circumstances, how can we speak of justice and forgiveness as the source and condition of peace? We can and we must, no matter how difficult this may be a difficulty which often comes from thinking that justice and forgiveness are irreconcilable. But forgiveness is the opposite of resentment and revenge, not of justice. In fact, true peace is "the work of justice" (Is 32:17). As the Second Vatican Council put it, peace is "the fruit of that right ordering of things with which the divine founder has invested human society and which must be actualized by man thirsting for an ever more perfect reign of justice" (*Gaudium et Spes*, 78). For more than 1,500 years the Catholic Church has repeated the teaching of St. Augustine of Hippo on this point. He reminds us that the peace which can and must be built in this world is the peace of right order — *tranquillitas ordinis*, the tranquility of order (cf. *De Civitate Dei*, 9, 13).

True peace therefore is the fruit of justice, that moral virtue and legal guarantee which ensures full respect for rights and responsibilities, and the just distribution of benefits and burdens. But because human justice is always fragile and imperfect, subject as it is to the limitations and egoism of individuals and groups, it must include and, as it were, be completed by the forgiveness which heals and rebuilds troubled human relations from their foundations. This is true in circumstances great and small, at the personal level or on a wider, even international scale. Forgiveness is in no way opposed to justice, as if to forgive meant to overlook the need to right the wrong done. It is rather the fullness of justice, leading to that tranquility of order which is much more than a fragile and temporary cessation of hostilities, involving as it does the deepest healing of the wounds which fester in human hearts. Justice and forgiveness are both essential to such healing.

It is these two dimensions of peace that I wish to explore in this message. The World Day of Peace this year offers all humanity, and particularly the leaders of nations, the opportunity to reflect upon the demands of justice and the call to forgiveness in the face of the grave problems which continue to afflict the world, not the least of which is the new level of violence introduced by organized terrorism.

The Reality of Terrorism

4. It is precisely peace born of justice and forgiveness that is under assault today by international terrorism. In recent years, especially since the end of the Cold War, terrorism has developed into a sophisticated network of political, economic and technical collusion which goes beyond national borders to embrace the whole world. Well-organized terrorist groups can count on huge financial resources and develop wide-ranging strategies, striking innocent people who have nothing to do with aims pursued by the terrorists.

When terrorist organizations use their own followers as weapons to be launched against defenseless and unsuspecting people, they show clearly the death wish that feeds them. Terrorism springs from hatred, and it generates isolation, mistrust and closure. Violence is added to violence in a tragic sequence that exasperates successive generations, each one inheriting the hatred which divided those that went before. Terrorism is built on contempt for human life. For this reason, not only does it commit intolerable crimes, but because it resorts to terror as a political and military means it is itself a true crime against humanity.

5. There exists therefore a right to defend oneself against terrorism, a right which as always must be exercised with respect for moral and legal limits in the choice of ends and means. The guilty must be correctly identified, since criminal culpability is always personal and cannot be extended to the nation, ethnic group or religion to which the terrorists may belong. International cooperation in the fight against terrorist activities must also include a courageous and resolute political, diplomatic and economic commitment to relieving situations of oppression and marginalization which facilitate the designs of terrorists. The recruitment of terrorists in fact is easier in situations where rights are trampled upon and injustices tolerated over a long period of time.

Still, it must be firmly stated that the injustices existing in the world can never be used to excuse acts of terrorism, and it should be noted that the victims of the radical breakdown of order which terrorism seeks to achieve include above all the countless millions of men and women who are least well positioned to withstand a collapse of international solidarity — namely, the people of the developing world, who already live on a thin margin of survival and who would be most grievously affected by global economic and political chaos. The terrorist claim to be acting on behalf of the poor is a patent falsehood.

You Shall Not Kill in God's Name!

6. Those who kill by acts of terrorism actually despair of humanity, of life, of the future. In their view, everything is to be hated and destroyed. Terrorists hold that the truth in which they believe or the suffering that they have undergone is so absolute that their reaction in destroying even innocent lives is justified. Terrorism is often the outcome of that fanatic fundamentalism which springs from the conviction that one's own vision of the truth must be forced upon everyone else. Instead, even when the truth has been reached — and this can happen only in a limited and imperfect way — it can never be imposed.

Respect for a person's conscience, where the image of God Himself is reflected (cf. Gn 1:26-27), means that we can only propose the truth to others, who are then responsible for accepting it. To try to impose on others by violent means what we consider to be the truth is an offense against human dignity and ultimately an offense against God, whose image that person bears. For this reason, what is usually referred to as fundamentalism is an attitude radically opposed to belief in God. Terrorism exploits God: It ends by making Him an idol to be used for one's own purpose.

7. Consequently, no religious leader can condone terrorism, and much less preach it. It is a profanation of religion to declare oneself a terrorist in the name of God, to do violence to others in His Name. Terrorist violence is a contradiction of faith in God, the creator of man who cares for man and loves him. It is altogether contrary to faith in Christ the Lord, who taught His disciples to pray: "Forgive us our debts, as we also have forgiven our debtors" (Mt 6:12).

Following the teaching and example of Jesus, Christians hold that to show mercy is to live out the truth of our lives: We can and must be merciful because mercy has been shown us by a God who is love (cf. 1 Jn 4:7-12). The God who enters into history to redeem us, and through the dramatic events of Good Friday prepares the victory of Easter Sunday, is a God of mercy and forgiveness (cf. Ps 103:3-4; 10-13). Thus Jesus told those who challenged His dining with sinners: "Go and learn what this means, 'I desire mercy and not sacrifice.' For I came not to call the righteous, but sinners" (Mt 9:13). The followers of Christ, baptized into His redeeming death and resurrection, must always be men and women of mercy and forgiveness.

The Need for Forgiveness

8. But what does forgiveness actually mean? And why should we forgive? A reflection on forgiveness cannot avoid these questions. Retuning to what I wrote in my message for the 1997 World Day of Peace ("Offer Forgiveness and Receive Peace"), I would reaffirm that forgiveness inhabits people's

hearts before it becomes a social reality. Only to the degree that an ethics and a culture of forgiveness prevail can we hope for a "politics" of forgiveness, expressed in society's attitudes and laws, so that through them justice takes on a more human character.

Forgiveness is above all a personal choice, a decision of the heart to go against the natural instinct to pay back evil with evil. The measure of such a decision is the love of God, who draws us to Himself in spite of our sin. It has the perfect exemplar in the forgiveness of Christ, who on the cross prayed, "Father, forgive them; for they know not what they do" (Lk. 23:34).

Forgiveness therefore has a divine source and criterion. This does not mean that its significance cannot also be grasped in the light of human reasoning; and this, in the first place, on the basis of what people experience when they do wrong. They experience their human weakness, and they want others to deal leniently with them. Why not therefore do toward others what we want them to do towards us? All human beings cherish the hope of being able to start all over again and not remain forever shut up in their own mistakes and guilt. They all want to raise their eyes to the future and to discover new possibilities of trust and commitment.

9. Forgiveness therefore, as a fully human act, is above all a personal initiative. But individuals are essentially social beings, situated within a pattern of relationships through which they express themselves in ways both good and bad. Consequently, society too is absolutely in need of forgiveness. Families, groups, societies, states and the international community itself need forgiveness in order to renew ties that have been sundered, go beyond sterile situations of mutual condemnation and overcome the temptation to discriminate against others without appeal. The ability to forgive lies at the very basis of the idea of a future society marked by justice and solidarity.

By contrast, the failure to forgive, especially when it serves to prolong conflict, is extremely costly in terms of human development. Resources are used for weapons rather than for development, peace, and justice. What sufferings are inflicted on humanity because of the failure to reconcile! What delays in progress because of the failure to forgive! Peace is essential for development, but true peace is made possible only through forgiveness.

Forgiveness, the High Road

10. Forgiveness is not a proposal that can be immediately understood or easily accepted; in many ways it is a paradoxical message. Forgiveness in fact always involves an apparent short-term loss for a real long-term gain. Violence is the exact opposite; opting as it does for an apparent short-term gain, it involves a real and permanent loss. Forgiveness may seem like weakness, but it demands great spiritual strength and moral courage, both in granting it and in accepting it. It may seem in some ways to diminish us, but in fact it leads us to a fuller and righter humanity, more radiant with the splendor of the Creator.

My ministry at the service of the Gospel obliges me, and at the same time gives me the strength, to insist upon the necessity of forgiveness. I do so again today in the hope of stirring serious and mature thinking on this theme, with a view to a far-reaching resurgence of the human spirit in individual hearts and in relations between the peoples of the world.

11. Reflecting on forgiveness, our minds turn naturally to certain situations of conflict which endlessly feed deep and divisive hatred and a seemingly unstoppable sequence of personal and collective tragedies. I refer especially to what is happening in the Holy Land, the blessed place of God's encounter with man, where Jesus, the Prince of Peace, lived, died and rose from the dead.

The present troubled international situation prompts a more intense call to resolve the Arab-Israeli conflict which has now been going on for more than 50 years, with alternate phases of greater or lesser tension. The continuous recourse to acts of terror and war which aggravate the situation and diminish hope on all sides must finally give way to a negotiated solution. The rights and demands of each party can be taken into proper account and balanced in an equitable way, if and when there is a will to let justice and reconciliation prevail. Once more I urge the beloved peoples of the Holy Land to work for a new era of mutual respect and constructive accord.

Interreligious Understanding and Cooperation

12. In this whole effort religious leaders have a weighty responsibility. The various Christian confessions as well as the world's great religions need to work together to eliminate the social and cultural causes of terrorism. They can do this by teaching the greatness and dignity of the human person and by spreading a clearer sense of the oneness of the human family. This is a specific area of ecumenical and interreligious dialogue and cooperation, a pressing service which religion can offer to world peace.

In particular, I am convinced that Jewish, Christian, and Islamic religious leaders must now take the lead in publicly condemning terrorism and in denying terrorists any form of religious or moral legitimacy.

13. In bearing common witness to the truth that the deliberate murder of the innocent is a grave evil always, everywhere and without exception, the world's religious leaders will help to form the morally sound public opinion that is essential for building an international civil society capable of pursuing the tranquility of order in justice and freedom.

In undertaking such a commitment, the various religions cannot but pursue the path of forgiveness, which opens the way to mutual understanding, respect, and trust. The help that religions can give to peace and against terrorism consists precisely in their teaching forgiveness, for those who forgive and seek forgiveness know that there is a higher truth, and that by accepting that truth they can transcend themselves.

Prayer for Peace

14. Precisely for this reason, prayer for peace is not an afterthought to the work of peace. It is of the very essence of building the peace of order, justice, and freedom. To pray for peace is to open the human heart to the inroads of God's power to renew all things. With the life-giving force of His

grace, God can create openings for peace where only obstacles and closures are apparent; He can strengthen and enlarge the solidarity of the human family in spite of our endless history of division and conflict. To pray for peace is to pray for justice, for a right ordering of relations within and among nations and peoples. It is to pray for freedom, especially for the religious freedom that is a basic human and civil right of every individual. To pray for peace is to seek God's forgiveness and to implore the courage to forgive those who have trespassed against us.

For all these reasons I have invited representatives of the world's religions to come to Assisi, the town of St. Francis, on Jan. 24, 2002, to pray for peace. In doing so we will show that genuine religious belief is an inexhaustible wellspring of mutual respect and harmony among peoples; indeed it is the chief antidote to violence and conflict. At this time of great distress, the human family needs to be reminded of our unfailing reasons for hope. It is precisely this hope that we intend to proclaim in Assisi, asking Almighty God — in the beautiful phrase attributed to St. Francis himself — to make each of us a channel of His peace.

15. *No peace without justice, no justice without forgiveness.* This is what in this message I wish to say to believers and unbelievers alike, to all men and women of good will who are concerned for the good of the human family and for its future.

No peace without justice, no justice without forgiveness: This is what I wish to say to those responsible for the future of the human community, entreating them to be guided in their weighty and difficult decisions by the light of man's true good, always with a view to the common good.

No peace without justice, no justice without forgiveness: I shall not tire of repeating this warning to those who, for one reason or another, nourish feelings of hatred, a desire for revenge or the will to destroy.

On this World Day of Peace, may a more intense prayer rise from the hearts of all believers for the victims of terrorism, for their families so tragically stricken, for all the peoples who continue to be hurt and convulsed by terrorism and war. May the light of our prayer extend even to those who gravely offend

God and man by these pitiless acts, that they may look into their hearts, see the evil of what they do, abandon all violent intentions and seek forgiveness. In these troubled times may the whole human family find true and lasting peace, born of the marriage of justice and mercy!

From the Vatican, Dec. 8, 2001

✝ PILGRIMAGE TO POLAND: DEDICATION OF THE SHRINE OF THE DIVINE MERCY, AUGUST 16-19, 2002

On Saturday morning, August 17, the Holy Father consecrated the Shrine of The Divine Mercy in Krakow-Lagiewniki. It is a large white, oval, tent-like church that seats 4,000 persons. On the grounds is the convent of the Sisters of Our Lady of Mercy and their reform school for girls, where St. Faustina lived the last years of her life. Behind the altar, above the tabernacle, as the central focus, is the image of the Merciful Jesus. During his homily, the Pope took the opportunity with a solemn papal act to entrust the world to the mercy of God and expressed his burning desire that the message of God's merciful love may be made known to all. His remarks follow:

> Today, therefore, in this Shrine, I wish solemnly to entrust the world to The Divine Mercy. I do so with the burning desire that the message of God's merciful love, proclaimed here through St. Faustina, may be made known to all the peoples of the earth and fill their hearts with hope. May this message radiate from this place to our beloved homeland and throughout the world. May the binding promise of the Lord Jesus be fulfilled: from here there must go forth "the spark which will prepare the world for his final coming." At many places in the liturgy, the choir and people sang in Polish the simple aspiration, "*Jezus, ufam tobie,* Jesus, I trust in You."

Here is a translation of the Pope's homily at the Mass of the Consecration of the Shrine of The Divine Mercy. At the end of the Mass, before the final blessing, the Holy Father commented on his joy and gratitude at being able to consecrate the Shrine and his gratitude to all who helped make this happen:

"O inconceivable and unfathomable Mercy of God,

Who can worthily adore You and sing Your praises?

O greatest attribute of God Almighty,

You are the sweet hope of sinners" (*Diary*, 951).

Dear Brothers and Sisters!

1. Today I repeat these simple and straightforward words of St. Faustina, in order to join her and all of you in adoring the inconceivable and unfathomable mystery of God's mercy. Like St. Faustina, we wish to proclaim that apart from the mercy of God there is no other source of hope for mankind. We desire to repeat with faith: *Jesus, I trust in You*!

Proclamation of trust in Divine Mercy needed in our time

This proclamation, this confession of trust in the all-powerful love of God, is especially needed in our own time, when mankind is experiencing bewilderment in the face of many manifestations of evil. *The invocation of God's mercy* needs to rise up from the depth of hearts filled with suffering, apprehension and uncertainty, and at the same time yearning for an infallible source of hope. That is why we have come here today, to this Shrine of Lagiewniki, in order to glimpse once more in Christ the face of the Father: "the Father of mercies and the God of all consolation" (2 Cor 1:3). With the eyes of our soul, we long to look into the eyes of the merciful Jesus, in order to find deep within

His gaze the reflection of His inner life, as well as the light of grace which we have already received so often, and which God holds out to us anew each day and on the last day.

Thanks to all who spread the message and helped build the Shrine to honor the Mercy of God

2. We are about to dedicate this new church to the Mercy of God. Before doing so, I wish to *offer heartfelt thanks* to those who contributed to its construction. In a special way I thank Cardinal Franciszek Machrski, who has put so much effort into this undertaking as a sign of his personal devotion to The Divine Mercy. My thoughts turn with affection to the Sisters of Our Lady of Mercy, whom I thank for their work in spreading the message left behind by Saint Sister Faustina. I greet the Cardinals and Bishops of Poland, headed by the Cardinal Primate, as well as the Bishops coming from various parts of the world. I rejoice in the presence of the diocesan and religious priests, and the seminarians.

My cordial greeting goes to all those taking part in this celebration, especially the representatives of the Foundation of the Shrine of The Divine Mercy who oversaw the work of construction, as well as the builders involved in the various projects. I know that many of those present offered generous material support to the work of construction. I pray that God will reward their magnanimity and their commitment by His blessing!

May God bless the special place that He has chosen to sow the grace of His mercy

3. Brothers and Sisters! As we dedicate this new church, we too can ask the question which troubled King Solomon when he consecrated the Temple of Jerusalem as the house of God: "But will God indeed

dwell on the earth? Behold, heaven and the highest heaven cannot contain You; how much less this house which I have built!" (1 Kgs 8:27). Yes, at first glance, to bind certain "places" to God's presence might seem inappropriate. We can never forget that time and space belong to God in their entirety. Yet even though time and the entire world may be considered His "temple," God has chosen certain times and places to enable people to experience in a special way His presence and His grace. Impelled by their sense of faith, people journey to these places, confident that there they will truly find themselves in the presence of God.

In this same spirit of faith I have come to Lagiewniki to dedicate this new church. I am convinced that this is the special place chosen by God to sow the grace of His mercy. I pray that this church will always be a place where the message of God's merciful love is proclaimed; a place of conversion and repentance; a place for the celebration of the Eucharist; a fountain of mercy; a place of prayer and of constant appeals for mercy for ourselves and for the whole world. I pray in the words of Solomon: "Have regard to the prayer of Your servant and to his supplication, O Lord my God, hearkening to the cry and to the prayer which Thy servant prays before You this day; that Your eyes may be open night and day towards this house. … Hearken to the supplication of Your servant and of Your people Israel, when they pray in this place. Hear in heaven, Your dwelling place; and when You hear, forgive" (1 Kgs 8:28-30).

The Holy Spirit enables us to view sin in the light of the merciful and forgiving love of God

4. "*But the hour is coming, and now is when true worshipers will worship the Father in spirit and truth, for such the Father seeks to worship Him*" (Jn 4:23). When we read these words of the Lord Jesus here in

the Shrine of The Divine Mercy, we are particularly aware that *no one can come here except in Spirit and truth*. It is the Holy Spirit, the Comforter and the Spirit of Truth, who guides us along the ways of Divine Mercy. By convincing the world "concerning sin and righteousness and judgement" (Jn 16:8), He also makes known the fullness of salvation in Christ. This "convincing" concerning sin is *doubly related to the Cross of Christ*. On the one hand, the Holy Spirit enables us, through Christ's Cross, to acknowledge sin, every sin, *in the full dimension of evil which it contains and inwardly conceals*. On the other hand, the Holy Spirit permits us, again through the Christ's Cross, to see sin *in the light of the mysterium pietatis*, that is, of the merciful and forgiving love of God (cf. *Dominum et Vivificantem*, 32).

Consequently, this "convincing concerning sin" also becomes a conviction that *sin can be laid aside* and that man can be restored to his dignity as a son beloved of God. Indeed, the Cross "is the most profound condescension of God to man [...]. The Cross is like a touch of eternal love upon the most painful wounds of man's earthly existence" (*Dives in Misericordia*, 8).

Cornerstone comes from Mount Calvary

The cornerstone of this Shrine will always be a reminder of this truth, for it was brought here from Mount Calvary, as if from beneath the Cross on which Jesus Christ triumphed over sin and death.

I firmly believe that this new church will always be a place where people will come before God in Spirit and truth. They will come with the trust which accompanies all those who humbly open their hearts to the working of God's merciful love, to that love which is stronger than even the greatest sin. Here, in the fire of divine love, human hearts will burn with desire for conversion, and whoever looks for hope will find comfort.

Mercy is needed to ensure that every injustice in the world will come to an end in the splendor of truth

5. "Eternal Father, I offer You the Body and Blood, Soul and Divinity of Your beloved Son, our Lord Jesus Christ, for our sins and those of the whole world; for the sake of His sorrowful Passion, have mercy upon us and upon the whole world" (*Diary*, 476). *Upon us and upon the whole world.* ... How greatly today's world needs God's mercy! In every continent, from the depth of human suffering, a cry for mercy seems to rise up. Where hatred and the thirst for revenge dominate, where war brings suffering and death to the innocent, there the grace of mercy is needed in order to settle human minds and hearts and to bring about peace. Wherever respect for life and human dignity are lacking, there is need of God's merciful love, in whose light we see the inexpressible value of every human being. Mercy is needed in order to ensure that every injustice in the world will come to an end in the splendor of truth.

✝ PILGRIMAGE TO POLAND: SOLEMN ENTRUSTMENT OF THE WORLD TO DIVINE MERCY, AUGUST 17, 2002

Today, therefore, in this Shrine, I wish *solemnly to entrust the world to Divine Mercy.* I do so with the burning desire that the message of God's merciful love, proclaimed here through St. Faustina, *may be made known to all the peoples of the earth* and fill their hearts with hope. May this message radiate from this place to our beloved homeland and throughout the world. May the binding promise of the Lord Jesus be fulfilled: From here there must go forth "the spark which will prepare the world for His final coming" (*Diary*, 1732). This spark needs to be lighted by the grace of God. This fire of mercy needs to be passed on to the world. *In the mercy of God the world will find peace and mankind will find happiness!* I entrust this task to you, dear Brothers and Sisters, to the Church in Krakow and Poland, and to all the votaries of Divine Mercy who will come here from Poland and from throughout the world. *May you be witnesses to mercy!*

SOLEMN ACT OF ENTRUSTMENT OF THE WORLD TO THE DIVINE MERCY:

6. God, merciful Father,
in Your Son, Jesus Christ,
You have revealed Your love
and poured it out upon us
in the Holy Spirit, the Comforter.
We entrust to You today the destiny of the world
and of every man and woman.
Bend down to us sinners,
heal our weakness, conquer all evil,
and grant that all the peoples of the earth
may experience Your mercy.
In You, the Triune God,
may they ever find the source of hope.
Eternal Father,
by the Passion and Resurrection of Your Son,
have mercy on us and upon the whole world!
Amen.

✝ PILGRIMAGE TO POLAND: THE HOLY FATHER'S PERSONAL REMARKS AT THE END OF THE MASS, AUGUST 17, 2002

At the end of this solemn liturgy, I desire to say that many of my personal memories are tied to this place. During the Nazi occupation, when I was working in the Solvay factory near here, I used to come here. Even now I recall the street that goes from Borek Falecki to Debniki that I took every day going to work on the different turns with the wooden shoes on my feet. They're the shoes that we used to wear then. How was it possible to imagine that one day the man with the wooden shoes would consecrate the Basilica of The Divine Mercy at Lagiewniki of Krakow?

I rejoice for the construction of this beautiful shrine dedicated to The Divine Mercy. I entrust to the care of Cardinal Macharski and to the whole Archdiocese of Krakow and to the Sisters of Our Lady of Mercy the material, and especially, the spiritual upkeep of the Shrine. May this collaboration in the work of spreading the devotion of the merciful Jesus give blessed fruit in the hearts of the faithful in Poland and in the whole world.

May the merciful God bless abundantly all the pilgrims who come and who will come here in the future.

✝ PILGRIMAGE TO POLAND: FOUR NEW BLESSEDS, AUGUST 18, 2002

"Creative Messengers of Mercy": Modern Forms of Poverty Call for "Creativity" in Charity

On Sunday, August 18, at Blonie Park in Krakow, the Holy Father celebrated the Mass of Beatification to raise to the glory of the altars four Servants of God, Sigismund Felinski, Jan Balicki, Jan Beyzym, and Santia Szymkowiak. The Pope held them up as heroic witnesses to God's mercy in their generous outreach to their neighbour in need in the most difficult circumstances of modern history. The Holy Father could then insist on the need to respond today to the limitless generosity of Divine Mercy:

> Once we recognize this truth, we become aware that Christ's call to love others even as He has loved us calls all of us to that same measure. We feel in some sense impelled to make our lives a daily offering by showing mercy to our brothers and sisters, drawing upon the gift of God's merciful love.

The Holy Father called for a new creativity in charity:

Faced with the modern forms of poverty that, as we all know, are not lacking in our country, what is needed today is — as I called it in my apostolic letter Novo Millennio Ineunte — "a new 'creativity' in charity" (50), in a spirit of solidarity towards our neighbour, so that the help we lend will be a witness of "sharing between brothers and sisters" (ibid.). May this "creativity" never be lacking in the residents of Krakow and in all the people of our homeland. It represents the pastoral plan of the Church in Poland. May the message of God's mercy be reflected always in works of human mercy!

Here is translation of the homily of the Mass of Beatification:

"*This is My commandment, that you love one another as I have loved you*" (Jn 15:2).

Dear Brothers and Sisters!

1. The words of Jesus which we just heard are closely related to the theme of today's liturgical assembly in Blonie in Krakow: "*God, rich in mercy*." This phrase in a way captures the entire truth about the love of God which has redeemed humanity. "*God, who is rich in mercy, out of the great love with which He loved us, even when we were dead through our trespasses, made us alive together with Christ*" (Eph 2:4-5). The fullness of this love was revealed in the sacrifice of the Cross. For "greater love has no man than this, that a man lay down his life for his friends" (Jn 15:13). *Here is the measure of God's love! Here is the measure of God's mercy!*

God calls us to witness to mercy in today's world

Once we recognize this truth, we become aware that Christ's call to love others even as He has loved *us calls all of us to that same measure*. We feel in some sense impelled to *make our lives a daily offering by showing mercy to our brothers and sisters*, drawing upon the gift of God's merciful love. We realize that God, in showing us mercy, calls upon us to become witnesses to mercy in today's world.

From Krakow with its rich tradition of mercy, I greet Poland and all the pilgrims who have joined us

2. The call to be witnesses of mercy resounds with particular eloquence here, in my beloved Krakow, dominated by the Shrine of The Divine Mercy of Lagiewniki and its new church which yesterday I had the joy of consecrating. Here this call sounds familiar, for it appeals to the age-old tradition of the City, which has always been known for its *readiness to assist those in need*. We cannot forget that this tradition includes the numerous Saints and Beati — priests, consecrated persons and laity — who devoted their lives to works of mercy. Beginning with Bishop Stanislaus, Queen Hedwig, John of Kelty and Piotr Skarga, and continuing to Brother Albert, Angela Salawa and Cardinal Sapieha, this heritage of mercy has been passed down by generations of Christians in this City over many centuries. *Today this heritage has been placed in our hands and it must not be forgotten.*

I thank Cardinal Franciszek Macharski whose words of greeting have reminded us of this tradition. I am grateful for the invitation to visit my dear Krakow and for the hospitality offered to me. I greet everyone present, beginning with the Cardinals and the Bishops, and all those who share in this Eucharist through radio and television.

I greet the whole of Poland. In spirit I retrace the luminous journey by which St. Faustina Kowalska was being prepared to receive the message of mercy —

from Warsaw, on to Plock, Vilnius and finally Krakow — and I recall all those who cooperated with the Apostle of Mercy on that journey. I embrace with affection my countrymen, particularly the suffering and the sick; those struggling with various difficulties, the unemployed, the homeless, the elderly and the lonely, and families with many children. I assure them of my spiritual closeness and I accompany them constantly in my prayer. My greeting also goes to my countrymen throughout the world. I also offer a heartfelt greeting to the pilgrims who have come here from various countries in Europe and from throughout the world.

A pressing call now to proclaim the message of mercy to the world in a new way

3. From the beginning of her existence the Church, pointing to the mystery of the Cross and the Resurrection, has preached the mercy of God, a pledge of hope and a source of salvation for man. Nonetheless, it would appear that *we today have been particularly called* to proclaim this message before the world. We cannot neglect this mission, if God Himself has called us to it through the testimony of St. Faustina.

God has chosen our own times for this purpose. Perhaps because the twentieth century, despite indisputable achievements in many areas, was marked in a particular way by the "*mystery of iniquity.*" With this heritage both of good and of evil, we have entered the new millennium. New prospects of development are opening up before mankind, together with hitherto unheard-of dangers. Frequently man lives as if God did not exist, and even puts himself in God's place. He claims for himself the Creator's right to interfere in the mystery of human life. He wishes to determine human life through genetic manipulation and to establish the limit of death. Rejecting divine law and moral principles, he openly attacks the family. In a variety of ways he attempts to silence the voice of God in human hearts; he wishes to make God the "great absence" in the culture and the conscience of peoples. The "mystery of iniquity" continues to mark the reality of the world.

In experiencing this mystery, man lives in fear of the future, of emptiness, of suffering, of annihilation. Perhaps for this very reason, it is as if Christ, using the testimony of a lowly Sister, entered our time in order to indicate clearly the source of relief and hope found in the eternal mercy of God.

The message of merciful love needs to resound forcefully anew. The world needs this love. The hour has come to bring Christ's message to everyone: to rulers and the oppressed, to those whose humanity and dignity seem lost in the *mysterium iniquitatis.* The hour has come when the message of Divine Mercy is able to fill hearts with hope and to become the spark of a new civilization: the civilization of love.

These four Blesseds proclaim mercy with their lives

4. The Church desires tirelessly to proclaim this message, not only by convincing words, but by the ready practice of mercy. This is why she ceaselessly holds up stupendous examples of individuals *who out of love for God and for man "went forth and bore fruit."* Today she adds four new Beati to their number. They lived at different times and led very different lives. But they are united by that particular feature of holiness which is *devotion to the cause of mercy.*

Blessed Sigismund Felix Felinski

Blessed Sigismund Felix Felinski, Archbishop of Warsaw, during a difficult period marked by the lack of national freedom, urged everyone to persevere in generous service to the poor and to establish educational institutions and charitable works. He himself founded an orphanage and a school; he also brought the Sisters of the Blessed Virgin Mary of Mercy to Warsaw and supported the work they began. After the failure of the insurrection of 1863, in a spirit of mercy towards his brothers and sisters he openly defended the persecuted. This fidelity cost him deportment to the interior of Russa, which lasted twenty years. Even there he continued to be mindful of the poor and distressed, showing them great love, patience, and understanding. It has been written of him that "during his exile, oppressed on every side, in the poverty of prayer, he remained always alone at the foot of the Cross, commending himself to Divine Mercy."

His was an example of pastoral ministry which today in a special way *I wish to entrust to my Brothers in the Episcopate.* Dear Brothers, Archbishop Felinski supports your efforts to *create and carry out a pastoral program of mercy.* May this program be the expression of your commitment, primarily in the life of the Church and then, as fitting and necessary, in the social and political life of the Nation, of Europe and of the world.

Inspired by this spirit of social charity, Archbishop Felinski gave himself fully in defending the freedom of the nation. This is necessary today also, when different forces — often under the guidance of a false ideology of freedom — try to take over this land. When the noisy propaganda of liberalism, of freedom without truth or responsibility, grows stronger in our country too, the Shepherds of the Church cannot fail to proclaim the one fail-proof philosophy of freedom, which is the truth of the Cross of Christ. This philosophy of freedom finds full motivation in the history of our nation.

Blessed Jan Beyzym

5. The desire to bring mercy to the neediest led Blessed Jan Beyzym to far-away Madagascar, where, out of love for Christ, he devoted himself to caring for lepers. Day and night he served those who had been marginalized and separated from social life. By his works of mercy on behalf of the abandoned and despised, he bore extraordinary witness. This was a witness that rung out first in Krakow, then in Poland, and afterwards among Poles overseas. Funds were collected to construct the hospital named after Our Lady of Czestochowa, which still stands today. One of those who promoted this help was St. Br. Albert.

I am pleased that this *spirit of solidarity in mercy continues to be active in the Church in Poland*; this is seen in the many programs lending assistance to the communities struck by natural catastrophes in different parts of the world. It is also seen in the recent initiative to purchase surplus grain and send it to those suffering hunger in Africa. I hope that this project will come to fruition.

The charitable work of Blesssed Jan Beyzym was an integral component of his fundamental mission: bringing the Gospel to those who do not know it. *This is the greatest gift of mercy*: bringing people to Christ and giving them the opportunity to know and savour His love. Therefore I ask you: pray for the birth of missionary vocations in the Church in Poland. Support missionaries unceasingly with your prayers.

Blessed Jan Balicki

6. Blessed Jan Balicki's life was marked by his service of mercy. As a priest, his heart was always open to the needy. His ministry of mercy, besides offering help to the sick and the poor, found a particularly energetic expression in *the confessional*, where he was filled with

patience and humility, always open to bringing the repentant sinner back to the throne of divine grace.

With this in mind, I turn to the priests and seminarians: I beseech you, Brothers, do not forget that, *insofar as you are dispensers of Divine Mercy, you have a great responsibility*; remember also that *Christ Himself comforts you with His promise* handed on through St.Faustina: "Tell My priests that hardened sinners will soften at their words, when they speak of My boundless mercy and of the compassion that I feel for them in My Heart" (*Diary*, 1521).

Blessed Santia Janina Szymkowiak

7. The work of mercy traced out a path in the religious vocation of Blessed Santia Janina Szymkowiak, Sister "Seraphica." She had already received from her family an ardent love for the Sacred Heart of Jesus, and in this spirit she was filled with goodness towards others, especially the poor and the needy. She began to lend help to the poor first as a member of the Marian Guild and of the Saint Vincent Mercy Association; then, having embraced the religious life, she devoted herself to the service of others with greater fervour. She accepted the difficult times of the Nazi occupation as an occasion to give herself completely to the needy. She considered her religious vocation a gift of Divine Mercy.

As I greet the Congregation of the Daughters of Our Lady of Sorrows, the "Seraphic" Sisters, I turn to all religious and consecrated persons. Let Blessed Santia be your patron. Make your own her spiritual witness, summarized in a simple phrase: "To give yourself to God, you have to give yourself to the point of totally losing yourself."

Live the mystery of Divine Mercy in our lives by a new 'creativity in charity'

8. Brothers and Sisters, as we contemplate these Beati, I wish to recall once more what I wrote in the encyclical *Dives in Misericordia*: "Man attains to the merciful love of God, His mercy, *to the extent that he himself is interiorly transformed in the spirit of that love towards his neighbor*" (14). On this path, may we rediscover ever more profoundly the mystery of Divine Mercy and live it in our daily lives!

Faced with the modern forms of poverty that, as we all know, are not lacking in our country, what is needed today is — as I called it in my apostolic letter *Novo Millennio Ineunte* — "a new 'creativity' in charity" (50), in a spirit of solidarity towards our neighbour, so that the help we lend will be a witness of "sharing between brothers and sisters" (*ibid.*). May this "creativity" never be lacking in the residents of Krakow and in all the people of our homeland. It represents the pastoral plan of the Church in Poland. May the message of God's mercy be reflected always in works of human mercy!

We must take a loving look around ourselves if we are to be aware of the neighbour by our side, who — because of the loss of work, home, the possibility to maintain his family in a decent manner and to educate his children — feels a sense of abandonment, of being lost, of distrust. This "creativity in charity" is needed to provide material and spiritual assistance to neglected children; to refrain from turning one's back on the boy or girl who has gotten lost in the world of addiction or crime; to give advice, consolation, spiritual support to those engaged in an internal struggle with evil. May this "creativity" never be lacking when a needy person pleads: "Give us this day our daily bread!" Thanks to brotherly love, this bread will not be lacking. "Blessed are the merciful, for they shall obtain mercy" (Mt 5:7).

Never separate from the love of God the cause of man who needs to experience Divine Mercy

9. During my 1979 pilgrimage to Poland, here in Blonie I said that "when we are strong with the Spirit of God, we are also strong with faith in man — strong with faith, hope and love, which are inseparable — and we are ready to bear witness to the cause of man before those who really have this cause at heart" (Homily at Mass at Blonie Kraskowie, June 10, 1979, 4). Therefore, I asked you: "Never disdain charity, which is 'the greatest of these' and which shows itself in the Cross. Without it, human life has no roots and no meaning" (*ibid.*, 5).

Brothers and Sisters, today I repeat this invitation: open yourselves to God's greatest gift, to His love that, through the Cross of Christ, has revealed itself to the world as merciful love. Today, living in different times, at the dawn of the new century and millennium, continue to be "ready to bear witness to the cause of man." Today, with all my strength, I beseech the sons and daughters of the Church, and all people of good will: *never, ever separate "the cause of man" from the love of God.* Help modern men and women to experience God's merciful love! This love, in its splendour and warmth, *will save humanity!*

✝ PILGRIMAGE TO POLAND: *ANGELUS,* AUGUST 18, 2002

Be appealing witnesses of mercy in our day. Christ embraces you with His merciful love

On Sunday, August 18, before the blessing at the end of the Mass of Beatification, the Holy Father introduced the *Angelus* with a special greeting for young people, singling out for special mention the "Light and Life" youth movement which he endorsed very strongly. He also greeted the groups of pilgrims who came to honor one or other of the new Beati. Then he greeted the pilgrims from around the world in their languages. The Pope challenged the young people to take St. Faustina's message of Divine Mercy everywhere by being witnesses to and messengers of mercy:

> The witness of men and women who live the Beatitudes is needed in every age. It is needed today too. I ask God to grant that your lives, according to this demanding divine measure, will be an appealing witness of mercy in our day.

Here is a translation of the Holy Father's remarks that introduced the *Angelus*:

> Before concluding this liturgy by praying the *Angelus*, I wish to speak to the young people. Unfortunately it was not possible to have a special meeting with them during this visit, but I saw them everywhere I went on my pilgrimage.

Special Greetings

> I Know that there is a large group of members of the "Light and Life" movement present here; they spent the night in prayer at the Church of Saints Peter and Paul in All Saints Parish in order to meet the Pope at this solemn Mass. I remember that exactly thirty years ago, on August 16, in Blyszcz near Tylmanowa, I was able to take part in the so-called "Days of Communion." At that time I would comment that I felt personally very close to the lifestyle begun and proposed to the young people by the Servant of God Fr. Franciszek Blachnicki. And my feelings have not changed.

> I thank God for this movement, which in the difficulties of past years has borne so much spiritual fruit in the hearts of young people and which today represents a stimulating environment for their spiritual growth and that of their families. Beloved members of "Oasis," when I was Bishop of Krakow I sought to show you my support by my presence; as Bishop of Rome I

continue to accompany you endlessly with my prayer and my spiritual closeness. May love for the Eucharist and for the Bible always shine divine light upon the paths of your lives.

I greet the members of the Catholic Youth Association and the Scouts. I constantly entrust you to the protection of the Mother of God. God bless you all.

Dear young friends! Recently in Toronto, Canada, a special meeting of youth from throughout the world took place, a meeting that occurs every two years called World Youth Day. It was a marvellous event, filled with a spirit of faith; faith is the solid foundation for the enthusiasm of young people's aspirations and plans. As I said on the shores of Lake Ontario, we have relived the experience of the people of Galilee, to whom Jesus entrusted the message of the Beatitudes beside the Lake Tiberias. Today I return from that experience, keeping in mind the message of Divine Mercy. Through St. Faustina, God entrusts this message to you, so that in its light you can better understand what it means to be poor in spirit, to be merciful, to be peacemakers, to hunger and thirst for justice, and finally to suffer persecution for Jesus' name. The witness of men and women who live the Beatitudes is needed in every age. It is needed today too. I ask God to grant that your lives, according to this demanding divine measure, will be an appealing witness of mercy in our day. Remember that Christ surrounds you constantly with His merciful love. May this consciousness fill you with peace and guide you on the difficult paths of daily life.

I also wish to greet in a special way the members of the "Friends of Lepers" Association of Fr. Jan Beyzym, who continues his effective mission of helping lepers. I urge you: do not let your work of mercy ever cease, and may your patron sustain you.

Through Cardinal Armand Gaétan Razafindatandra, Archbishop of Atananarivo, I greet the Church in Madagascar. I greet those who have found a place at the foot of Kosciuszko hill and also in Aleje.

I cannot forget the Archdiocese of Przemysl, which rejoices today because Superior Jan Balicki has been raised to the glory of the altars. I greet Archbishop Józef, the clergy and faithful, and I ask God to grant that devotion to the new Patron will bring abundant fruits of grace into the hearts of all.

I greet the Jesuit Fathers with their Father General. Today you have a new *Beatus*: Jan Beyzym. May his dedication to God and to the needy be an example for you, and may it inspire you always to undertake new tasks according to the demands of the times.

I have already remembered the "Seraphic Sisters," the Sisters of Our Lady of Mercy: once more I greet them, expressing the hope that they grow in number and in virtue before God and men.

Greetings to pilgrims from around the world

Finally, we must show our respect for the guests who have come from various parts of the world. Let me then greet the pilgrims from Lithuania, Russia, Ukraine, Belarus, Uzbekistan, Slovakia, the Czech Republic, Hungary, Italy, Austria, Canada, England, France, Germany, Sweden, Switzerland, the United States, and other countries. Their presence is testimony that the devotion to Divine Mercy is spreading throughout the world. And thanks be to God! I am convinced that they will carry this message to their families and to the places where they live. I pray that this will be a gift of hope and peace for all people of good will.

And now we commend our intentions to the Mother of God, the Mother of Mercy.

[*After the Apostolic Blessing, the Holy Father responded to a song the young people of the Oasis were singing:*]

To conclude, I would like to add that this same song of the "Oasis" accompanied me 24 years ago outside my country. I heard it all the time. It was the time of the conclave. I have not forgotten this song of the "Oasis" all these years. It was like a hidden breath of our homeland. It was my guide on the variety of paths of the Church. It was this song that often led me spiritually here, to Blonie of Krakow, to the foot of the Kosciuszko Hill. I thank you, song of the "Oasis." I thank you Blonie of Krakow for the hospitality you have shown so many times, especially today. May God reward you, I would like to add: See you again. But this is completely in God's hands. I entrust this entirely to the mercy of God.

✝ PILGRIMAGE TO POLAND: DEPARTURE CEREMONY, AUGUST 19, 2002

May my compatriots welcome the message of Divine Mercy and take it everywhere

On Monday afternoon, August 19, at 5:30 p.m., the Departure Ceremony took place at the airport. The Pope gave warm thanks to the religious and civil authorities who did so much to make his visit so magnificent. In reviewing the events, he mentioned how he took with him the vision of the people who joined him in all the events. He said:

I shall not forget the crowds of the faithful gathered in prayer — living testimony of the faith of the Church in Poland and of your trust in the power of God's mercy. Taking leave of Poland, I wish to bid you all farewell, dear Compatriots. Many have waited for my coming. Many have wished to meet me, although not all were able to do so.

He asked the Poles to act responsibly in the time of transition by sharing one another's burdens. His last word was a call to trust:

> Grateful for everything, and with the entire ecclesial community in Poland, I repeat before the merciful Jesus: "Jesus, in You I trust!" May these heartfelt words bring comfort to future generations in the new millennium. May God who is rich in mercy bless you!

He opened his heart as he left: "What can I say in the end? I am sorry to leave." Here is a translation of the conclusion of his farewell address:

> I congratulate the Archdiocese of Krakow and all of Poland for the church which I had the opportunity to dedicate. I am convinced that the Shrine of Lagiewniki will become a significant point of reference and a powerful centre of devotion to The Divine Mercy. May the rays of light coming down from the tower of the temple of Lagiewniki, reminiscent of the rays emanating from the image of the merciful Jesus, cast their spiritual reflection on the whole of Poland — from the Tatra Mountains to the Baltic Sea, from the Bug River to the Oder — and on the whole world!

> *"Jesus, I trust in You."*

> "God, rich in mercy." These are the words that sum up this visit. We have heard them as a call to the Church and to Poland in the new millennium. I pray that my Compatriots will welcome with open hearts this message of mercy and will succeed in carrying it to wherever men and women are in need of the light of hope.

I cherish in my heart every good thing that has happened and in which I have taken part during these days of my pilgrimage. Grateful for everything, and with the entire ecclesial community in Poland, I repeat before the merciful Jesus: "Jesus, in You I trust!" May these heartfelt words bring comfort to future generations in the new millennium. May God who is rich in mercy bless you.

✝ REGINA CAELI MESSAGE FOLLOWING EUCHARISTIC CELEBRATION FOR THE REPOSE OF THE SOUL OF POPE JOHN PAUL II, Divine Mercy Sunday, April 3, 2005

Pope John Paul II died peacefully on the evening of April 2, 9:37 p.m. Rome time. The last gift of the Holy Father for Divine Mercy Sunday, April 3, (also the Second Sunday of Easter), was the *Regina Caeli*, read by Archbishop Leonardo Sandri, Substitute of the Secretariat of State, at the end of the Holy Mass celebrated that day in St Peter's Square for the deceased Pope. "I have been charged," Archbishop Sandri said, "to read you the text that was prepared in accordance with his explicit instructions by the Holy Father John Paul II. I am deeply honoured to do so, but also filled with nostalgia":

Dear Brothers and Sisters,

1. Today the glorious Alleluia of Easter resounds. Today's Gospel from John emphasizes that on the evening of that day He appeared to the Apostles and "*showed them His hands and His side*" (Jn 20:20), that is, the signs of the painful passion with which His Body was indelibly stamped, even after the Resurrection. Those glorious wounds, which He allowed doubting Thomas to touch eight days later, reveal the mercy of God who "*so loved the world that He gave His only Son*" (Jn 3:16).

This mystery of love is at the heart of the liturgy

today, the Second Sunday of Easter, dedicated to the devotion of Divine Mercy.

2. As a gift to humanity, which sometimes seems bewildered and overwhelmed by the power of evil, selfishness, and fear, the Risen Lord offers His love that pardons, reconciles, and reopens hearts to love. It is a love that converts hearts and gives peace. How much the world needs to understand and accept Divine Mercy!

Lord, [You] who reveal the Father's love by Your death and Resurrection, we believe in You and confidently repeat to You today: Jesus, I trust in You, have mercy upon us and upon the whole world.

3. The liturgical solemnity of the Annunciation that we will be celebrating tomorrow urges us to contemplate with Mary's eyes the immense mystery of this merciful love that flows from the Heart of Christ. With her help, we will be able to understand the true meaning of Easter joy that is based on this certainty: the One whom the Virgin bore in her womb, who suffered and died for us, is truly risen. Alleluia!

✝ BEATIFICATION OF THE VENERABLE JOHN PAUL II, Homily by Pope Benedict XVI, Divine Mercy Sunday, May 1, 2011

Dear Brothers and Sisters,

Six years ago we gathered in this Square to celebrate the funeral of Pope John Paul II. Our grief at his loss was deep, but even greater was our sense of an immense grace which embraced Rome and the whole world: a grace which was in some way the fruit of my beloved predecessor's entire life, and especially of his witness in suffering. Even then we perceived the fragrance of his sanctity, and in any number of ways God's People showed their veneration for him. For this reason, with all due respect for the Church's canonical norms, I wanted his cause of beatification to move forward with reasonable haste. And now the longed-for day has come; it came quickly because this is what was pleasing to the Lord: John Paul II is blessed!

I would like to offer a cordial greeting to all of you who on this happy occasion have come in such great numbers to Rome from all over the world — cardinals, patriarchs of the Eastern Catholic Churches, brother bishops and priests, official delegations, ambassadors and civil authorities, consecrated men and women, and lay faithful, and I extend that greeting to all those who join us by radio and television.

Today is the Second Sunday of Easter, which Blessed John Paul II entitled Divine Mercy Sunday. The date was chosen for today's celebration because, in God's providence, my predecessor died on the vigil of this feast. Today is also the first day of May, Mary's month, and the liturgical memorial of St. Joseph the Worker. All these elements serve to enrich our prayer, they help us in our pilgrimage through time and space; but in heaven a very different celebration is taking place among the angels and saints! Even so, God is but one, and one too is Christ the Lord, who like a bridge joins earth to heaven. At this moment we feel closer than ever, sharing as it were in the liturgy of heaven.

"Blessed are those who have not seen and yet have come to believe" (Jn 20:29). In today's Gospel Jesus proclaims this beatitude: the beatitude of faith. For us, it is particularly striking because we are gathered to celebrate a beatification, but even more so because today the one proclaimed blessed is a Pope, a Successor of Peter, one who was called to confirm his brethren in the faith. John Paul II is blessed because of his faith, a strong, generous and apostolic faith. We think at once of another beatitude: "Blessed are you, Simon, son of Jonah! For flesh and blood has not revealed this to you, but My Father in heaven" (Mt 16:17). What did our heavenly Father reveal to Simon? That Jesus is the Christ, the Son of the living God. Because of this faith, Simon becomes Peter, the rock on which Jesus can build His Church. The eternal beatitude of John Paul II, which today the Church rejoices to proclaim, is wholly contained in these sayings of Jesus: "Blessed are you, Simon" and "Blessed are those who have not seen and yet have come to believe!" It is the beatitude of faith, which John Paul II also received as a gift from God the Father for the building up of Christ's Church.

Our thoughts turn to yet another beatitude, one which appears in the Gospel before all others. It is the beatitude of the Virgin Mary, the Mother of the Redeemer. Mary, who had just conceived Jesus, was told by St. Elizabeth: "Blessed is she who believed that there would be a fulfilment of what was spoken to her by the Lord" (Lk 1:45). The beatitude of faith has its model in Mary, and all of us rejoice that the beatification of John Paul II takes place on this first day of the month of Mary, beneath the maternal gaze of the one who by her faith sustained the faith of the Apostles and constantly sustains the faith of their successors, especially those called to occupy the Chair of Peter. Mary does not appear in the accounts of Christ's resurrection, yet hers is, as it were, a continual, hidden presence: she is the Mother to whom Jesus entrusted each of His disciples and the entire community. In particular we can see how St. John and St. Luke record the powerful, maternal presence of Mary in the passages preceding those read in today's Gospel and first reading. In the account of Jesus' death, Mary appears at the foot of the cross (cf. Jn 19:25), and at the beginning of the Acts of the Apostles she is seen in the midst of the disciples gathered in prayer in the Upper Room (cf. Acts 1:14).

Today's second reading also speaks to us of faith. Saint Peter himself, filled with spiritual enthusiasm, points out to the newly-baptized the reason for their hope and their joy. I like to think how in this passage, at the beginning of his First Letter, Peter does not use language of exhortation; instead, he states a fact. He writes: "*you rejoice*," and he adds: "you *love* Him; and even though you do not see Him now, you believe in Him and rejoice with an indescribable and glorious joy, for you *are receiving* the outcome of your faith, the salvation of your souls" (1 Pet 1:6, 8-9). All these verbs are in the indicative, because a new reality has come about in Christ's resurrection, a reality to which faith opens the door. "This is the Lord's doing," says the Psalm (118:23), and "it is marvelous in our eyes," the eyes of faith.

Dear brothers and sisters, today our eyes behold, in the full spiritual light of the risen Christ, the beloved and revered figure of John Paul II. Today his name is added to the host of those whom he proclaimed saints and blesseds during the almost twenty-seven years of his pontificate, thereby forcefully emphasizing the universal vocation to the heights of the Christian life, to holiness, taught by the conciliar Constitution on the Church *Lumen Gentium*. All of us, as members of the people of God — bishops, priests, deacons, laity, men and women religious — are making our pilgrim way to the heavenly homeland where the Virgin Mary has preceded us, associated as she was in a unique and perfect way to the mystery of Christ and the Church. Karol Wojtyla took part in the Second Vatican Council, first as an auxiliary Bishop and then as Archbishop of Kraków. He was fully aware that the Council's decision to devote the last chapter of its Constitution on the Church to Mary meant that the Mother of the Redeemer is held up as an image and model of holiness for every Christian and for the entire Church. This was the theological vision which Blessed John Paul II discovered as a young man and subsequently maintained and deepened throughout his life. A vision which is expressed in the scriptural image of the crucified Christ with Mary, His Mother, at His side. This icon from the Gospel of John (19:25-27) was taken up in the episcopal and later the papal coat-of-arms of Karol Wojtyla: a golden cross with the letter "M" on the lower right and the motto "*Totus tuus*," drawn from the well-known words of St. Louis Marie Grignion de Montfort in which Karol Wojtyla found a guiding light for his life: "*Totus tuus ego sum et omnia mea tua sunt. Accipio te in mea omnia. Praebe mihi cor tuum, Maria* — I belong entirely to you, and all that I have is yours. I take you for my all. O Mary, give me your heart" (*Treatise on True Devotion to the Blessed Virgin*, 266).

In his Testament, the new Blessed wrote: "When, on October 16, 1978, the Conclave of Cardinals chose John Paul II, the Primate of Poland, Cardinal Stefan Wyszynski, said to me:

'The task of the new Pope will be to lead the Church into the Third Millennium.'" And the Pope added: "I would like once again to express my gratitude to the Holy Spirit for the great gift of the Second Vatican Council, to which, together with the whole Church — and especially with the whole episcopate — I feel indebted. I am convinced that it will long be granted to the new generations to draw from the treasures that this Council of the twentieth century has lavished upon us. As a Bishop who took part in the Council from the first to the last day, I desire to entrust this great patrimony to all who are and will be called in the future to put it into practice. For my part, I thank the Eternal Shepherd, who has enabled me to serve this very great cause in the course of all the years of my Pontificate." And what is this "cause"? It is the same one that John Paul II presented during his first solemn Mass in St. Peter's Square in the unforgettable words: "Do not be afraid! Open, open wide the doors to Christ!" What the newly-elected Pope asked of everyone, he was himself the first to do: society, culture, political, and economic systems he opened up to Christ, turning back with the strength of a titan — a strength which came to him from God — a tide which appeared irreversible. By his witness of faith, love, and apostolic courage, accompanied by great human charisma, this exemplary son of Poland helped believers throughout the world not to be afraid to be called Christian, to belong to the Church, to speak of the Gospel. In a word: he helped us not to fear the truth, because truth is the guarantee of liberty. To put it even more succinctly: he gave us the strength to believe in Christ, because Christ is *Redemptor hominis*, the Redeemer of man. This was the theme of his first encyclical, and the thread which runs though all the others.

When Karol Wojtyla ascended to the throne of Peter, he brought with him a deep understanding of the difference between Marxism and Christianity, based on their respective visions of man. This was his message: man is the way of the Church, and Christ is the way of man. With this message, which is the great legacy of the Second Vatican Council and of its "helmsman," the Servant of God Pope Paul VI, John Paul II led the People of God across the threshold of the Third

Millennium, which thanks to Christ he was able to call "the threshold of hope." Throughout the long journey of preparation for the great Jubilee he directed Christianity once again to the future, the future of God, which transcends history while nonetheless directly affecting it. He rightly reclaimed for Christianity that impulse of hope which had in some sense faltered before Marxism and the ideology of progress. He restored to Christianity its true face as a religion of hope, to be lived in history in an "Advent" spirit, in a personal and communitarian existence directed to Christ, the fullness of humanity and the fulfillment of all our longings for justice and peace.

Finally, on a more personal note, I would like to thank God for the gift of having worked for many years with Blessed Pope John Paul II. I had known him earlier and had esteemed him, but for twenty-three years, beginning in 1982 after he called me to Rome to be Prefect of the Congregation for the Doctrine of the Faith, I was at his side and came to revere him all the more. My own service was sustained by his spiritual depth and by the richness of his insights. His example of prayer continually impressed and edified me: he remained deeply united to God even amid the many demands of his ministry. Then too, there was his witness in suffering: the Lord gradually stripped him of everything, yet he remained ever a "rock," as Christ desired. His profound humility, grounded in close union with Christ, enabled him to continue to lead the Church and to give to the world a message which became all the more eloquent as his physical strength declined. In this way he lived out in an extraordinary way the vocation of every priest and bishop to become completely one with Jesus, whom he daily receives and offers in the Church.

Blessed are you, beloved Pope John Paul II, because you believed! Continue, we implore you, to sustain from heaven the faith of God's people. You often blessed us in this Square from the Apostolic Palace: Bless us, Holy Father! Amen.

CHRONOLOGY OF THE GREAT MERCY POPE

1942: Karol Wojtyla enters the clandestine seminary in Krakow. During this time, Andrew Deskur, now retired Cardinal in the Vatican, introduces him to the message of Divine Mercy, revealed to the mystic nun, now St. Faustina Kowalska (1905-1938).

1958: Bishop Karol Wojtyla often visited the motherhouse of the Sisters of Our Lady of Mercy, where Sr. Faustina died and was buried. He came for his own time of retreat and to conduct retreats for the Sisters (verbally related in 1989 by Mother Pauline, Superior General).

OCT. 1965: Archbishop Karol Wojtyla of Krakow confers with Cardinal Ottaviani about the desire of the faithful in Poland to have Sr. Faustina raised to the honors of the altar, despite a notification from the Vatican prohibiting "the spread of images and writings that propose the devotion of The Divine Mercy in the form proposed by the same Sr. Faustina."

OCT. 21, 1965: Twenty-seven years after the death of Sr. Faustina, Bishop Julian Groblicki, specially delegated by Archbishop Karol Wojtyla, begins with a solemn session, in the Archdiocese of Krakow, the Informative Process relating to the life and virtues of Sr. Faustina. From this moment, Sr. Faustina is worthy of the title "Servant of God."

JUNE 26, 1967: Archbishop Karol Wojtyla becomes Karol Cardinal Wojtyla.

SEPT. 20, 1967: The Archbishop of Krakow, Karol Cardinal Wojtyla officially closes the first informative stage in the process for the beatification of the Servant of God, Sr. Faustina Kowalska.

The outcome of the Process of Information shows that the action in Rome with regard to Sr. Faustina was taken (at the least) on insufficient evidence. (Official communications between Rome and the Church in Poland during those post-war years, especially with regard to religious matters, were very difficult. Relevant, authentic documents could not be made available to the investigating authorities who were being pressed to make a judgment on the matter presented to them.)

JAN. 31, 1968: By a Decree of the Sacred Congregation for the Causes of Saints, the Process of Beatification of the Servant of God, Sr. Faustina H. Kowalska is formally inaugurated.

Because of the positive outcome of the Informative Process concerning the life and virtues of Sr. Faustina, inquiries from many places, especially from Poland and, in particular, from the Archbishop of Krakow, Cardinal Wojtyla, are received by the Sacred Congregation for the Doctrine of Faith, asking whether the prohibitions of the 1959 "Notification" are still in effect.

OCT. 16, 1978: Karol Cardinal Wojtyla of Krakow, Poland, becomes Pope John Paul II.

MARCH 14, 1979: In his first encyclical, *Redemptor Hominis*, John Paul II describes the divine and human dimension of the mystery of redemption as the revelation of love, which is also described as mercy. "This revelation of love and mercy has taken a form and a name: that of Jesus Christ." He is the redeemer of "each and every" man — fully revealing man to himself.

JUNE 3, 1979: John Paul II addresses the vast assembly before the Image of the Merciful Savior, Warsaw, Poland. Cardinal Macharski asks the Marian Helpers Center in Stockbridge, Massachusetts, to print a prayercard for this event for him to distribute.

JULY 12, 1979: The Congregation of Marians, having asked for an authoritative explanation of the "Notification" of 1978 that lifted the ban on the message and devotion, receives a reply from the Prefect of the Sacred Congregation, stating that:

> ... with the new "Notification," — ... arrived at in the light of original documentation examined also by the careful informative intervention of the then Archbishop of Krakow, Karol Cardinal Wojtyla, it was the intention of the Holy See to revoke the prohibition contained in the preceding "Notification" of 1959 — ... there no longer exists, on the part of this Sacred Congregation, any impediment to the spreading of the devotion to The Divine Mercy in the authentic forms proposed by the Religious Sister mentioned above [the Servant of God, Sr. Faustina Kowalska].

NOV. 30, 1980: Pope John Paul II publishes his second encyclical letter *Rich in Mercy (Dives in Misericordia) in which he stresses that Jesus Christ has revealed God, who is rich in mercy, as Father. He speaks of mercy as "the most stupendous attribute of the Creator and Redeemer"* (13). Describing the mercy of God as the presence of love which is greater than evil, greater than sin, and greater than death, he summons the Church to plead for God's mercy on the whole world (15).

In this encyclical on the mercy of God, John Paul II opens with a statement and a summary of the message: "*God who is rich in mercy, Jesus Christ reveals as Father.*" He appeals to the Church to plead for God's mercy as the only answer to our present human condition. He devotes one section of the encyclical to Mary, as Mother of Mercy.

MAY 13, 1981: Pope John Paul II, wounded by an attempted assassination, forgives his assassin on the way to the hospital. The *Diary of Sr. Faustina* is read to him in Polish during his convalescence.

NOV. 22, 1981: Pope John Paul II makes his first public visit outside of Rome following his lengthy recuperation, on the Feast of Christ the King, to the Shrine of Merciful Love in Collevalenza near Todi, Italy, where, within a few days, an international congress is to be held to reflect on the encyclical *Dives in Misericordia* (*Rich in Mercy*) one year after its publication.

After celebrating the Holy Sacrifice of the Eucharist, he makes a strong public declaration about the importance of the message of mercy:

> A year ago I published the encyclical *Dives in Misericordia*. This circumstance made me come to the Sanctuary of Merciful Love today. By my presence I wish to reconfirm, in a way, the message of that encyclical. I wish to read it again and deliver it again.
>
> Right from the beginning of my ministry in St. Peter's See in Rome, I considered this message my special task. Providence has assigned it to me in the present situation of man, the Church and the world. It could be said that precisely this situation assigned that message to me as my task before God.

FEB. 25, 1983: The Holy See is approached with the petition to authorize, during the Holy Year of Redemption, the celebration of a Votive Mass of The Divine Mercy in the Diocese of Rome with the formulary already approved for the Archdiocese of Krakow. The request is granted.

DEC. 27, 1983: Pope John Paul II visits Ali Agca in his prison to extend his forgiveness. This worldwide witness to mercy is recorded in the film *Time for Mercy*.

FEB. 11, 1984: In the apostolic exhortation *Salvifici Doloris*, John Paul II describes Jesus transforming suffering by His love and mercy into the work of our salvation, and how Jesus invites us to join with Him in our suffering by our love and mercy, bringing salvation to souls. We learn from Jesus a two-fold approach of mercy to suffering: to do good *with* our suffering, and to do good *to* the suffering.

MAY 18, 1986: In the third encyclical of a trilogy on the Holy Trinity, *Dominum et Vivificantem,* John Paul II describes how the Holy Spirit continues the work of Jesus and he pictures Him as mercy "personified and actualized in a transcendent way …" (39). The Holy Spirit also convinces the world of sin, not to condemn it, but to bring it to the source of all love, mercy, and salvation: the Cross, in order that we may have life. John Paul II exhorts us to implore the Holy Spirit to renew the face of the earth.

NOV. 13, 1986: Pope John Paul II is presented an icon of The Divine Mercy from the Congregation of Marian Fathers of the Immaculate Conception "as an expression of our thanksgiving for your proclaiming to the world the message of Divine Mercy." (Filmed for the movie, *Divine Mercy — No Escape,* in the apartment of the Holy Father.)

MARCH 25, 1987: In his encyclical *Redemptoris Mater* on the Blessed Virgin Mary in the life of the pilgrim Church, John Paul II describes Mary as the faithful virgin and mother at Christ's first coming and as "Mediatrix of Mercy" at His final coming.

DEC. 7, 1990: In the encyclical *Redemptoris Missio,* John Paul II describes the mission of Christ as making the kingdom of God present, which is to make God's mercy present and believable. It is the Holy Spirit that makes mercy present. The mission of Christ is the mission of the Church.

FEB. 12, 1991: All the documents concerning the heroic virtue of Sr. Faustina are completed and sent to the Sacred Congregation.

APRIL 10, 1991: Pope John Paul II, at his General Audience, speaks about Sr. Faustina, showing his great respect for her, relating her to his encyclical *Rich in Mercy,* and emphasizing her role in bringing the message of mercy to the world:

> The words of the encyclical on Divine Mercy (*Dives in Misericordia*) are particularly close to us. They

recall the figure of the Servant of God, Sr. Faustina Kowalska. This simple woman religious particularly brought the Easter message of the merciful Christ closer to Poland and the whole world ... .

And today? ... Is it perhaps not necessary to translate into the language of today's generations the words of the Gospel, "Blessed are the merciful, for they shall obtain mercy"? (Mt 5:7).

MARCH 7, 1992: In the presence of the Holy Father, the Congregation for the Causes of Saints promulgates the Decree of Heroic Virtues, by which the Church acknowledges that Sr. Faustina practiced all the Christian virtues to a heroic degree. As a result, she receives the title "Venerable" Servant of God, and the way is opened for verification of a miracle attributed to her intercession.

OCT. 11, 1992: In *Fidei Depositum*, John Paul II introduces the *Catechism of the Catholic Church* which is a compendium and "symphony" of our faith. It begins with God's mercy and continues throughout describing God's mercy and our response of trust in Him.

DEC. 21, 1992: The Holy Father publishes the Church's acceptance of the miracle as granted through the intercession of Sr. Faustina and announces the date for her solemn beatification.

APRIL 18, 1993: Sister Faustina is beatified by Pope John Paul II in Rome on the Second Sunday of Easter (which Our Lord had revealed to her as the "Feast of Mercy"):

I clearly feel that my mission does not end with death, but begins," Sr. Faustina wrote in her diary. And it truly did! Her mission continues and is yielding astonishing fruit. It is truly marvelous how her devotion to the merciful Jesus is spreading in our contemporary world and gaining so many human hearts! This is doubtlessly a *sign of the times — a sign of our 20th century*. The balance of this century which is now ending, in addition to the advances which have often surpassed those of preceding eras, presents a deep restlessness and fear of the future. Where, if not in The Divine Mercy, can the world find refuge and the light of hope? Believers understand that perfectly.

Give thanks to the Lord, for He is good.

Give thanks to the Lord, for He is merciful.

AUG. 6, 1993: In his encyclical *Veritatis Splendor*, John Paul II deals with certain fundamental questions of the Church's moral teaching. He concludes the encyclical by entrusting all the questions and the research of moralists to Mary, Mother of God and Mother of Mercy. He then explains how she is Mother of Mercy.

AUG. 14, 1993: The helicopter carrying John Paul II hovers over the 100-ft. high Image of The Divine Mercy upon departing World Youth Day, Denver, Colorado.

SEPT. 4, 1993: Pope John Paul II prays the Rosary at the Shrine of Ostra Brama in Vilnius, Lithuania, before the icon of the Mother of Mercy.

SEPT. 5, 1993: John Paul II kneels and prays at the Image of Divine Mercy (painted under the direction of Sr. Faustina) in the Church of the Holy Spirit in Vilnius, Lithuania.

APRIL 10, 1994: Second Sunday of Easter, *Regina Caeli* Address:

> What is mercy if not the boundless love of God, who confronted with human sin, restrains the sentiment of severe justice and, allowing Himself to be moved by the wretchedness of His creatures, spurs Himself to the total gift of self, in the Son's cross? 'O happy fault ... which gained for us so great a Redeemer!' (Easter Proclamation).

Who can say he is free from sin and does not need God's mercy? As people of this restless time of ours, wavering between the emptiness of self-exaltation and the humiliation of despair, we have a greater need than ever for a regenerating experience of mercy.

APRIL 1994: In *Crossing the Threshold of Hope*, Pope John Paul II answers questions submitted to him using the theme "Do not be afraid" — because the Son of God has become a man. How do we cross the threshold of hope? By trust in Jesus. He is mercy — "Love that became man, Love crucified and risen, Love unceasingly present among men. It is Eucharistic Love."

NOV. 10, 1994: In the apostolic letter *Tertio Millenio Adveniente*, John Paul II sets out an action plan to prepare for the third millennium. He challenges us to intense prayer to the Holy Spirit for the mercy to forgive, especially overcoming obstacles to unity, in order that our witness to evangelization be real and believable.

JAN. 23, 1995: Pope John Paul II grants to the Polish bishops that the Sunday after Easter be called the Sunday of Divine Mercy — because of the need and desire of the faithful.

MARCH 25, 1995: In the encyclical *Evangelium Vitae*, John Paul II calls us to mobilize our consciences and unite to build a new *culture of life* in our dramatic struggle with the culture of death. The culture of life is one of mercy — a mercy that is both love-giving life and life-giving love.

APRIL 23, 1995: Pope John Paul II celebrates Divine Mercy Sunday in Holy Spirit Church, the Shrine of The Divine Mercy in Rome. (*L'Osservatore Romano*, English Edition, April 26, 1995). In his homily, he challenges us to "trust in the Lord and be Apostles of Divine Mercy."

In his *Regina Caeli* address, he speaks of the whole Octave of Easter as a single day, and the Octave Sunday as the day of thanksgiving for God's mercy, called the Sunday of Divine Mercy. He challenges us to personally *experience* this mercy in order to be merciful and forgive — and so break the spiral of violence by the miracle of forgiveness.

MAY 17, 1995: On the eve of his 75th birthday, John Paul II reflects during his Wednesday General Audience on the central role of Divine Mercy in his life:

> I am encompassing years of service on the Vatican post. I do it being aware of my human weaknesses, yet, at the same time [being] full of great faith in the magnitude of The Divine Mercy. First of all, I renew before Christ the offer of my readiness to serve the Church as long as He wants, surrendering myself completely to His holy will. I leave to Christ the decision of how and when He wants to relieve me of this service.

MAY 25, 1995: In his encyclical *Ut Unum Sint*, Pope John Paul II, in the section on the "Ministry of Unity of the Bishop of Rome," describes his ministry as a service of unity rooted in the action of Divine Mercy (94) and heir to the ministry of Peter:

> As the heir to the mission of Peter in the Church, which has been made fruitful by the blood of the Princes of the Apostles, the Bishop of Rome exercises a ministry originating in the *manifold mercy of God*. This mercy converts hearts and pours forth the power of grace where the disciple experiences the bitter taste of his personal weakness and helplessness. The authority proper to this ministry is completely at the service of *God's merciful plan*, and it must always be seen in this perspective. Its power is explained from this perspective (92).

> Associating himself with Peter's threefold profession of love, which corresponds to the earlier threefold denial, his successor knows that *he must be a sign of mercy. His is a ministry of mercy, born of an act of*

Christ's own mercy. This whole lesson of the Gospel must be constantly read anew so that the exercise of the Petrine ministry may lose nothing of its authenticity and transparency.

The Church of God is called by Christ to manifest to a world ensnared by its sins and evil designs that, despite everything, *God in His mercy* can convert hearts to unity and enable them to enter into communion with Him (93).

NOV. 1, 1996: In *Gift and Mystery*, John Paul II calls his memoirs of 50 years of priesthood: "Singing the mercies of the Lord."

JUNE 7, 1997: Pope John Paul II makes a pilgrimage to the Shrine of The Divine Mercy in Lagiewniki, Poland (outside of Krakow) and witnesses to his personal involvement in The Divine Mercy message and devotion.

NOV. 29, 1998: John Paul II in *Incarnationis Mysterium* announces the Jubilee Year of 2000, calling it a "year of mercy."

APRIL 11, 1999: John Paul II calls the Octave day of Easter, Divine Mercy Sunday.

DEC. 20, 1999: Pope John Paul II accepts the healing of the heart of Fr. Ronald Pytel of Baltimore, Maryland, as the miracle needed for the canonization of Sr. Faustina.

MARCH 12, 2000: John Paul II, as a Jubilee Year act of mercy, celebrates the "Universal Prayer of Confession of Sins and Asking for Forgiveness."

APRIL 30, 2000: Pope John Paul II canonizes St. Maria Faustina Kowalska and proclaims Divine Mercy Sunday for the universal Church.

JAN. 6, 2001: John Paul II publishes his apostolic letter *Novo Millennium Inuente (At the Beginning of the New Millenium).*

MARCH 25, 2001: John Paul II's Letter to Priests is published on Holy Thursday: "Priests of God, You Embody the Mystery of Mercy."

APRIL 22, 2001: Pope John Paul II celebrates the universal feast of Divine Mercy Sunday and the first anniversary of the canonization of St. Faustina in St. Peter's Square.

MAY 31, 2001: Dario Cardinal Castrillon Hoyos, prefect of the clergy writes a six-page summary (Aug. 8/15, 2001, *L'Osservatore Romano*) of The Divine Mercy message and devotion in response to John Paul II's Holy Thursday 2001 Letter to Priests.

MAY 2001: John Paul II reaches out to Orthodox Christians in Syria and Greece.

OCT. 24, 2001: John Paul II reflects on Psalm 51, emphasizing that mercy is stronger than our misery.

JAN. 1, 2002: John Paul II proclaims on World Day of Peace: "No Peace without Justice, No Justice without Forgiveness."

MARCH 17, 2002: Pope John Paul II publishes his Letter to Priests on Holy Thursday. He focuses on the Sacrament of Reconciliation, exhorting priests to be ministers of mercy.

APRIL 7, 2002: As directed by John Paul II, Divine Mercy Sunday is declared a day of prayer for peace in the Middle East.

JUNE 29, 2002: Under the direction of John Paul II, the Apostolic Penitentiary proclaims plenary and partial indulgences for Divine Mercy Sunday.

AUG. 16-19, 2002: Pilgrimage to Poland: Dedication of the Basilica of Divine Mercy, Entrustment of the World to Divine Mercy, Beatification of four "creative messengers of Divine Mercy."

APRIL 17, 2003: John Paul II's encyclical *The Church of the Eucharist* is published as his Holy Thursday 2003 Letter to Priests, calling the Eucharist "The Mystery of Mercy."

APRIL 27, 2003: On Divine Mercy Sunday, John Paul II beatifies six Servants of God who showed God's mercy to the world.

OCT. 16, 2003: Pope John Paul II entrusts his 25-year pontificate to Divine Mercy.

2004: *Rise, Let Us Be on Our Way,* which is the second-to-last book of John Paul II, is published.

APRIL 2004: Influenced by John Paul II, the Knights of Columbus provide parishes in U.S. and Canada with The Divine Mercy Hour of Prayer and The Divine Mercy Image.

MARCH 28, 2004: John Paul II's Letter to Priests is published on Holy Thursday. It is titled "On the Mystery of the Eucharist and the Mystery of the Priesthood."

APRIL 18, 2004: On Divine Mercy Sunday, John Paul II meditates on the testimony of forgiveness and Jesus as the perfect manifestation of mercy.

JUNE 10, 2004: On the feast of Corpus Christi, John Paul II announces the Year of the Eucharist, beginning October 2004 and running through October 2005.

AUG. 14, 2004: John Paul II makes a pilgrimage to Our Lady of Lourdes Shrine in France.

2005: *Memory and Identity,* which is the last book written by John Paul II, is published.

MARCH 12, 2005: John Paul II says to the Chapter of the Marian Fathers of the Immaculate Conception, "Be for everyone apostles and witnesses of Divine Mercy."

APRIL 2, 2005: On the Vigil of Divine Mercy Sunday, John Paul II dies after his final "AMEN."

APRIL 3, 2005: John Paul II's posthumous message for Divine Mercy Sunday is shared with the faithful in St. Peter's Square.

APRIL 8, 2005: The *"Rogito"* document is placed in the Pope's coffin at his funeral.

APRIL 8, 2005: Cardinal Joseph Ratzinger gives the homily at John Paul II's Funeral Mass.

APRIL 20, 2005: Pope Benedict XVI gives his first message as Pope to the Cardinals.

MAY 13, 2005: Pope Benedict XVI announces "exceptional circumstances" and waives the five-year waiting period for beginning the beatification process for John Paul II.

JUNE 2-3, 2005: Sister Marie Simon-Pierre Normand, a French nun who was confined to her bed by Parkinson's disease, asks the late John Paul II to intercede for her and says she has experienced a complete healing.

JUNE 28, 2005: Cardinal Camillo Ruini, vicar general for the Diocese of Rome, officially opens the diocesan inquiry in order to gather testimonies and documents related to the life and virtues of Pope John Paul II.

OCT. 16, 2005: Polish TV interviews Pope Benedict XVI about John Paul II's legacy.

EARLY 2006: The Vatican begins investigating Sr. Marie Simon-Pierre Normand's claim of a healing as a possible miracle attributed to the intercession of the Servant of God John Paul II.

MARCH 26, 2006: Nearly a year after John Paul II's death, on the Fourth Sunday of Lent, Pope Benedict XVI remembers his predecessor's last text, including the line "How much the world needs to understand and accept Divine Mercy!" Pope Benedict describes it as "a testament" of mercy for John Paul II, who had written his last text for Divine Mercy Sunday in 2005.

APRIL 23, 2006: On Divine Mercy Sunday, Pope Benedict XVI mentions John Paul II's desire to have the Sunday after

Easter be dedicated in a special way to Divine Mercy, his connection to St. Faustina, and his devotion to the mystery of God's merciful love.

MAY 27, 2006: Pope Benedict XVI prays at the tomb of St. Faustina Kowalska in Krakow-Lagiewniki, Poland, and addresses the sick at the International Shrine of The Divine Mercy there.

MAY 28, 2006: Pope Benedict XVI celebrates Mass before an estimated 900,000 people in John Paul II's native Poland. During his homily, he encourages prayers for the early canonization of John Paul II and states that he hopes it will occur "in the near future."

MAY 31, 2006: Pope Benedict XVI shares Divine Mercy highlights of his pastoral visit to Poland during his General Audience.

APRIL 2, 2007: On the second anniversary of Pope John Paul II's death, his cause proceeds to the scrutiny of the committee of lay, clerical, and Episcopal members of the Vatican's Congregation for the Causes of Saints, who will conduct an investigation of their own.

APRIL 15, 2007: On Divine Mercy Sunday, two years after Pope John Paul II's death, Pope Benedict XVI remembers his predecessor, saying that he has "entered the light of Divine Mercy" and "speaks to us in a new way. Have faith, he tells us, in Divine Mercy!"

MAY 4, 2007: The decree on the validity of the diocesan inquiry for John Paul II's cause is published by the Congregation for the Causes of the Saints.

MARCH 30, 2008: On Divine Mercy Sunday, Pope Benedict XVI remembers John Paul II, especially his connection to Divine Mercy and St. Faustina. The Pontiff says the Servant of God John Paul II made himself an apostle of Divine Mercy when he established that the Sunday after Easter should be called Divine

Mercy Sunday throughout the Church and also canonized Sr. Faustina Kowalska.

APRIL 2, 2008: Pope Benedict XVI opens the First World Apostolic Congress on Mercy on the third anniversary of Pope John Paul II's death. The Pontiff says God's mercy is the key to interpreting the Servant of God John Paul II's life and pontificate. He points to John Paul II's desire for the message of God's merciful love to be made known to all and for the faithful to witness to it.

APRIL 19, 2009: On Divine Mercy Sunday, Pope Benedict XVI speaks of how John Paul II's deep conviction regarding the Risen Christ's message of forgiveness and inner renewal had inspired him to call the Second Sunday of Easter Divine Mercy Sunday. He also highlights how John Paul accepted the message of Divine Mercy that the Lord gave to St Faustina, a message summed up in the words "Jesus, I trust in You."

NOV. 16, 2009: A panel of reviewers at the Congregation for the Causes of Saints votes unanimously that Pope John Paul II had lived a life of heroic virtue.

DEC. 19, 2009: Pope Benedict XVI signs the first of two decrees needed for the beatification of John Paul II. The first recognizes that he lived a heroic, virtuous life. He can now be called "Venerable."

JAN. 14, 2011: Pope Benedict XVI signs the second decree recognizing the healing of Sr. Marie Simon-Pierre Normand from Parkinson's disease as a miracle through the intercession of the Venerable Servant of God John Paul II. Further, the Vatican announces that Pope Benedict XVI will beatify John Paul II on May 1, Divine Mercy Sunday, in St. Peter's Square.

JAN. 16, 2011: After the January 14th announcement concerning the date for John Paul II's beatification, Pope Benedict XVI says of the news:

On May 1, I'll have the joy of beatifying Venerable Pope John Paul II, my beloved predecessor. The date that has been chosen is very significant: It will be the Second Sunday of Easter, which he himself entitled "Divine Mercy." ... Those who knew him, those who esteemed and loved him, cannot but rejoice with the Church for this event. We are happy!

MAY 1, 2011: The Great Mercy Pope, the Venerable Servant of God John Paul II — who died on the Vigil of Divine Mercy Sunday in 2005 — is beatified in St. Peter's Square on Divine Mercy Sunday by his successor, Pope Benedict XVI. An overflow crowd, estimated at more than 1.5 million people, attends the beatification in Rome in 2011, which comes in record-breaking time, only six years after John Paul's death in 2005. In fact, it is the largest crowd Rome has seen since John Paul's funeral. Further, it is significant that Blessed John Paul II entitled the Second Sunday of Easter as Divine Mercy Sunday, which Pope Benedict highlights at the beatification. Pope Benedict says in his homily for the occasion:

> Six years ago we gathered in this Square to celebrate the funeral of Pope John Paul II. Our grief at his loss was deep, but even greater was our sense of an immense grace which embraced Rome and the whole world: a grace which was in some way the fruit of my beloved predecessor's entire life, and especially of his witness in suffering. Even then we perceived the fragrance of his sanctity, and in any number of ways God's People showed their veneration for him. For this reason, with all due respect for the Church's canonical norms, I wanted his cause of beatification to move forward with reasonable haste. And now the longed-for day has come; it came quickly because this is what was pleasing to the Lord: John Paul is blessed! ...

Today is the Second Sunday of Easter, which Blessed John Paul II entitled Divine Mercy Sunday. The date was chosen for today's celebration because, in God's providence, my predecessor died on the vigil of this feast.

OCT. 1-5, 2011: The second World Apostolic Congress on Mercy is celebrated in Krakow-Lagiewniki, Poland. The location of the congress highlights the connection between Blessed John Paul II, St. Faustina, and the message of Divine Mercy. Not only is it held in the beloved homeland of John Paul and St. Faustina but at Krakow-Lagiewniki, where St. Faustina lived and was buried and where the Great Mercy Pope entrusted the world to Divine Mercy. "This is the place from which the message full of hope that Jesus gave to mankind through St. Faustina and Blessed John Paul II was sent to the world," says Cardinal Stanislaus Dziwisz, Archbishop of Krakow, at the congress. Cardinal Dziwisz spent 40 years working side by side with Pope John Paul II as his personal secretary.

INDEX OF PAPAL WRITINGS AND ADDRESSES

ADDRESSES OF JOHN PAUL II

APOSTOLIC LETTERS

BOOKS OF JOHN PAUL II

DIVINE MERCY SUNDAY: HOMILIES AND REGINA CAELI MESSAGES

ENCYCLICALS

INFLUENCE OF JOHN PAUL II

VATICAN DOCUMENTS

BEATIFICATION

© Br. Albin Milewski, MIC

Cardinal Karol Wojtyla in 1969 attends an event in Michigan. Brother Albin Milewski, MIC, used this photo to show the staff at the Marian Helpers Center what their new Pope looked like after his election in 1978.

© Joseph Romagnano

The tapestry of Blessed John Paul II hangs on the front of St. Peter's Basilica at his beatification on May 1, 2011, Divine Mercy Sunday.

On November 13, 1986, Fr. George Kosicki, CSB, and Fr. Donald Van Alstyne, MIC, present Pope John Paul II with an icon of The Divine Mercy from the Congregation of Marians of the Immaculate Conception "as an expression of our thanksgiving for your proclaiming to the world the message of Divine Mercy." (The presentation was filmed for the movie *Divine Mercy — No Escape* in the apartment of the Holy Father.)

On November 27, 1996, on behalf of the Marian Congregation, Fr. Walter Dziordz, MIC, presents Pope John Paul II with a commemorative copy of the new Spanish-language edition of St. Faustina's *Diary* and a plaque congratulating him on the 50th anniversary of his ordination to the priesthood.

Father Kazimierz Chwalek, MIC (far left), Fr. Walter Dziordz, MIC, and Br. Andrew Maczynski, MIC (far right), are among the Marians showering Pope John Paul II with affection and appreciation after he addressed their General Chapter in Rome in 1999.

The Marians gather around Pope John Paul II at their private audience with him during their General Chapter meeting in Rome in 1999.

On June 8, 1999, Pope John Paul II joins the largest assembly of Marians in history — about 300 — during his visit to the Marians' Shrine in Lichen, Poland. It was the first papal visit to a Marian location.

**Solemn Act of Entrustment of the World to The Divine Mercy
by Pope John Paul II on August 17, 2002**

*God, merciful Father,
in Your Son, Jesus Christ, You have revealed Your love
and poured it out upon us in the Holy Spirit, the Comforter.
We entrust to You today the destiny of the world
and of every man and woman.*

*Bend down to us sinners, heal our weakness, conquer all evil,
and grant that all the peoples of the earth may experience
Your mercy. In You, the Triune God,
may they ever find the source of hope.*

*Eternal Father, by the Passion and Resurrection of Your Son,
have mercy on us and upon the whole world! Amen.*

Pope John Paul II's entrustment of the world to The Divine Mercy on August 17, 2002, at the Shrine in Krakow-Lagiewiniki has inspired World Apostolic Congresses on Mercy in the life of the Church. Congress organizers have particularly underscored his prophetic charge on the occasion when he said, "From here there must go forth 'the spark which will prepare the world for [Jesus'] final coming' (*Diary of St. Faustina*, 1732). This spark needs to be lighted by the grace of God. This fire of mercy needs to be passed on to the world."

The faithful wave banners reading *"Santo subito!"* (Saint now) to call for the immediate canonization of Pope John Paul II during his funeral in St. Peter's Square on April 8, 2005. An estimated 4 million mourners came to Rome for the funeral.

Some pilgrims carry signs with the image of The Divine Mercy and John Paul II as the Great Mercy Pope at his beatification on May 1, 2011.

"NON ABBIATE PAURA SPALANCATE LE PORTE A CRISTO" Comunione e Liberazione

A crowd of more than 1.5 million pilgrims filled the streets and piazzas of Rome to celebrate the beatification of John Paul II on May 1, 2011. Shown here in St. Peter's Square are images of John Paul II throughout his papacy. The large banner translates to: "Do not be afraid to open wide the doors to Christ." These words of Pope John Paul II from his inauguration on October 22, 1978, epitomize the spirit of his papacy.

Above, during the Mass for beatification, Sr. Marie Simon-Pierre Normand (right), of the Little Sisters of Catholic Motherhood, carries the reliquary containing the blood of John Paul II. At right, Sr. Simon-Pierre was cured from Parkinson's disease through the intercession of John Paul II two months to the day after his death. Her healing was recognized as the miracle for his beatification.

Pilgrims wave to Pope Benedict XVI as he makes his way through the crowd in St. Peter's Square for the beatification of John Paul II on May 1, 2011, Divine Mercy Sunday. Many of the pilgrims carry images of The Divine Mercy during the celebration.

Hovering over St. Peter's Square at the beatification of John Paul II on May 1, 2011, balloons carry a sign with the Latin phrase, *"Deo Gratias,"* which translates as: "Thanks be to God."

As Pope Benedict XVI declares John Paul II blessed on May 1, 2011, Divine Mercy Sunday, the tapestry of the new blessed is unveiled on the facade of St. Peter's Basilica.

At the concluding Mass for the second World Apostolic Congress on Mercy, October 5, 2011, Cardinal Christoph Schönborn, president of the congress, incenses an image of Blessed John Paul II. Below the image is a first-class relic of the blessed. The Mass was celebrated at the International Shrine of The Divine Mercy in Krakow-Lagiewniki, Poland, where the image and relic have been displayed for public veneration since John Paul II was declared blessed on Divine Mercy Sunday, May 1, 2011. Pope John Paul II's entrustment of the world to The Divine Mercy in 2002 in this Shrine inspired the Church to celebrate World Apostolic Congresses on Mercy.

PROMOTING DIVINE MERCY SINCE 1941

Marian Press, the publishing apostolate of the Marian Fathers of the Immaculate Conception of the B.V.M., has published and distributed millions of religious books, magazines, and pamphlets that teach, encourage, and edify Catholics around the world. Our publications promote and support the ministry and spirituality of the Marians worldwide. Loyal to the Holy Father and to the teachings of the Catholic Church, the Marians fulfill their special mission by:

- Fostering devotion to Mary, the Immaculate Conception.

- Promoting The Divine Mercy message and devotion.

- Offering assistance to the dying and the deceased, especially the victims of war and disease.

- Promoting Christian knowledge, administering parishes, shrines, and conducting missions.

Based in Stockbridge, Mass, Marian Press is known as the publisher of the *Diary of Saint Maria Faustina Kowalska,* and the Marians are the leading authorities on The Divine Mercy message and devotion.

Stockbridge is also the home of the National Shrine of The Divine Mercy, the Association of Marian Helpers, and a destination for thousands of pilgrims each year. Globally, the Marians' ministries also include missions in developing countries where the spiritual and material needs are enormous.

To learn more about the Marians, their spirituality, publications or ministries, visit **marian.org** or **thedivinemercy.org**, the Marians' website that is devoted exclusively to Divine Mercy.

Below is a view of the National Shrine of The Divine Mercy and its Residence in Stockbridge, Mass. The Shrine, which was built in the 1950s, was declared a National Shrine by the National Conference of Catholic Bishops on March 20, 1996.

MARIAN PRESS
STOCKBRIDGE · MA 01263

For our complete line of books, DVDs, CDs, and other trustworthy resources on Divine Mercy and Mary, visit thedivinemercy.org or call 1-800-462-7426 to have our latest catalog sent to you.

 Find us on Facebook
Facebook.com/DivineMercyOfficial
Facebook.com/MarianHelpers

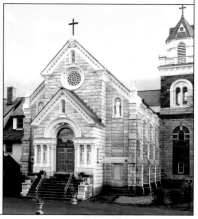

© MARIE ROMAGNANO

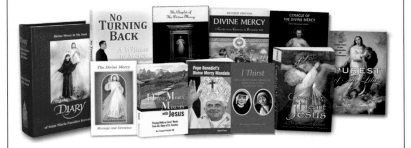

ESSENTIAL DIVINE MERCY RESOURCES

DIARY OF ST. MARIA FAUSTINA KOWALSKA

This extraordinary book sparked The Divine Mercy movement among Christians. Written in the 1930s, it exemplifies God's miracles in our world and His love and mercy toward mankind.

DELUXE, SOFT LEATHER-BOUND EDITION

24-page photo section with gilded edges, a ribbon marker, and full color photo section. 772 pages.

Hardcover, Trade Paper, and Compact Editions also available in English and Spanish.

Burgundy
DDBURG 9781596141896

Navy blue
DDBLUE 9781596141902

AUDIO DIARY OF ST. FAUSTINA

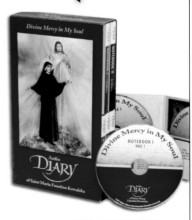

You'll feel like you are actually listening to St. Faustina speak in a gentle Polish accent as she writes in her *Diary*. Hear this dramatic portrayal of the voices of Jesus and Our Lady. Gain deeper insight into Faustina's mission to share the message of Divine Mercy with the world. Includes all passages from the printed *Diary*, prayerful music, and three renditions of the Chaplet of The Divine Mercy. 33 hours on 27 CDs.

ADCD 9781596142299

GROW CLOSER TO THE MERCIFUL HEART OF JESUS THROUGH THE IMMACULATE HEART OF MARY

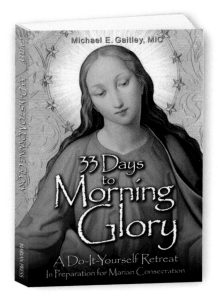

33 DAYS TO MORNING GLORY

From Fr. Michael E. Gaitley, MIC, author of the popular book *Consoling the Heart of Jesus*, comes an extraordinary 33-day journey to Marian consecration with four giants of Marian spirituality: St. Louis de Montfort, St. Maximilian Kolbe, Blessed Mother Teresa of Calcutta, and Blessed John Paul II. Fr. Michael masterfully summarizes their teaching, making it easy to grasp and simple enough to put into practice. More specifically, he weaves their thought into a user-friendly, do-it-yourself retreat that will bless even the busiest of people. So, if you've been thinking about entrusting yourself to Mary for the first time or if you're simply looking to deepen and renew your devotion to her, *33 Days to Morning Glory* is the right book to read and the perfect retreat to make.

9781596142442 / 33DAY

In these pages I met the gentle Mother I have loved for so long. In reading this book, I hope that you get the chance to meet her and come to rely on her as I do. ... I fully recommend it to you as one of the best books on Mary!

Immaculee Ilibagiza
Author of *Left to Tell* and
Our Lady of Kibeho